UNCONVENTIONAL CANDOUR

George Smitherman

UNCONVENTIONAL CANDOUR

DUNDURN
TORONTO

Cover image: Mitchel Raphael
Printer: Webcom, a division of Marquis Printing Inc.

Library and Archives Canada Cataloguing in Publication

Title: Unconventional candour / George Smitherman.
Names: Smitherman, George, author.
Description: Includes Index.
Identifiers: Canadiana (print) 20190051760 | Canadiana (ebook) 20190051779 | ISBN 9781459744653 (softcover) | ISBN 9781459744660 (PDF) | ISBN 9781459744677 (EPUB)
Subjects: LCSH: Smitherman, George. | LCSH: Legislators—Ontario—Biography. | LCSH: Gay legislators—Ontario—Biography. | CSH: Cabinet ministers—Ontario—Biography | LCSH: Ontario—Politics and government—1995-2003. | LCSH: Ontario—Politics and government—2003-
Classification: LCC FC3078.1.S65 A3 2019 | DDC 971.3/05092—dc23

1   2   3   4   5   23   22   21   20   19

 Conseil des Arts du Canada   Canada Council for the Arts    Canadä   ONTARIO ARTS COUNCIL CONSEIL DES ARTS DE L'ONTARIO an Ontario government agency un organisme du gouvernement de l'Ontario

We acknowledge the support of the **Canada Council for the Arts**, which last year invested $153 million to bring the arts to Canadians throughout the country, and the **Ontario Arts Council** for our publishing program. We also acknowledge the financial support of the Government of Ontario, through the **Ontario Book Publishing Tax Credit** and **Ontario Creates**, and the **Government of Canada**.

Nous remercions le Conseil des arts du Canada de son soutien. L'an dernier, le Conseil a investi 153 millions de dollars pour mettre de l'art dans la vie des Canadiennes et des Canadiens de tout le pays.

Care has been taken to trace the ownership of copyright material used in this book. The author and the publisher welcome any information enabling them to rectify any references or credits in subsequent editions.

The publisher is not responsible for websites or their content unless they are owned by the publisher.

Printed and bound in Canada.

VISIT US AT

dundurn.com | @dundurnpress | dundurnpress | dundurnpress

Dundurn
3 Church Street, Suite 500
Toronto, Ontario, Canada
M5E 1M2

To Michael and Kayla, who are my reason to live; to Canada, which made me possible; and to all of those who have been told they can't and did anyway.

Contents

	Prologue	9
	Introduction	11
1	Early Years	13
2	1980s	27
3	1990s	42
4	Health	79
5	So-Called Scandals	110
6	Health Reform	119
7	Energy	131
8	Christopher	149
9	Mayoral Race	156
10	Worse Than Defeat	185
11	Carrying On	192
12	Life After Politics?	199
13	Run Over by a Ford Again (Different Model)	206
	Acknowledgements	220
	Image Credits	222
	Index	223

Prologue

A memoir always risks being seen as a bit of a vanity project. How could I reasonably expect that my life, starting as a kid in Etobicoke, would ever be book worthy? It was something beyond my wildest dreams.

I have always had an inner conflict in which the self-confident me says, "Look what I got to do on a Grade 12 diploma," and the insecure me asks, "How could I warrant a book?"

I have watched others, people with lives certainly as interesting as mine, who have never managed to produce a memoir, often due to their own reticence or to their loyalty to those who might otherwise make the best fodder for their stories.

As you will see in my book, I have no reticence. And without it, I myself make the best fodder. That's deliberate, because I want the book to help, and to help it has to be candid and expose some real truths about power: how to get it, how to use it, and how to walk away from it. The book also reveals some real truths about my own character and peculiar brain chemistry, and I am prepared to be judged for my complete body of work.

For every salacious, heart-wrenching, or embarrassing anecdote you might encounter in this book that leaves you asking how I can live with myself, please don't ever forget that I choose to take my lumps and press forward despite the strong urge to toss in the towel, because I have experienced enough joy and hope to withstand and offset any downside.

I want this book to be a message to those people who feel that the circles of power are impenetrable: you can penetrate them.

I want this book to be a message to those people who struggle with addiction and can't see the other side: you can get to a place where despair does not have to be your constant companion.

I want this book to be a message to those people who have been struck by trauma once or one too many times: you are stronger than you know and the resilience you show now will hold you in good stead for the rest of your life.

This is the story of an unremarkable kid who, when asked at age six what he wanted to be when he grew up, said, "Blood donor." And who, thirty-three years later, as minister of health, was forbidden from giving blood because of his sexual orientation.

This is the story of a man who rose to the heights of power and risked it all.

This is the story of a man who loved and lost and loved again.

This is the story of a man who dreamed of having kids and had them.

This is a fairy tale without the candy coating.

But it is a personal journey interwoven with our politics, which have evolved over the four decades since I wandered into the Liberal party in Etobicoke Centre. During that time, I have served as a Liberal volunteer, a party staff member, an opposition MPP, a cabinet minister, and a candidate in two municipal elections, and I have seen an almost unbelievable change in how politics is practised. The friendly rivalry that characterized my early exposure to politics in the era of Bill Davis and David Peterson has deteriorated into a bitter partisanship that increasingly bypasses spin in favour of outright nonsense.

Back in the 1980s, it wouldn't have been that hard to imagine Peterson or Davis sitting at each other's cabinet table. Today, the disdain between Premier Doug Ford and his predecessor, Kathleen Wynne, is palpable, even in the legislative chamber.

Terrible as this transformation is, the fact remains that politics is a central part of our democracy. I have been privileged to participate in a significant way in the political process in Ontario and in Toronto. My book tells the story of our political evolution and my part in it, as well as that of my own personal evolution.

Introduction

I played golf on October 3, 2003. The night before, the Liberal Party had won the Ontario election and returned to power after a thirteen-year absence, and I had held my seat (Toronto Centre–Rosedale) in the Legislature. I remember it was a cold autumn day and I smoked a celebratory cigar during the round. Although I'm naturally competitive, the game didn't matter. It was a way to relax. Besides, the bigger game had already been won. And I was expecting things to get better still. I was confident that premier-elect Dalton McGuinty would put me in his cabinet. I didn't feel I had to lobby people in his inner circle for a seat at the table. They knew who I was.

Then I started reading all the speculation in the media about who would be in cabinet, and I began to get nervous. Some pundits ignored me altogether. One suggested I would be a minister without portfolio. So I called Gordon Ashworth, whom I knew from the days when David Peterson was premier and who was on McGuinty's transition team, to ask what was up. "All you need to know," said Ashworth, "is that when a tough assignment comes along and the question is raised about who can handle it, McGuinty always says: 'George.'"

I concluded from that conversation that I was going to make it into the cabinet. But in what portfolio? My dream job was minister of transportation, both because I was the son of a trucker and because transit was a big issue in my riding. Also, in opposition I had served as the party critic on gridlock in the Greater Toronto Area. So transportation made sense.

A few weeks later — on October 22 — Tracey Sobers, McGuinty's executive assistant, called me on my cellphone and asked me to hold for the premier-elect. I was on my way to the airport to pick up a friend who was coming into town to see the swearing-in ceremony the following day. (That shows you how confident I was that I would make it into cabinet.) McGuinty came on the line and said, "George, I want you to be minister of health."

I gasped but managed to compose myself. "I'm your man," I said.

McGuinty then added: "I want you to know that I've got your back and you can ignore the headlines."

I thanked him and the call ended. So began a roller-coaster ride in government.

At the ceremony the next day, with my friends and family in attendance, I took the oath of office. But as I exited the stage, I tripped and fell down the stairs. "It's an expectation-dampening moment," I joked to the media.

In a later interview, I said that I had put a Curious George doll on my desk in the minister's office. There was a photo of me with the doll in the *Star* the next day, and I was subsequently deluged with Curious Georges from people around the province.

"I'm looking forward very much to the opportunity to let my curiosities be satisfied, to really try to reach out and to add to the base of knowledge that I already have," I explained. "My first priority is to take the time necessary to understand the breadth and complexity of the [health] ministry ... I've got a pretty good appetite for hard work that I think is well suited to this place."

McGuinty echoed that comment with his own remarks. "I think George is chock-full of potential," he said. "I think he's a very hard-working guy. I'm absolutely convinced that he's the right person for this particular job. It's a huge responsibility, and I know that he is going to perform admirably."

A Queen's Park columnist opined afterward: "This could be an inspired choice, but it is also a risky one." The son of a trucker from Etobicoke was on a roll. In trucker talk, it would be shiny-side-up and rubber-side-down.

CHAPTER ONE

Early Years

I was born just ten weeks after the assassination of John F. Kennedy, coming into the world on February 12, 1964. My mother, Margaret, was a devotee of Kennedy. She saw him as the champion of the underdog — the poor, the dispossessed, racial and religious minorities. His assassination affected her profoundly. My sister recalls her reacting hysterically to the images on television. Subsequently, the family made not one but two pilgrimages to the Arlington National Cemetery in Washington to see his gravesite.

My mother's values came from her mother, my grandmother. My grandmother was born here and attended Jesse Ketchum school in Yorkville, a fact I learned from my mom on the day I was attending the school's hundredth anniversary. She and my grandfather were working-class people. He had emigrated from St. Anne's-on-the-Sea in Lancashire, England. They weren't particularly religious — they were mildly Anglican. Nor were they involved in politics, although after my grandfather's death, at a time when I was really young, I recall seeing a poster of Pierre Trudeau in their home.

But both my mother and grandmother possessed a social-justice streak. When my grandmother was working at my father's trucking business, she was transported there daily by taxis driven almost exclusively by immigrants from Lebanon, who politicized her with respect to the treatment of Palestinians. Similarly, my mother was imbued with a sense of the injustices visited on the Indigenous Peoples in Canada through her brother, who married a First Nations woman.

And although they had limited formal education, they both had an interest in learning. To a very large degree, I am who I am because of the influence of my mother and grandmother.

*   *   *

I was the fourth, and last, of the Smitherman children. My older brother was first, born in 1956 and named after my father, Arthur. My sisters, Joanne and Christine, followed in 1958 and 1962, respectively. Over that period, my family's economic circumstances improved markedly. I have always told everyone that I am the son of a trucker, and that is true. But by 1964 my father's single coal-hauling dump truck that served all purposes (including grocery shopping) had evolved into a growing fleet of tractor-trailers. Just months after my birth, the family moved from a combined home-and-truck-yard on Jay Street near Keele Street and Lawrence Avenue to a newly built bungalow in the West Deane Park neighbourhood of central Etobicoke. The house had a backyard swimming pool and bordered on the Mimico Creek ravine.

This was a big step up for my parents, especially my father. He had experienced extreme poverty as a child and was forced out of school in Grade 6 to work for a living. My mother's own background was barely better and remembered by my uncle (her brother) as a lot of living in basements with summers in shacks alongside the Credit River. My mother's father worked as a mechanic at Avro, the aircraft manufacturer that built the Lancaster, the famed Second World War bomber, and, after the war, the Avro Arrow, the Canadian interceptor jet cancelled by the Diefenbaker government in 1959. Over the years, he was regularly away servicing planes at air force bases across eastern Canada. His job paid him a good wage, but he gambled much of it away.

My father's father had the same gambling propensity, without a steady job to go with it. Perhaps in reaction, my father was driven to be a reliable provider for his family, although sometimes at the expense of being a nurturing parent. He worked seven days a week building up the trucking business. Up at six every morning, and not home before nightfall. So we didn't see much of him. The exceptions to this rule were Sunday breakfast (which he cooked), a yearly holiday in Florida (to which we drove both ways straight through), and summer Saturday afternoons entertaining customers around our pool.

*　*　*

Being the last-born child had its advantages. As time marched on, my father mellowed somewhat and found more time to spend with me. On weekends, he drove me regularly to the rink for my hockey games. (The fact that the games were often scheduled at six thirty or seven in the morning suited him, as he could still spend the rest of the day at work.) Hockey was a big deal for me. I started playing at age five or six in the West Mall league at an outdoor rink, right by the Etobicoke Civic Centre. I was inspired by stories of the Dryden boys, who hailed from the same area. While not a great talent hockey-wise, I really enjoyed the game and played right up until age eighteen (and again later in life). I was often the assistant captain of the team, mainly because my father's business, Sure-Way Transport, was usually the sponsor. My mother was also involved as a volunteer helping to run the league. I remember spending hours at the newly opened Centennial Arena running the stairs and frequenting the snack bars.

My father also used to take me down to Maple Leaf Gardens to watch the Leafs play. Through his business, he had season tickets to Leafs games. We progressed from front row greys (the upper level of the Gardens) to somewhere in the middle of the greens (the next level down). I actually preferred the greys because there was a railing where we could put peanut shells and flick them down on the reds (the posh seats). My father also had season tickets for the Blue Jays and for the Toronto Toros, a team in the short-lived World Hockey Association. The Toros tickets were a lot cheaper, but I enjoyed watching their games just as much because we were so much closer to the action and the referees were within the sound of my voice.

My father also had a strong interest in stock car racing, which he passed on to me. In his day, he was a member of the pit crew for Jack Greedy's super-modified, a class of open-wheel race car. They raced Saturday nights down at Exhibition Place. In 1972, during a trip to California, we "raced"

Striking a pose — and always with the Lange skates!

our full-size station wagon both on Jack Greedy's Delaware Speedway near London and on the famed Bonneville Salt Flats in Utah. The following year my father and his business partner rented a motorhome and took me and the other boys to an accident-plagued running of the Indianapolis 500. (In the late 1980s, I repaid my father in kind with some amazing seats for the Daytona 500, scored through a very senior businessman I had met through my then boss, Hugh O'Neil.)

I also inherited a love of off-road motorcycles from my father. Once he did a contra deal to get me a used Honda CT70 that was sitting on a front lawn on Jane Street north of Wilson, in exchange for a lot of painting. Having a motorcycle wasn't too foreign a concept in the Smitherman family. My sister Joanne had one and had perfected avoidance of the police in the Mimico Creek Valley, which in the early days of suburban sprawl remained accessible to motorized recreational vehicles.

For a period we also had snowmobiles, and we would trailer up to far-away farm fields and golf courses on Highway 10 and around Shelburne to ride them. What I mostly recall of these times was brand new SnowCruiser (cheap and unproven) snowmobiles smoking or on fire and my father experiencing a lot of frustration. Like me, while he had some mechanical knowledge, he lacked an aptitude for repairs.

It's no wonder that over the years I have had motorcycles ranging from a Honda CT70 to a 1200cc Honda GoldWing, along with three-wheelers, four-wheelers, and my own snowmobile. Later in life, I had some extraordinary experiences on snowmobiles, especially in the Algoma district of Ontario. I have a need for speed that can be quite intense.

* * *

Not only did I spend time with my dad snowmobiling and going to sports events, I also visited him at work. I went to work with my father frequently. It was "take-your-kid-to-work day" thirty to forty days a year for me. I recall lots of minor mishaps. I was a small kid wandering around a busy truck yard with a hundred pieces of moving equipment, an eleven-bay garage, arc-welding work, diesel smoke, and other attendant risks. From a very early age, I remember my father driving home a wide variety of "do not cross this line" messages.

I wasn't just wandering around, though. From an early age, I worked for my father. I was doing tasks beyond my age, such as snowplowing. I was just eleven when my father had his shop customize the bucket on an old Case farm tractor; he then trained me to push snow around the six-acre yard, usually in exchange for a twenty-five-cent hot chocolate. Sometimes, there were accidents. Once, for instance, I got soaked in diesel fuel as I was trying to refuel a truck and had to be rushed home for a quick bath. Another time, while I was scraping doors for repainting, I left the paint thinner too close to some blowtorches, which resulted in a mini-fire. So, the risk of injury was great, but my father made us well aware of that, and no serious mishaps occurred.

I was exposed to the colourful verbal exchanges that are common in a truck yard or any industrial workplace. And, as since this was in the 1970s, the language wasn't politically correct, to say the least. For example, my father employed two black truck drivers who were called "nigger one" and "nigger two." This is horrible in hindsight. It was also at the truck yard that I heard an anti-gay slur for the first time. It was directed at a driver, who was referred to by the others as a "gear jammer." This was a metaphor I understood only later in life. And no recall of a trucking environment would be complete without referencing the volume of naked portrayals of women.

* * *

The family tradition of driving to Florida for a March break vacation began the same year that I was born. All six of us would pile into the family car for the 1,200-mile trek to Daytona Beach or, more often, we'd tack on another 250 miles to Miami. For a Christmas present in 1969, my father gave my mother a brand new Mercury Meteor station wagon. But he could not make the annual Florida trip that year, so we set out in March of 1970 without him. It turned out to be an ill-fated trip.

During a freak intense rainstorm we ran into as we headed back home, an out-of-control car spun through the median and rammed straight into us. No one was hurt, but the brand new Mercury sustained heavy damage. So, we had a layover in Macon, Georgia, waiting for my father to come and drive us all back to Toronto. It was during these few days in Georgia that I had my first encounter with segregation. The motel where we were staying in Macon had a diner, and I started playing with the son of a black woman who worked in the kitchen. The senseless commotion that followed was deeply disturbing to me and still remains as a motivation for my commitment to equality.

My childhood wasn't all spent on family outings or at the truck yard. My friends and I also enjoyed playing in the ravine beside our house and frolicking in the Mimico Creek or in our backyard pool, which was a magnet for the whole neighbourhood. As young kids, we were afforded a tremendous amount of liberty. For example, we would set out on our own by bus to the Royal York subway station and from there to downtown. For a dollar, we could see Metro Croatia soccer games at Varsity Stadium.

And, of course, I went to school. My formal education began at West Deane Public School, just down the street from my home. (It has since been converted to a Catholic school named after Josyf Cardinal Slipyj, a former Ukrainian archbishop.) I was a keen participant in school-wide speaking contests. When I was in Grade 3, I made a speech to the whole school on "Ten Steps to Becoming a Millionaire." (My entrepreneurial role model for the speech was Eddie Shack, a former Maple Leaf who at that time was a big vendor of Christmas trees.) Experiences like this helped me overcome any aversions to public speaking. To this day, I can be nervous before a game of shinny hockey but not before speaking to an audience of a thousand people.

* * *

My parents divorced when I was about ten years old. One summer day, my mother said my father was coming home from work early and wanted to talk to me. This was most unusual, so I knew something was up. He took me to the rooftop of the Terminal One parking garage at Malton Airport (now Pearson International), where people often used to go to watch incoming or outgoing planes. There he told me that he and my mother were separating. It wasn't his idea, so there was no bad-mouthing of my mother. (For many months afterward, my father lived on the faint hope that they would get together again.) "Don't worry," he said. "Just because your mother and I are not going to be together, we love you just the same." On the way home, he bought me a chocolate bar.

It was not a big surprise to me that they were splitting. I had seen the signs of it. One night, my father had too much to drink and caused a big fuss. He didn't hit anyone, but he made a scene and the police were called. And on a family vacation with my two sisters and grandmother in Acapulco, where I shared a room with my parents, they did not sleep in the same bed. This was noteworthy.

After his airport announcement, my father shared my basement bedroom with me for a few months until he got his own modest accommodation nearby. After the reality of his situation had sunk in, he moved again to a luxury apartment that had the feel of a bachelor pad. My parents told me I could choose whom I wanted to stay with. But given that my father was a little light on the nurturing side, there was no real choice. My sisters and I stayed with our mother.

The family bungalow was soon sold and my mother moved in with a new man, D'Arcy Kelley, who was both my scouting leader and president of my minor hockey league. The three of us (my mother, my sister Christine, and I) shared a brand new condo in Etobicoke with D'Arcy and his son, Michael. So, my mother went from a house with a backyard and a pool to a more modest apartment on the other side of Highway 427. And she traded in her flashy Corvette Stingray for a down-market Mercury Bobcat. In other words, she took a hit to her standard of living to get out of a relationship she knew was not right for her. I deeply respect her for that.

The saddest moment of the divorce for me was Halloween in 1975. I was eleven, and Halloween was still a big deal for me. We had not yet moved out of the family bungalow, but I came home from school to find the house was dark. My sisters were out and my mother was in pursuit of her new relationship. I was crestfallen. But Christmas 1975 was a different story. We had just moved into the condo with my stepfather and his son. The new family dynamic proved to be extraordinarily beneficial for the children, insofar as one measures happiness on Christmas Day by material possessions. The parents went on a spending spree in an attempt to atone for the obvious disruption they caused. To this day, I remember getting from my father a pair of customized disco platform shoes that made a loud click as I walked down the hallway at school. This was the fashion highlight of my entire life. Never since have I been more in style, and that year I made my second speech to the entire school.

At the risk of underestimating the trauma of divorce for children, I have to say that I feel that in my case there were positive outcomes from my parents' split, and not just at Christmas. Both of my parents ended up with partners that were much better suited to them. D'Arcy was a good match for my mother. He shared her thirst for knowledge and sparked her interest in nature. They went canoeing in Algonquin Park, drove a fifth-wheel trailer all over North America, and raised honey bees at their beloved farm (named Darmarg, after the two of them) atop the Niagara Escarpment.

The divorce also forced my father to take on more of a home-making role, a task that had previously been delegated entirely to my mother. For the first few years after the divorce, my father had a bachelor pad with enough space to accommodate me and my sister Christine on weekends, which the divorce settlement stipulated we would spend with him. So, he had to make sure we brushed our teeth and washed our hands and all the other mundane things parents struggle to get their kids to do.

Eventually, my father was remarried to Marilyn, an Orillia farm girl who went to the same high school as Gordon Lightfoot and whose parents were very active in the Progressive Conservative Party. She brought stability to my father's life — although there was still a sense of adventure. They bought a cabin cruiser and toured around Lake Ontario together. My father has long since passed, but I still see my stepmother, or "Grandma Marilyn" to my kids. Each year, just after Christmas, we drive her down to her winter escape in south Florida. She has been a big influence on me and my own children. Originally, I had her pegged as a conservative person, because her parents were. But she turned out to be a lot more progressive in her views than I had imagined and we enjoy an unpredictably close connection.

* * *

Then there is my brother, Art, eight years older than me and with a rebellious streak. As a teenager, he wore his hair long and sold drugs. His car reeked of hash. He was in constant conflict with my father

The rest of the family had serious problems with Art, too. Once, when I was a little kid, he pushed me into wet cement at a construction site. Later, when my sexual identity began to emerge, Art physically assaulted me. It was really hard for me to deal with this attack. Difficult as it was, though, I later learned my hurt was minor compared to what my sisters suffered. My mother regretted until the day she died that Art's assaults had caused so much emotional harm to my sisters.

When my father died in 1992, his will left my brother less than my sisters and me. This reflected the fact that my father had already bailed Art out of so many financial jams. But Art was so offended that he cut us all off, and we have had no relationship with him since. At first I was concerned. But after speaking with my sisters, I realized we were all relieved.

* * *

In middle school, we all had to take a standardized aptitude test to aid in our streaming. The results told me that I should be a truck mechanic. It was as if the test read my mind and discovered my experiences in my father's truck yard. At that point in my life, a career as a mechanic was not my personal ambition, but changing a car tire seemed like a good skill to have. I ended up attending Burnhamthorpe Collegiate in Etobicoke, a school with a strong vocational program that included auto mechanics, electronics, welding, plumbing, and drafting courses. I enjoyed all of that but struggled with some of the academic courses, especially math and the sciences. In my first term at Burnhamthorpe, I got failing grades in math, even though I am actually good with numbers and can juggle them with ease in my head — a skill that came in handy later in my life. (When I was minister of health, I frequently demonstrated a remarkable recall for numbers, sometimes to the chagrin of deceptive bureaucrats.) But advanced mathematics stumped me, and that narrowed the options for me farther down the academic stream.

While I was an academically unfocused student in high school, I was not a shy one. I enjoyed lively debates with my teachers and mixing with my fellow students, although the outcomes were not always positive. Once in Grade 9, I tried to sit at a table in the school cafeteria and was told to get the hell away by a jock. He said the table was reserved for football players. Decades later, when I was health minister, the same guy came to my office to lobby me for something. I reminded him of that incident in the cafeteria; unsurprisingly, he did not recall it as vividly as I did.

Precociously, I ran for student council president in Grade 10. My campaign consisted of going from classroom to classroom handing out candy.

There were no real issues, but my team took the campaign very seriously, and I thoroughly enjoyed the opportunity to put my recently discovered political skills to work. I beat the incumbent (a girl who had the same birthday as me) with 83 percent of the vote.

Extracurriculars were not a big part of my high-school days because I tended to have after-school work. I did try out for the football team in Grade 11. By then, I was about 220 pounds, or lineman size. I lasted one practice. I fared better in the dramatic arts. Burnhamthorpe had an eccentric but inspiring drama teacher who organized an annual event called the "feast of fools," a potpourri of student-written plays and performances staged at venues throughout the school over several nights. One year before the fall of the Berlin Wall, I played the role of Leonid Brezhnev, the corpulent Soviet leader, in a play based on the Cold War and the John Lennon song "Imagine." I remember enjoying myself on stage. It was an experience that I carried over to politics, where performance is part of the job of convincing people.

Mostly, however, I used my after-school hours not for extracurricular activities but for making money in various jobs. This began in middle school, when I had a paper route. With the help of my mother, I delivered the *Toronto Star* daily to 150 households in Etobicoke. (If I wasn't delivering papers with my mother, we were going to Blue Jays games together. She was a big fan. We would buy grandstand seats for $2 apiece. In the team's first year of existence, we saw forty-two games, including the opener!)

My after-school work continued during my high-school years, mainly because I needed the money to pay for my car, a used 1973 Datsun that I had bought in the spring of 1980, at age sixteen. It cost $1,650, and the money was fronted by my father. The car paid for itself, in a way, as I used it to do deliveries for Clem and Joan Neiman, who had a law practice in Brampton. (Joan was a senator, appointed by Pierre Trudeau, and she and Clem ran the first election campaign I ever worked on.) They hired me to deliver documents to registry offices and clients downtown. (I used my position as school president to have secretaries field my calls from the law office until I got a pager.) I earned much more doing that than in my other job as a truck-washer at my father's yard.

*   *   *

My social life in high school was less adventurous. That is, my sexual awakening was delayed. The awareness was there, but the manifestations were slow to come. Contributing to this were my insecurity about my weight and my inklings about my sexual orientation.

I think my love of sugar and penchant for binge-eating began in the womb. There my system was shocked because my mother was stressed out by the assassination of John Kennedy. I was always a chubby kid, which meant I had to endure lots of teasing and bullying. Plus there is a whole basket of stuff that comes with being named George and being pudgy. I must have had the nursery rhyme repeated to me several thousand times: "Georgie Porgie, pudding and pie / Kissed the girls and made them cry." Why are the girls running away? What did I do? Is this why I am gay? Probably not, but it's definitely been built into the mix of who I am and it influenced my instinct for hectoring.

In my father's shop, the mechanics called me the Pillsbury Doughboy. I have also often been compared to "Bib" the Michelin man, which is ironic because I actually sold Michelin tires for a year or so. At one point, my high-school gym teacher thoughtfully intervened and referred me to a program at Sick Kids Hospital, where I was monitored and counselled on better eating habits and the like. Mostly what I remember is eating candy on the way there and back. Even today, while my eating habits have improved, I think like a fat guy. That is, I think I am fatter than I really am. To some, I might appear out of shape, but I can still walk nine miles. No matter how fat I have been, I have always been physically active — playing hockey and tennis, running, and cycling. This is not to say that one completely offsets the other. But were it not for my physical activity, the strong probability is that I would have type 2 diabetes by now. That's why I promote the idea that walking is freedom.

So, weight was an issue, and as I said, my sexual orientation was also one. I went on a few dates with girls, including school proms, but there was never any romantic connection. Nor was there a lightbulb moment when I realized I was gay, but there were lots of hints and signals all through my adolescence. Through high school and into my early twenties, I was topsy-turvy. I was transitioning but not on a consistently clear path. In high school, I was not sexually active, with either boys or girls. In my final year, I heard about AIDS for the first time. I have always considered myself fortunate that I only later became sexually active, doing so then with a full awareness of the risk involved.

In my final year of high school, my mother discovered some gay magazines in my room. She and D'Arcy sat me down for a talk. I don't remember it as a difficult conversation, although I am sure it was. I assured her I was just reading the magazines, not acting on my feelings. I'll never forget my mother's response: "We love you no matter what, and all we want for you is to be happy and healthy." These are words every LGBTQ questioning kid ought to hear. Subsequently, I actively dated a few women. It was a confusing time for both me and my mother.

I never had the same sort of conversation with my father when I was a teenager. But about a decade later, when I was twenty-six or so, I had something close to it on a brief motor trip to Florida to visit his in-laws. He raised the issue of marriage (to a woman), and I made it clear to him that was not in the cards for me. The penny dropped for my father; he never raised the issue again. (This is a quite common story in the gay community: the conversations with mothers are very different from the ones with fathers.) But the conversation did not damage our relationship.

* * *

I got my Grade 12 diploma at Burnhamthorpe Collegiate despite being called a "dropout," but I obtained just four of the six credits I needed for Grade 13. This put a crimp in my dreams of going to university and then law school. I set out to complete my high-school education through correspondence courses, but I never did finish them. Instead, I did what Smithermans do and joined the work force.

My father didn't think it would be a good idea for me to work for him. Although I was a bit pissed off, I could see the picture clearly enough. So, he arranged a deal with one of his primary competitors, which, like my father's business, did a lot of hauling for Algoma Steel in Sault Ste. Marie. I began as a rating clerk at Trans Provincial Freight Carrier's terminal in Mississauga. Within a few months of my starting, the terminal manager in Sault Ste. Marie died and I was sent to replace him, at the ripe age of twenty. Despite my lack of experience and my youth, my pedigree, presence, and profanity must have been enough, because I only remember being well received in the role.

I would return home most weekends, riding south with a Trans Pro truck on a Friday and returning to the Soo as a passenger in one of my father's trucks on a Sunday. I soon got tired of this and took a job back in Toronto selling Michelin truck tires, mostly to my father's business.

This was a listless time for me, but I wasn't exactly standing still. Rather, I was getting deeply involved in politics. My involvement can be traced to February 16, 1980, just days after my sixteenth birthday. On that day, I secured from Pierre Trudeau one of the two roses that adorned his lapel. "Mr. Trudeau," I said, as he squeezed through the doorway of Joe Cruden's Liberal campaign office in Etobicoke, "my grandmother is a great admirer of yours. May I have that flower for her?" I think he was glad to be rid of the second one, no doubt pinned on him at his previous event. But for me it remains my most prized political possession. My grandmother pressed that flower in a book and, upon her death just two years later from breast cancer, my mother and my aunt returned it to me, framed with an image of Trudeau that I acquired at my first national Liberal convention in Winnipeg in the summer of 1980. Thus my career in politics was launched.

CHAPTER TWO

1980s

Pierre Trudeau was in Etobicoke that February day in 1980 in his quest to become prime minister again, less than a year after he had been defeated by Joe Clark and the Progressive Conservatives. Trudeau had resigned the party leadership after the Liberals' loss to the PCs but then staged a fantastic comeback to fight a rematch against Clark, whose government had surprisingly lost a budget vote in Parliament. Two days after handing me the rose, Trudeau won a majority.

His victory speech that evening still sends chills up my spine. "Well, welcome to the 1980s," he began. He went on to claim a mandate "to speak for all the people of Canada" and declared: "Canada has been, Canada is, and Canada will remain more than the sum of its parts." (Bear in mind that this was just three months before the first Quebec referendum.) He concluded with the oft-quoted lines from Robert Frost's poem: "I have promises to keep, / And miles to go before I sleep." He went on to win the referendum and then repatriate the Constitution with a Charter of Rights that would open previously forbidden passages for me and many others.

While the Liberal Party won nationally in 1980, the local campaign in my riding of Etobicoke Centre, in which I worked as a volunteer, was not successful. We did better than in 1979, but we still lost by more than three thousand votes to the incumbent Conservative, Michael Wilson, the trade minister in Clark's government. So, I learned the sting of defeat in my first involvement in politics.

I worked as a volunteer in the campaign of Joe Cruden, a long-time Bell Canada executive and active Liberal fundraiser. The campaign was run by Clem Neiman and his wife, Senator Joan Neiman. I had been noticed when I showed up at Cruden's nomination around Christmas, and this fresh new recruit was on hand days later to help set up the campaign headquarters on Dundas Street West, just up the hill from the iconic Montgomery's Inn. I made my reputation quickly as I was not averse to hard work. Among other things, I recall schlepping heavy office chairs from a nearby realty office to the headquarters. The campaign proved to be a welcoming environment for a kid, and it showed me that politics, with its extreme organizational challenges, provided an opportunity for talent to shine. It was a turning point in my life. Indeed, the Liberal Party became a surrogate family for me. "This is my thing," I thought. Other kids could stand out in academics or athletics; I could ace politics.

Beyond Cruden and Neiman, three women nurtured me in that 1980 campaign. Bea Yakimoff was by day a school secretary but had a key role in campaign organization by night. She was my guide for fifty-six of the most important days of my life (the length of federal campaigns back then). Marian Maloney, who later served with distinction as a senator, also showered me with attention. And Simone Flahiff's nearby house at Kipling and Burnhamthorpe became a second home for me. All three of them exemplified the talented women who once dominated campaign offices. In my opinion, they have never been effectively replaced, since today more of the talents of women are deployed in the paying workplace.

I got very caught up in the 1980 campaign. I vividly recall how terrible I felt the one night I couldn't go to the campaign office because I had to study for an exam or some other useless academic exercise. I think that says a lot about the allure and attraction of politics — for me, at least. I also discovered that I had some useful expertise to offer. For example, I had an after-school job as a pizza delivery driver. The deliveries were in the same territory where I was tasked to put up election signs. As a result, my sign team was very fast because I already knew where all the houses were on those streets.

On election night, I recall walking home from the election night party at St. George's on the Hill Anglican church to get some air. I came upon some Conservative campaign signs. I thought of kicking them down, but I restrained myself then, as I have on every other occasion since. I think that driving stakes and metal posts into the frozen tundra of Etobicoke in the cold winter election of 1980 taught me a lot of respect for volunteer labour.

When it came to heckling, however, I did not show such restraint. Despite a childhood bout with pneumonia and a lengthy stay at Sick Kids, my lungs were capable of producing plenty of volume. I quickly learned to heckle and used that skill to advantage during all-candidates meetings. You know you are good at something when you come home from a hard day of campaigning to a message from your mother letting you know that somebody from another riding association has called to see if you would be available to heckle at *their* all-candidates meeting. (My mother took it all in stride, perhaps given the kinds of hobbies my older siblings had taken up.) Until recently, having passed away in February 2019, Michael Wilson would greet me with a question about whether he was going to be heckled once again.

Soon after the new Liberal government was formed in Ottawa in 1980, I took to staying up late and watching the 11:30 p.m. replay of Question Period. Despite my lack of French, I could emulate the accents of my favourites, Marc Lalonde and Monique Bégin. As well, I corresponded frequently with Liberal MPs and even cabinet ministers. My family had purchased one of the earliest Apple computers, and by Grade 9 I had acquired strong typing skills. I put these two elements to work, and for years I received tons of communications back from Ottawa. One response was particularly surprising. Soon after the 1980 election, Ed Lumley, the new Liberal trade minister, took his predecessor, Wilson, on a foreign trade mission. I was incensed that this guy I had worked so hard to defeat was being shown such a courtesy. A few days later, our home phone rang. The Honourable Ed Lumley was on his speaker phone looking to speak to George Smitherman. He explained to me that there was a parliamentary tradition that matches opposition members with travelling ministers to avoid the risk of losing votes in the House of Commons. On many occasions throughout my political life, I have retold that story, often in Lumley's presence or in his adopted hometown of Cornwall.

* * *

One notable feature of political campaigns is that they keep on coming, especially in a federation, like Canada. In March of 1981, Ontario premier Bill Davis called an election in search of an elusive majority, and I went to work for the Liberals in the provincial riding of York West, which overlapped with the federal riding of Etobicoke Centre. For me, it was a hard lesson on the differences between the provincial and federal Liberals — especially in organizational terms. I will always remember that the posters of the Ontario Liberal leader, Stuart Smith, arrived in the last week of the campaign, while the Trudeau posters had come early and often.

Organization aside, Davis was also a far more difficult opponent than Clark. So, a relatively close loss to Michael Wilson in the federal election became a provincial shellacking at the hands of the incumbent Conservative, Nick Leluk. He was a lacklustre pharmacist and MPP, but he beat the Liberal candidate, Michael Eagen, a thoughtful high-school teacher, by more than eight thousand votes. I knew the Conservatives were going to have a good night when my own mother confessed to me that she was going to vote for Bill Davis. I don't believe that ever happened again.

Stuart Smith resigned following his defeat in the 1981 provincial election. The ensuing Liberal leadership race introduced me to David Peterson, the man I still think of as my leader. I remember the convention well. It was held in the Grand Ballroom of the Sheraton Centre in downtown Toronto. The five-person race featured an interesting cast of characters, ranging from a guy known mostly for his voice in ads hawking food (Richard Thomas) to veteran MPPs who represented a much more conservative era for Ontario Liberals (Jim Breithaupt and John Sweeney). However, Peterson's main rival was Sheila Copps, who had won a seat in the Legislature in the 1981 election and was just twenty-nine at the time. While Sheila ran a spirited campaign, Peterson won fairly easily on the second ballot.

Luckily for me, Joe Cruden had a role that day working the floor for Peterson, and I was the guy beside him on the radio. That weekend I got to meet media titans like local CBC anchor Fraser Kelly and Larry Zolf, who told me how he had rented the back side of billboards very cheaply in his campaign to be appointed to the Senate.

Around then, I also encountered Ernest "Pete" Farrow, a long-time Etobicoke councillor whose campaign signs said, "I work for people not votes." He was one of the most genuine people I have ever met and one of

the greatest influences on my life in terms of service to people. An accountant and a Second World War veteran who had served in the RAF and,
after being shot down, was held captive as a POW, shared ownership of
a private plane. One day, Pete offered to take me flying. We drove out to
the Brampton Flying Club and got airborne. It quickly became clear to me
that Pete's best days as a pilot had passed. Once safely back on the ground,
I thanked Pete and told myself, "Never again."

* * *

Back then, municipal elections were held every two years, with the next
one due in the fall of 1982. All of eighteen at the time and still a student in
high school, I actually considered running against an incumbent Etobicoke
councillor, Dick O'Brien. I spent most of my discretionary hours mocking
up my first campaign brochure and getting set to run. But O'Brien enlisted
Pete Farrow to persuade me not to. I followed the advice. At the time, I
found it astonishing that a veteran pol like O'Brien would have the least bit
of concern about some kid running against him. But the incident informed
my view that the politicians who last are the ones who maintain at least a
trace of paranoia.

* * *

Instead of running for municipal office, I became president of the provincial
Liberal association in York West. My relative youth and lack of education
didn't seem to stand in my way, perhaps because I looked older than my age
and I was accustomed to working with adults. (It also must be said that, given
the low standing of the provincial Liberals of that era, the position of president of a riding association was not something that was highly sought after.)

I drafted the aforementioned Marian Maloney to run the 1985 provincial campaign for our candidate, Leonard Braithwaite. He was seeking a return to the Legislature, where he already enjoyed the distinction
of having been Ontario's first black MPP. We lost the riding to Leluk
again, although we cut his margin from 8,273 votes in 1981 to just 715
votes. However, province-wide, the Liberals under David Peterson added
fourteen seats, the Conservatives lost eighteen, and the net result was a

minority Legislature. Peterson then joined forces with Bob Rae and the New Democrats to send the Conservatives packing after forty-two years in power. It was a historic moment.

After the shift in power, Bob Elgie, a prominent Conservative, resigned his seat in York East and caused a by-election to be called in early 1986. Taking a big risk, I quit my job selling tires to work as an unpaid volunteer in that campaign, won by the Liberal candidate Christine Hart. There I was noticed by Pat Sorbara, who worked in Premier Peterson's office. She arranged some paid assignments for me at Queen's Park, beginning with the backup receptionist job in the Premier's Office during the 1986 doctors' strike over extra-billing by doctors. The government's initiative to end the practice prompted a high volume of calls, almost all of them negative. (I suspected at the time that most of the callers were doctors' spouses.) The desk where I worked was less than ten feet from the premier's door. I could see the likes of Robert Nixon (treasurer) and Murray Elston (health minister) coming and going before Question Period. It was heady stuff for a twenty-two-year-old.

After my stint doing that, I was put in charge of coordinating the appointment of new returning officers. The riding boundaries had changed after the 1985 election, which gave the Liberals an opportunity to sweep aside returning officers deemed too partisan or incompetent. After that, I was sent over to the provincial Liberal headquarters on St. Mary Street, a few blocks from Queen's Park, where I became a full-time field organizer for the party as it prepared for the next election. My territory included Hamilton, Niagara, Mississauga, and the Simcoes. I had my own Ford Ranger by then and logged a lot of miles driving around the ridings to monitor nomination meetings.

Given that the Liberals were expected to win massively in the upcoming election (which was eventually held in 1987), there was a lot of competition for those nominations. And with competition come accusations of skullduggery. Candidates would arrive at party headquarters to hand over thousands of paid memberships just before the deadline. I am proud to say that none of the ridings on my list resulted in the party having to arbitrate a dispute, although Mississauga South came close. The party had a star candidate in mind: Claudette MacKay-Lassonde, the first female president of the Association of Professional Engineers. She was dynamic, vivacious, energetic, and a natural-born leader. But she was late getting into the race, and a local candidate was already well positioned to take the nomination. In the end, MacKay-Lassonde won, but there were allegations of ballot-stuffing and the like. The resulting bitterness and division hampered us in the general election in Mississauga South, where I was second-in-command in the campaign. Accordingly, the Conservative candidate, Margaret Marland, held the seat by a slim 599 votes. It was one of just sixteen seats the Tories won across the province in the 1987 election as Peterson's Liberals swept to a big majority.

After that election, I was transferred back to the Premier's Office as a legislative assistant in the policy unit. I was working under Hershell Ezrin (Peterson's principal secretary) and under the influence of Gordon Ashworth (executive director of the Premier's Office). These were two giants of Liberal politics, and just being near them was a great experience for me. My direct boss was Phil Dewan, who a dozen years later became Dalton McGuinty's chief of staff. My assignment included working up profiles of the province's ridings. This put me in conflict with another power centre at Queen's Park, the caucus office, headed up by the redoubtable Isobel Finnerty, later appointed to the Senate. So I learned something about office politics, as well.

Another of my responsibilities was to sit behind the Speaker's chair during Question Period and pass notes to Peterson as he fielded tricky inquiries from the opposition parties. Sunday shopping was a major issue at the time, and united in opposition to it were a wide array of groups that were not normally on the same side: unions, churches, small businesses, and rural Ontario. This, too, was a learning experience for me. But I did not stay long in the job — barely five months — before moving to a minister's office.

I was recruited by Pam Gutteridge to work as a policy adviser in the office of the minister of tourism and recreation, Hugh O'Neil. Pam, whom I knew from previous campaigns, was Hugh's executive assistant. Working there was a tremendous break for me, as O'Neil was an experienced and able politician. A former teacher and real estate broker, he had been the MPP for Quinte for twelve years by the time I arrived. He taught me skills and habits that I employed years later in my own time as an elected politician and cabinet minister. Hugh was also like a second father to me.

We often dined together at the end of a long work day. The tourism office was at 77 Bloor Street West, close to Yorkville, so that meant we were eating at such renowned (then) establishments as Il Posto, Fenton's, and

Bellini. I also travelled with him. This gave me better access to the minister than was enjoyed by my boss, Pam Gutteridge. Pam, ever the champion for me, blessed the relationship and moved on to give me an even bigger opportunity. She has been so loyal to the party; yet the party has never really repaid her appropriately.

Tourism and Recreation was also an interesting experience for me. We called it the "ministry of fun, fun, fun," since it was perceived as dealing with a lot of discretionary spending. Under its umbrella were the Ontario Lottery Corporation, Ontario Place, the Niagara Parks Commission, Old Fort Henry, Sainte-Marie Among the Hurons in Midland, the Big Thunder ski jump in Thunder Bay, and many other agencies with high profiles in their regions. There were a lot of "announceables" — grants and programs to be announced by the minister — plus meetings with interesting people. Among them was "Eddie the Eagle," the British ski jumper who finished last at the 1988 Olympics but became an international celebrity in the process. I remember getting his autograph in Thunder Bay and look forward to finding it someday among my forty-odd boxes of "stuff."

O'Neil taught me a political lesson: every Friday afternoon, he would "enhance the government's prospects" by travelling to various parts of Ontario on a government aircraft. He would fly in to announce something or the other and then fly back late at night or more likely the next day, when I would drop him off at CFB Trenton and head for Toronto. There was a bar on the plane, so I always arrived in Toronto well refreshed and ready for Friday evening activities at Bemelmans, Chaps, Colby's, or Woody's.

It wasn't all wine and roses at the ministry of fun, however. One of our agencies (damn agencies!) — Ontario Place — was chaired by Patti Starr, who became the centre of a fundraising scandal. (She made illegal campaign donations to the Liberal Party and its various candidates in her role as head of the Toronto section of the National Council of Jewish Women, a charity.) The story, and its various spinoffs (including Starr's relationship with the development industry), was front-page news at the time, especially in the *Globe and Mail*, which was delivering almost daily scoops on it. One of my jobs was to get the *Globe*'s "bulldog" edition late at night at Yonge and Bloor to get an advance look at the latest instalment in the scandal. Starr eventually had to resign as chair of Ontario Place, but the scandal stuck with the Peterson government and helped to bring it down in 1990.

Starr was eventually charged with fraud and breach of trust, convicted, and served time. Somewhere in my forty boxes of stuff, I have the original of her resignation letter.

O'Neil survived that upheaval but was moved in a subsequent cabinet shuffle from Tourism and Recreation to the Mines ministry. It was interpreted at the time as a demotion, but O'Neil didn't see it that way — in part because eastern Ontario had a proud mining history. On his watch, the Mining Act was rewritten to open up more Crown land for prospecting. Also attached to the portfolio was an added bonus of foreign travel. At the urging of Hugh's ex-colleague Pat Reid, a former Liberal MPP who had become head of the Ontario Mining Association, O'Neil went on a tour of nickel refineries in Norway and Wales, with a side trip to Finland to promote mining investment. To make the trip more palatable to the Premier's Office, we were forced to take on the additional task of delivering the bid book for the 1996 Summer Olympics to an IOC representative in the Netherlands. It was my first trip to continental Europe, and I took full advantage of it. To this day, I remember Dutch gold medalist Anton Geesink (judo) touring us about Utrecht. First stop was a great beer hall, where I drank mine and Hughie's too, and then came the harbourside, where I enjoyed the raw herring so well it earned me a second helping.

While we were attending a reception in Helsinki a few days later, a call came in from the Premier's Office. Christine Hart (whose by-election win I had assisted on in 1986) had been dumped as minister of culture and communications over a possible conflict of interest with a telecommunications company that had donated to her campaign. The premier needed to hand her responsibilities off to someone — Hugh. So, in addition to being minister of mines, O'Neil now had the Ministry of Culture and Communications added to his portfolio. It was an incongruous pairing, but we made the most of it, and Hugh and his wife, Donna, were early and vigorous promoters of the arts scene in Quinte.

This situation didn't last long, however, because Peterson was about to call a snap election, over the objections of some of his ministers (including O'Neil, although he was too loyal to say it out loud). The government was not due to face the electorate until 1991, but Peterson decided to go to the polls a year early, notwithstanding signs of growing voter discontent. Among other things, Peterson was one of the champions of the Meech

Lake Accord, signed with Prime Minister Brian Mulroney in 1987. The accord was unpopular on the ground in Ontario, for a variety of reasons. I had witnessed some of the backlash myself while advancing a bus tour for Peterson through O'Neil's eastern Ontario backyard in the summer of 1989. I recall an event in Kingston — a breakfast in a tent that was ringed with protesters, many of them shouting anti-French slogans.

Peterson's government was seen by many as being obsessed with Meech Lake and constitutional reform, to the detriment of everything else. And Peterson himself was seen as too closely linked to Mulroney ("Lyin' Brian"). This image was magnified when Peterson, in a futile last-ditch effort to save the accord, offered to give up six of Ontario's twenty-four Senate seats, to be redistributed among other provinces east and west to win their agreement to Meech Lake. It was a magnanimous gesture that helped to cement a deal at the bargaining table. But the deal fell apart, and Peterson was left holding a bag of nothing. It was tough for me because Trudeau the elder, who was my hero, and Peterson, who had given me my first full-time job in politics, were at such odds.

O'Neil took cabinet confidentiality seriously and kept his opinions close to his chest, but I knew that he had a foreboding sense that the 1990 election was not going to end well. As it turned out, the campaign didn't start well, either. At Peterson's kick-off press conference on July 30, his message was drowned out by a tape recorder protesting the government's "failure to protect the environment." (The tape recorder was placed on the podium by Gord Perks, a Greenpeace activist then, now a Toronto city councillor.)

A week later, I was tasked with organizing the nomination meeting for Peterson himself in his London Centre riding. It was a fiasco. The premier's local team failed to produce a crowd, so the hall looked half-empty. And the event was crashed by John Clarke, an anti-poverty activist. "You're the poverty premier," Clarke shouted at Peterson.

"Someday you're going to grow up and find a responsible job," retorted the premier.

Clarke was ushered out of the hall by two large Liberal supporters, but the damage had been done. And my team was blamed for it. After that, we were banished to northern Ontario, where we organized campaign events for Peterson in Wawa, Kapuskasing, Hearst, and North Bay. I remember the event in North Bay well. It was a Friday night, and just before going to speak, Peterson was informed that, for the first time, tomorrow's press would report that the NDP was ahead in the polls. His back to the wall, Peterson delivered a heckuva speech that night. But it was too late. Not even a proposed sales tax cut could turn the tide.

On election night, I was in Simcoe West riding where we had come within a hair of winning in 1987. The first results there showed the Liberal candidate running third and the NDP in front. In a rural area, that was unheard of. So we knew our goose was cooked. Elsewhere in Ontario, the results were equally poor, although O'Neil was re-elected in Quinte. Province-wide, the NDP won a majority and the Liberals fell from ninety-five seats to just thirty-six. Immediately afterward, I drove all the way from Stayner back to Queen's Park for a midnight meeting with other political aides in O'Neil's office. The meeting was more about commiserating than plotting our futures, but I felt the need to share the pain.

On September 6, 1990, the people of Ontario did not set out to put the NDP in power with Bob Rae as premier. Rather, the voters decided to give Peterson and the Liberals a bitch-slap. The slap's unintended consequences included Peterson losing his own seat. He handled his defeat with dignity and humility, and he has since re-established himself as a statesman in the province and in the country. I hearkened back to this moment when I suffered my own humbling defeat in the 2010 Toronto mayoral election. More about that later.

* * *

The Peterson government has its critics. But there were many significant reforms during its five years in power, from blue boxes to the French Languages Services Act. One that stood out for me was Bill 7. It was a simple bill, adding sexual orientation as prohibited grounds for discrimination in Ontario. But it had a complex history.

The bill began under the outgoing Conservative government in 1985 as part of a package of legislation to bring Ontario's laws into conformity with the Charter of Rights. It was considered non-controversial at the time. But as it wound through committee hearings, an amendment brought forward by Evelyn Gigantes, an NDP MPP, changed all that by prohibiting discrimination on the basis of sexual orientation. With the stroke of a pen,

Bill 7 was changed from a piece of housekeeping legislation to a lightning rod. Suddenly, the bill faced considerable opposition, including a group called the Coalition for Family Values and the Catholic Church. Vehemently critical letters and phone calls began flooding into MPPs' offices. A counter campaign in favour of the amendment began in the gay community and drew support from some of the province's key unions.

This all came to a head in the Legislature on December 2, 1986. I was there, seated in the members' gallery, as Premier Peterson rose to close the debate. I remember his words to this day:

> Supposing that when one of my children was sixteen or eighteen he came to me and said, "Dad, I am a homosexual," what would I do then? Would I give my child some of the speeches we have heard in this House in the past six days and throw him out the door? Obviously, I would be concerned. Obviously, there would be repercussions. Obviously, I would look at myself and ask, "What did I do wrong?"
>
> My guess is that most of us, after we had got over the shock, would embrace that child and try to incorporate him into our own family. We would say we did not want anyone to discriminate against him in terms of his job or housing just because of a lifestyle that, for some reason unknown to any of us, he had adopted. If you could put it in the context of a loving parent for all the children of the province, that might make it a little easier for some of the people who have difficulty with this.
>
> I am proud to support this amendment today. I do not believe we can put it off and off and off.*

---

* One of the speakers just before Peterson that day was Nick Leluk, the Tory I had campaigned against in the 1981 and 1985 elections. He opposed the sexual orientation amendment, arguing that it would "legitimize an alternative lifestyle on the same level as the traditional family. Should we expect chronic drinkers and smokers to be added to the Human Rights Code as a group because their behaviour may adversely affect their chances of employment? Where does one draw the line? Should criminal behaviour also be enshrined in the code?"

With such strong backing from the premier, the amendment passed that day, by a vote of sixty-four to forty-five. I teared up and caught the eye of my colleague Pam Gutteridge. I wasn't "out" by then, but I think she knew. Over the next few years, I would use the safe haven the premier created for me within the party and government to come out to various people at various times. One such early confession came after a painful by-election in London North. (The incumbent Liberal, Ron Van Horne, had quit the Legislature after being dumped from cabinet.) The by-election was won by Dianne Cunningham for the Conservatives. Pat Sorbara drove me home to Toronto on that night. I was totally drunk. I said something like: "I'm gay, but I think I am going to throw up, so please pull over."

I didn't reveal my sexual orientation to many people back then. For instance, I didn't tell Hugh O'Neil. Nor was I sending out a lot of clues. Instead, I bit my tongue on more than one occasion when gay slurs (common back then) were uttered in my presence. For instance, I remember dining with O'Neil at Bigliardi's, a steak house that happened to be situated in the heart of the Gay Village. (It's now a high-end gay strip club.) This was at the time of one of the early Pride parades. The proprietor, George Bigliardi, approached our table and declared: "How dare they say they're proud." I nearly gagged. (Later, Bigliardi evolved, as so many others did. He became a regular customer of mine at my film shop, and I came to know him and his family well.)

But beyond the confines of my political life, I was exploring the boundaries. I can remember as if it were yesterday my first visit to a gay bar, Buddies, which was located down a laneway off Church at Gerrard. Little did I know that the guy sitting at the end of the bar was the owner of the place, none other than George Hislop, the unofficial mayor of the Gay Village. He was well known for his runs for elected office in 1980 (Toronto city council) and 1981 (Ontario Legislature). He was also charged — as a part-owner — in the infamous 1981 bath-house raids. I first heard his name spat out in disgust that a gay man would dare to be open about his sexuality, let alone seek elected office. It's one of the great joys in my life that I came to know and love George, and I could only wish that I had known him longer.

Another time, I was inside Chaps bar on Isabella on Halloween. New to the scene, I was shocked to the core when I exited only to find that a massive throng of onlookers had gathered to watch the costumed set arrive. Looking into a camera, I said, "Hi, Mom," while hoping like hell that it wasn't rolling.

Occasionally, I would run into other Queen's Parkers at the gay bars I attended. Ian Scott, then the attorney general, was a frequent visitor to Chaps, although he was not publicly "out" at that time. Indeed, when confronted on his sexuality by a *Toronto Sun* reporter, Scott replied, "Publish at your peril." The *Sun*, perhaps surprisingly, never did. Nor did any of the other newspapers in the city, although their reporters knew full well that Scott was gay. It was as if the local media had adopted their own version of "Don't ask, don't tell."

One sympathetic ear for me in those days was Bill Yetman, a staffer in Lily Munro's office, which was in the same building as O'Neil's ministry. A gay man himself, Yetman was a key factor in drawing me out of my shell and enlarging my network. He would take me to Bemelmans on Bloor Street, a straight bar but one with a big mixed crowd after work on Friday nights.

So I was living the gay life and systematically bringing people into the loop on a need-to-know basis. When people ask me when I came out, I say: "I am always coming out." But I suppose the signature moment for me was in 1994, when Lyn McLeod, then leader of the provincial Liberals, reversed herself in the vote on same-sex benefits in the Legislature. In response, Gordon Floyd (who had been a senior aide in Stuart Smith's office) and I formed an organization called Liberals for Equality Rights. As a spokesperson for the group, which numbered dozens and dozens, I did a series of TV interviews on the day of the vote. I remember calling my mother to give her a heads-up. "If there is anyone you haven't told already, now is the time." She understood and, as was customary, expressed no dismay at the implication for herself.

* * *

In September 1990, however, that moment was long in the future. My mind was elsewhere in the days following the government's defeat. In fact, I was in a bit of a daze. As a distraction, I attended some movies at the Toronto International Film Festival. (I got the tickets thanks to O'Neil's position as the minister of culture.) At the opening screening of *Bethune* at the Eglinton theatre, I approached the premier-elect, Bob Rae. "I'm one of your victims,"

I told him. I don't recall his exact words in response, but his eyes clearly said "Fuck you, who cares!" as mine would have if our roles were reversed.

How could I be angry at him? So ill-prepared were the New Democrats to form a government that they asked for an extra week or two of transition. That gave all of us political staffers more paid time to practise "Would you like fries with that" as we joked about our coming employment at Swiss Chalet.

CHAPTER THREE

1990s

I was adrift after the 1990 election, not immediately sure where to turn. I needed to find employment, that much was sure. But let's just say that I had not won many competitions for a normal job by that point in my life. Small business was the future career path I had settled on, so I began a passive search for opportunities alongside my recently retired father. I spent the better part of the first year post-election involved in volunteer efforts while relying on my government severance to pay the rent.

Fortunately for me, I joined an organizing committee at the AIDS Committee of Toronto (ACT), where the annual From All Walks of Life fundraiser was being planned. For several years, I had made the walk my primary community activity, and until today I have made AIDS my voluntary and philanthropic priority. In those days, the public awareness of the disease saw crowds of more than ten thousand gather for the walk, raising $1 million or more.

In the 1990s, I was deeply touched by the public response to the AIDS crisis. And it was a real crisis. As an "out" person living in the Gay Village, it was impossible not to know people who succumbed, often rapidly, to AIDS. These people truly came from all walks of life, including work colleagues, political allies, lovers, and friends. A peaceful memorial in Barbara Hall Park, next to the 519 Community Centre in the village, honours their memory.

In this same period, my high-school friend Richard Maeda and I bought a film-processing shop in the Gay Village with some help from my father, who was both our partner and banker. The store was atop the "Steps," an iconic location at the corner of Church and Wellesley that served as a magnet and safe haven for gay people across Canada. Our store was named Prints on Church. The shop was located directly beside the Second Cup coffee shop, which led the entire chain in sales thanks to a largely gay customer base. I would say that the biggest challenge our customers faced was making their way to our front door through a wonderful assortment of the gaybourhood's finest.

The purchase of the store was partially financed by my father, who had sold his trucking business in 1989 and had begun investing some of the proceeds. Beyond providing financing, my father really got involved in the business. As was customary for my dad, he rolled up his sleeves to help refurbish the shop and install new equipment. We were just building up steam toward opening more kiosk stores that would feed film volume to our well-equipped shop when, on New Year's Day in 1992, my father suffered a massive stroke. He hung on for another seven months at Brampton Peel Memorial, with the ability to only move his eyes. But he finally succumbed on August 5, 1992. He was just sixty-two years old; I was twenty-eight. His death hit me hard. We had not been estranged in previous years, but there is no question that our relationship had flourished with his involvement in the film-shop business. For once I had him free of the preoccupations that come with a business that involves several thousand rolling wheels. And then he was gone.

It was an open-casket funeral, and I remember that just before the casket was finally closed, my stepmother took me aside, removed my father's custom-made diamond ring from his finger and handed it to me. I wore that ring with pride and a sense of responsibility for my family, and later, when the laws of the country changed to allow me to marry another man, it became my wedding ring, a function it would serve not once but twice.

The film-shop business prospered, thanks to the steady hand of Richard, my Burnhamthorpe Collegiate schoolmate. Richard was an auto mechanic, and I guess you could say I was a political mechanic. But both of us were keen to run a small business. His personality and genuine warmth made him a natural for the retail business. Our customers, who came from across a wide base, liked and trusted Richard a lot. He is a good athlete and gifted hockey player and for several years represented our business in the gay hockey league, despite his obvious deficiencies as a straight person.

We had looked at a variety of businesses around the GTA, from downtown coffee shops to suburban tire stores. Then, by pure serendipity, we learned that a film shop was up for sale in my own neighbourhood, the Gay Village. I ended up in the rare situation where my out identity was an asset, not an impediment. We offered discretion to gay customers who didn't want prying eyes to see their photographs. The shop we bought was already established as the trusted place to go, but we expanded the business and attracted customers from further afield, including regulars who came from as far away as Barrie. We had a clear understanding of the Criminal Code and did not test its boundaries, but there were lots of nude photos to be processed.

One roll I never believed I would process quickly got very personal. The profile of an image could be made out many minutes before the visual proof presented itself at the other end of the machine in the form of a processed picture. Astonishingly, it was a then-lover of mine in full birthday suit with party favours deployed. Unmistakable. When the gentleman who had brought the film to my store returned less than an hour later, he found some of his pictures were missing. He likely assumed it was censorship on my part and not reputation management.

At best, the film shop provided us with a modest livelihood. Richard stayed with it for a long time. For me, it provided some community name recognition, which is useful for an aspiring politician. So were the lessons about maintaining good relations with customers and meeting a payroll and paying huge rent and commercial property taxes. But the gradual digitization of film in the late 1990s began to erode the business and eat into our profit margin. We finally closed it in 2001, one month before the 9/11 terrorist attacks. The experience has given me a lot of sympathy for the plight of the store owner today and important insights into the strength of retail-level relationships. My understanding of the power of those relationships later influenced government policies in areas such as pharmacy.

* * *

The 1990s were also marked by my introduction to the drug scene. For much of the decade, I was high, or I wanted to be, although I can vividly recall my disgust the time I first saw cocaine at a party, with my boyfriend of the time keen to partake. Fast forward less than two years to the period after my father's death and my aversion to drugs like cocaine had diminished, shall we say. In the years that followed, I used a whole range of drugs, both ingested and inhaled, but I never injected anything other than a flu shot. Prescription drugs or over-the-counter pain relief pills have never been my thing, either. Somewhat surprisingly, I also refrained from using sleeping pills to hasten the transition to sleep after a night of bingeing on drugs. It was the druggie take on the advice my father once gave me about drinking: "If you are going to be a man at night, you'd better be a man in the morning."

The so-called gay party scene consisted of raves with hot-and-cold running nubile young men. Mostly everyone was egged on by ecstasy, the preferred drug of the scene. But for me cocaine was never too far away. Sadly, as much as I might try to conjure up some exciting notion of sex, drugs, and rock-and-roll, I have to admit that the lion's share of all the cocaine I ever took was consumed alone in search of escape. Perhaps surprisingly, throughout this time I maintained a variety of day jobs that required me to function at a high level.

Quitting anything can be tough, and cocaine had a real grip on me. The lowest point came when my cocaine tastes trended from powder to crack. (Ironically, this also turned out to be the drug of choice for my opponent in the 2010 mayoral campaign, Rob Ford, although he denied it even when he was caught smoking crack on video.) In my experience, the crack-cocaine high is unrivalled in its euphoria. Unfortunately, the other big characteristic of crack is that the high doesn't last. So, while it might be true that you can *get* high cheap on crack, you can't *stay* high cheap. "They should just call this stuff MORE," a fellow user cracked to me. Crack has a decidedly addictive allure; the high comes quickly, and it puts the brain on notice for more, more, and still more. If you have the money, you could easily smoke through a thousand dollars a day chasing the euphoria of that first high.

My good fortune came in the form of an intervention from my "little brother," Sean Kirkey, whom I first met when we were matched through Big Brothers much, much earlier when he was eleven. As an adult in the 1990s, he reminded me that marijuana could be an off-ramp drug. While not coming anywhere close to matching the euphoria of crack, it could at least settle the brain's restlessness. Kicking the powder cocaine habit was also difficult for me. I had many false starts on the path to sobriety, aided by professional help, willpower, and cardio exercise in numerous forms. I discovered running and realized a liberation previously unknown to me. For a period of more than half a year, I also refrained from alcohol, as a couple of martinis would prove to be triggers. For the first time in my life, I also found the appeal of religion, especially the concept of forgiveness. Although I never took to organized religion, I have to thank Rev. Brent Hawkes, senior pastor at Metropolitan Community Church of Toronto, for his comfort and support and his abiding calm.

While my drug usage was known somewhat to my friends and some of my family, it was a well-kept secret from the rest of the world until 2006, when, in my role as minister of health, I attended the annual Courage to Come Back awards ceremony, sponsored by the Centre for Addiction and Mental Health (CAMH). The awards honoured people in recovery from mental health issues and addiction. As I reviewed profiles of those to be honoured later that evening, I knew that, if I was going to be true to myself, I had to come out about my own past drug use. I knew it was a big moment because I got jumpy, a bit nervous in the way I always did before a hockey game but rarely ever before a speech. Sitting at the centre table and looking up at the stage and especially those giant letters spelling out COURAGE, I was nearly bouncing in my seat, at once excited and trepidatious about the great unburdening and wanting to get on with it. "As one who has seen the wrong side of too many sunrises," I began. The declaration was admittedly obscure; to the untrained ear, it just blended in with the standard three or four minutes of political bumph that a fellow like me is expected to deliver in an opening act role. But since I was speaking to an audience of one thousand or more and the moment was captured live on Rogers 10, I fully expected the story to emerge. I just didn't know quite how. Call it a soft launch, if you will.

As it happened, one of those attending that night was veteran and savvy *Toronto Star* reporter Robin Harvey. So I wasn't surprised — a bit nervous, yes, but not surprised — when she contacted me the next day. With a sensitivity rarely shown by the media, she asked if I would like to expand on my words the night before. In the interview, I admitted to her that I had used "party drugs" in the past, without being specific, and I added: "When

I saw that word 'COURAGE' so large behind on the screen, it really made me realize it would really not be right to mount the podium and make the traditional greeting. So I said what was in my heart. I left the room a better person. It was liberating. If it comes back to haunt me, so be it."

I have frequently told closeted gay people that they need to come out to feel the liberation that comes with it. Telling the world my secret about my past drug usage would prove no less cathartic. And it was all the more powerful because I did it entirely of my own accord, under no threat of exposure or innuendo.

That was all fine and well for me. But what about my boss and his government? Luckily for me, Dalton McGuinty is one of the most decent and thoughtful people I have ever met. If people get bored of hearing that about him, too bad. It's true. On this occasion and a couple of others where he might have been ticked off about my distracting disclosures or behaviour, he called me only to ask about my well-being. It was one of the fewer than ten phone conversations we ever had. Afterward, he issued this statement: "I hope that [Smitherman] will serve as an inspiration to others in Ontario and wherever else who find themselves in a grip of drug addiction."

The early reviews were for the most part positive, with journalists and others applauding my courage. But the greatest rewards for me were the very personal expressions from those who took strength from my story in their own battles with addiction, and since I had been down that road I was glad to help even one person. Each story of recovery nourishes mine.

A certain cross-section of the media wasn't satisfied with my use of the vague expression "party drugs" to define my choice of stimulants, but I took full advantage of the *Toronto Sun*'s Christina Blizzard to brush aside gnarly follow-up questions. Blizzard, not my biggest fan at the best of times, was pissed off about the sympathetic press I was getting. She said enough was enough and we didn't need the gory details. Every time I was subsequently asked to elaborate on my drug usage, I merely told people I was with Christina Blizzard on this one.

I recall one person getting in my grill because I had shaded my past drug use with a gay connection. It was at a small group session organized by my friend Andreas Souvalotis, at McKinsey's Toronto headquarters. McKinsey, the multinational consulting firm, was hosting a reception for visitors to Toronto for a meeting of the Young Presidents Organization, and

Andreas, an avid YPOer, brought a cluster of gay CEOs together. Among them was Joel Simkhai, founder of Grindr, the gay hook-up app. (He has since sold it and is now undoubtedly a gazillionaire.)

"I see no reason why you had to hide behind the gay community to mask your addiction," Simkhai said very pointedly. I enjoyed the exchange. I like to think I would have done a similar thing if I were in his shoes. He was right to note that in order to deflect attention from a conversation about specific substances I used language to define a scene. And, as I noted earlier, the reality is that I mostly used drugs alone.

I certainly think my willingness to ask the unasked questions has been a valuable asset for me, and in turn I usually tried to answer penetrating questions with candour. But not in this case, where I was calculated and used vagueness and Christina Blizzard to neatly zip the bag back up. Calculating as it may have been, I still think it was the right thing to do. Other than feeding my enemies and providing a few minutes of chum for the press, if I had been more specific, I would have been subjected to unhelpful distractions and unwittingly exposed others. Worse yet, my mother would have had to live down a few more tough days.

People speak about regrets, and elsewhere in this book I address some of mine. Indeed, there's lots about my drug use that I wish I could undo, especially the pain I put myself and my loved ones through. But it must also be said that, by and large, even when dealing with people on the so-called margins of society, I found them to be honourable. As strange as it may seem, there were elements of the drug community that supported one another. There is, after all, a lot of trust involved when a mobile drug delivery service drops by your house, sometimes twice in the same evening.

* * *

Even while I was helping to run a small business in the 1990s, politics was never far from my mind. One of my sideline efforts, with Gordon Floyd, was Liberals for Equality Rights, the group we started in response to the Legislature debate over same-sex benefits and Lyn McLeod's flip-flop from support to opposition on the equality principle. Premier Bob Rae's government had introduced Bill 167, which would accord the same benefits, rights, and obligations to gay couples as were already enjoyed by straight couples;

yet Rae cynically chose not to whip his majority behind the bill because he saw an opportunity to blame its failure on McLeod's Liberals. At that point in his mandate (near the end of his fourth year), Rae was more interested in stopping the then-ascendant Liberals than in advancing the cause of equality. And he succeeded.

McLeod had campaigned in favour of gay rights during a by-election in Ian Scott's downtown Toronto riding, which would later become my riding. (Tim Murphy was elected to replace Scott, keeping the riding for the Liberals.) But McLeod's resolve softened under terrible attacks from various old-timers in her caucus. These attacks intensified after the Conservatives used gay equality as a wedge issue to pummel the Liberals in another by-election in Victoria-Haliburton.

At a public meeting on Valentine's Day 1994 convened by NDP gay activist Bob Gallagher, who was working with Rae on the bill, I stood and made the point plainly to all of those who had gathered: "There are no Liberal votes in this bill." I was giving them fair warning that, if the government wasn't committed to passing its own bill and subjected it to a free vote in the Legislature instead, it was destined to fail.

Bob Rae's political calculations aside, I was of course deeply disappointed, both in my own party and its leader. But I also learned a valuable lesson about how communities can be cynically exploited even when the matter at hand is a question of principle. During the gay-rights debate, I went to Queen's Park to lobby Liberal MPPs on the bill, including Murray Elston, health minister in Peterson's government and one of a bunch of "grumpy old men" who actively undermined McLeod within the caucus. Elston didn't take kindly to my commentary about what was going on. He angrily pulled me into his office, where we engaged in a forceful back-and-forth. I think I called him a "fucker," and I sure hope he remembers it like that, too. The bill was defeated on second reading in the Legislature on June 9, 1994, with only three Liberal MPPs in support of it. I will always remember the tension in the air when Hugh O'Neil, my old mentor, visited me that day in the members' gallery only minutes before he would cast a No vote. "Sorry, I can't be there for you on this one, brother," O'Neil said.

After the bill's defeat, thousands of gay people took to the streets of Toronto, egged on at least in part by their mistreatment inside Queen's Park.

At the annual Pride Parade, the Liberal presence included me, Bill Graham, Dr. Carolyn Bennett, and Sheila Copps.

(To this day, I am rankled by the image of Legislative security staff putting on rubber gloves before clearing the galleries.) The Liberals, having failed to put the onus on Rae and the New Democrats to use their majority to pass the bill, were the target of the crowd's rage. Cries of "Equality Now, Lyn's a Cow" rang out from the corner of Bay and Wellesley streets.

I seriously considered quitting the party after that, but I first called David Peterson to explain my dilemma. He urged me to stay in the party and fight the good fight from inside. "You've been a member of the party long before Lyn and will be a member long after her," he said. I took the advice and put my energy to work as election day chair for Dr. Carolyn Bennett, then involved in a by-election that got rolled into the 1995 general election, which swept Mike Harris and the Conservatives to power. Bennett lost. So did Tim Murphy in Toronto Centre–Rosedale, which opened the door to my own debut as a candidate four years later.

Just prior to this, I had also gotten very involved in Bill Graham's successful campaign for Parliament in 1993. (Finally, after two tries — a drubbing at the hands of David Crombie in 1984, and a heartbreaking squeaker loss in the free trade election of 1988 — Graham beat the Conservative incumbent, Hon. David MacDonald, by almost fifteen thousand votes.) I had high hopes I would get an offer to move to Ottawa afterward as Graham's executive assistant. But, not too surprisingly, that job went to one of Graham's former law students, the talented Bill Charnetski.

* * *

Luckily for me, however, in a similar time frame, John Webster, a prominent Liberal whom I had known during the Peterson days, introduced me to Barbara Hall, a city councillor who was planning to run for mayor in 1994 against the incumbent, June Rowlands. I knew Hall's husband, Max Beck; he and I had worked together as co-chairs of the From All Walks of Life fundraising event for AIDS. But I had not met Hall herself before then. Indeed, as a New Democrat, she was on the other team. She had run against Ian Scott in the 1985 provincial election.

But for the 1994 mayoral election, she was trying to build a bigger tent, encompassing Liberals and Conservatives as well as New Democrats. "Everyone tells me I have to do things differently if I am going to run for mayor," she said during our first meeting, in her warm and comfortable Cabbagetown home. "And you're part of the different way of doing things."

I signed on as her campaign aide, a combination of scheduler, driver, and psychologist. It was an immersive experience in local politics, and I learned a lot from her. We were like participants in an arranged marriage where each of us knew our place. But, by good fortune, our very different personalities managed to click. It helped that Barbara and I have two things in common: a taste for hard work and for jujubes. Otherwise, we couldn't have been more different. Until today, I still struggle while waiting for Barbara to finish her sentences. But when she does offer her thoughts, they are always considered, caring, and wise. I think of Barbara as a big sister. She and Max have been a consistent and loving presence in my life and in the lives of my children. Max was also my husband Christopher's most treasured resource in figuring out the role of the politician's spouse.

The Hall campaign had a superstructure of senior advisers reflecting the three political parties — the likes of Senator Keith Davey (Liberal), Libby Burnham (Progressive Conservative), and Michael Lewis (New Democrat, brother of Stephen and son of David). As a staffer, I was on a rung well below these folks. But as the campaign evolved and my commitment showed, my influence grew. I recall Hall proposing a short walk through

Cabbagetown to get a bag of jujubes. In addition to sharing the candy, she wanted to share the news that tomorrow's papers would show her trailing behind both Rowlands and Gerry Meinzer, a venture capitalist with zero political experience, in the mayoral race. "Don't overreact to this, George," she counselled me. She was right.

The campaign began to turn in our favour in the last few weeks. Rowlands, a great progressive in her earlier days, had not been a popular mayor. She approached the job like a bureaucrat, and she often appeared clueless and out of touch during her three years in office. On her watch, for example, the pop group Barenaked Ladies was banned from performing at City Hall Square on New Year's Eve because a bureaucrat decided their name "objectified women." Worst of all, Rowlands appeared not to notice the racially inspired Yonge Street riot that took place virtually outside her office door. In short, Rowlands came across as an old fuddy-duddy, while Hall appeared more modern. Hall was a progressive, even a lefty, but she also supported the Olympic bid, which was out of favour with the left. That point of distinction was symbolic and significant.

Rowlands also failed to understand that a big part of the mayor's job is to get out in the community to celebrate ethnic and neighbourhood events. Hall never shirked that duty; she called on more events in Toronto than previously thought possible. We also got a boost from an editorial endorsement in the *Toronto Star* on the final weekend. We printed tens of thousands of the editorial and distributed the copies around the city, especially in North Toronto, literally before the ink even had a chance to dry. In the end, Hall won with 43 percent of the vote to Rowlands's 36 percent. (Meinzer was third with 13 percent.)

After the election, I accepted a job on Hall's staff as director of operations, splitting duties with the fantastic Jennifer Morris, who served as director of policy. I stayed for two years, during which time Hall helped to redefine our city. Among her notable achievements was the "Two Kings" policy, which rezoned some four hundred acres of "employment lands" around the King and Parliament and King and Spadina intersections and allowed residential and commercial development. This helped to attract $8 billion in investment to the city and transformed an area of derelict factories and warehouses, leftovers from the Industrial Revolution. While some argued that we should be trying to attract industrial employment back to the city, Hall recognized that those days were never coming back.

Elsewhere, three different processes were concluded that led to the re-emergence of our city in historic ways. Hall was there the night Damon Stoudamire was drafted by the nascent Toronto Raptors basketball team, and she welcomed him and his family to Toronto. The Raptors played initially in the SkyDome, an unsuitable venue for basketball, while the search was on for a more permanent home. And Hall appointed me to lead the Raptors Stadium Project, as we called it. It helped that my former boss, David Peterson, was the Raptors' first chairman. Through him, I met Ralph Lean, Peterson's law partner and a key part of the fledgling Raptors organization. (Lean would later assist in my mayoral campaign.)

I was with Hall, who before her election as mayor had served as the chair of the land-use planning committee, when John Bitove, the Raptors' CEO, called and asked for her preference of the sites the Raptors were considering for construction of the new arena. Hall suggested she preferred the old post office building site at Bay and Lakeshore. The Raptors were also eyeing a site at Bay and Dundas (now the home of a Canadian Tire store and Ryerson University's business school). On my first visit with Hall to see the Lakeshore site, I remember having to run the car up a curb on the south side of the building by Lakeshore just to be able to find a place to stop. It's a far cry from what has emerged in the twenty years since.

Eventually, with an assist from the city through the transfer of a small triangle of land for a price of $1.8 million, the post office site was chosen. And when the Raptors were taken over by Maple Leaf Sports and Entertainment (MLSE), the new arena became home for both the Raptors and the Leafs. I was lucky to attend the last Leafs game at Maple Leaf Gardens and the first at the new arena, then called the Air Canada Centre.

Other highlights in Hall's mayoral term included the planning for the Bathurst Quay neighbourhood, the development around Fort York, and the future neighbourhood around the old Woodbine race track. Hall's legacy, achieved in only three years in office, is remarkable. Credit also belongs to the city's planning staff, led by Robert Millward, and council, which worked mostly as a team under Hall's leadership.

Besides having a direct hand in the physical transformation of the city, Hall also changed the *style* of politics at city hall. Prior to her mayoralty, city hall was sharply polarized between left and right, with many issues on the seventeen-person council decided by nine-to-eight votes. Hall set out to change this with a consultative approach. She believed that whatever time was seemingly lost at the beginning by talking to a wide range of people was compensated for at the other end by the benefits of consensus. That model lends itself to collective victories. Hall's adage, "I know of few good things that happened by one person working alone," rubbed off on those around her. She singlehandedly surmounted the philosophical divide on council that was reflected by Councillor Tom Jakobek, a weird right-winger who preferred confrontation to consensus. Hall outmanoeuvered him and, rather than nine-to-eight votes, she started to win eleven-to-six and even twelve-to-five. She accomplished this by winning over independents like Howard Joy, the eccentric Kay Gardner, and the colourful Chris Korwin-Kuczynski to vote alongside lefties like Pam McConnell, Kyle Rae, and Peter Tabuns, as well as Liberals like Mario Silva.

Hall also tackled the bureaucracy, which was incredibly siloed when she became mayor, with fourteen fiercely independent departments. The closest thing to someone being in overall charge was a guy named Herb Pirk, the long-time director of parks and recreation, who had acquired the power to set the regular agenda for the "meeting of equals." There was no city manager and very little co-operation between departments. Each one of them was free to build its own communications infrastructure, for instance. With approval and lots of engagement from council, Hall streamlined the whole operation with four overarching commissioners, themselves operating as a team. While the model was imperfect, it was at least a step in the right direction.

It was a difficult time for the city. We were just emerging from the recession of the early 1990s and city revenues were in decline. Then Mike Harris arrived at Queen's Park and began filling in unfinished subway tunnels, cancelling needed social housing, reducing rates of social support for the most vulnerable, and wreaking havoc with political boundaries. (We are watching a replay of this today with the Doug Ford government at Queen's Park.) Tom Jakobek, one of the craziest politicians I have ever met, was the budget chief at the time. He was a tremendously manipulative individual. Hall had to work the votes to protect against his proposed spending cuts on programs like seniors' dental care and the arts. One of the great joys of my time at city hall was serving as Hall's point person on the budget and conspiring with

At Gay Pride with Bill Graham and Pam McConnell, my local political colleagues and accomplices.

Councillor Pam McConnell, a woman who knew how to read a budget from her days at the school board. Hall's council made tough decisions in those budgets but always agonized over impacts to vulnerable people.

During Hall's mayoralty, I also got my first taste of the nastiness that comes with taking smoking out of public places. And when a Cabbagetown restaurateur refused to serve Hall in protest over the proposed ban, I took it personally. That event remained close to my thoughts a decade later when I was health minister and championed the Smoke-Free Ontario Act, which would bring an end to smoking in enclosed public spaces in Ontario.

One interesting footnote from the Hall era: during my time working for the mayor, I had responsibility for the Toronto Film and Television Office, which was responsible for coordinating location shooting around the city. Ordinarily, the purpose of the office is to facilitate filmmakers and help make Toronto an attractive place to make movies and television shows. But during my time at city hall, the Paul Bernardo trial took place just a few steps away at the provincial courthouse. It was a complete shit show, with major television networks from the United States as well as Canada camped out in ramshackle fashion in front of the courthouse. So I recommended to the mayor that we have the film office tackle the unseemly mess of satellite trucks by coordinating their positions and maintaining order. Of course, in doing so we incurred the wrath of critics who said we were legitimizing the sensationalism around the evil Bernardo. It was a good lesson for me: you can't please all the people, ever.

In 1996, one year before Hall's mayoral term ended, I was lured away from her office to work for David Collenette, then minister of national defence but also the "political minister" for Toronto. Collenette was a partisan guy who came up through the ranks, and it seemed like an exciting opportunity for me at the time. Plus, by nature I have a restlessness and curiosity that always makes me open to new things. Ironically, on the very day Barbara Hall and Max Beck were to host a going-away party for me at their home, Collenette resigned. (The reason given for the resignation was an ethical breach: he had written a letter on behalf of a constituent to the Immigration and Refugee Board. But the federal government was also embroiled in a scandal over the beating death of a Somali teenager at the hands of Canadian peacekeepers, so it was deemed convenient for Collenette to step aside, although he soon got back into cabinet.)

Getting the call about Collenette's resignation over lunch, I naively assumed I was sitting on some good inside info. So I placed a call to Senator David Smith, a political Mr. Fixit for Prime Minister Jean Chrétien. "Smitherman," he said without inviting a word, "you now work for Herb Gray." *Click.* I laugh out loud when I think about how wet behind the ears I was thinking I was going to tell the well-connected "Smitty," as he is known, something he didn't know! (Coincidentally, Smitty was also my father's nickname.)

Gray was the senior Ontario political minister, a role commensurate with his unmatched parliamentary longevity. Later, he was bestowed the honorific Right Honourable, a title typically reserved for a prime minister, in recognition of his being the third-longest-serving MP in Canada's history. He was also the first-ever Jewish cabinet minister in Ottawa. I lasted a total of only about six months working for Gray, but I learned a lot in that time. I saw how Collenette and Gray managed power differently, and I met people like Eugene Lang and Jason Grier, who made lasting impressions on me and became good friends. Grier went on to work for me and serve as president of my riding association. But the fact was that, through no fault of Gray's, back in the mid-1990s no one in Ottawa cared much about Toronto.

The country had just emerged from the near-death experience of the 1995 Quebec referendum, so all the focus was on that province.

I read the writing on the wall and returned to Hall's side to run her 1997 campaign for mayor of the new "megacity" against the media-anointed front-runner, North York mayor Mel Lastman. The megacity had been created by Premier Mike Harris with the forced amalgamation of the old City of Toronto and the other five lower-tier municipalities (Etobicoke, Scarborough, North York, York, and East York) that made up Metropolitan Toronto. The campaign pitted Hall, supported by most of the other outgoing lower-tier mayors, against Lastman. Because of his longevity in office (he had been mayor of North York for a quarter-century), his populist veneer, and his out-sized personality (embellished by appearances in ads for the appliance store he owned), Lastman had a huge profile as a cornball who gets stuff done. So it was an uphill battle for Hall from the start. But we campaigned hard, as only a candidate like Hall can, and we had no problem raising money.

Hall gained support from people involved in the arts, environmentalists, and others who appreciated the job she had done as mayor of the old City of Toronto. We could have raised $7 million for the campaign, but municipal regulations limited us to spending just $1.5 million, which ruled out a heavy advertising campaign. (That's a wonky throwback rule that always prevents mayoral campaigns befitting the scale of the amalgamated city.) Accordingly, we sought attention in other ways. For example, we decided to do our campaign kick-off not only in the morning but also right under Lastman's nose, at the North York Arts Centre (since renamed the Toronto Arts Centre), one of his legacies (actually a white elephant) as mayor of North York.

Hall arrived bright and energized for the morning event by subway and was greeted by more than five hundred cheering supporters. Among those introducing Hall that day was a young North York high-school student named Abid Malik, who later served as one of my most able and loyal staffers during my time as a cabinet minister.

It was a very complex campaign, the first of its kind to be run across the entire amalgamated city. As sentimentalists, we established offices in all six of the former lower-tier municipalities, and Hall attracted support from the previous mayors of Scarborough (Frank Faubert), York (Frances Nunziata), and East York (Michael Prue). Amalgamation was a *fait accompli* by then, so we did not explicitly campaign against it. But we picked up support from those who had opposed the idea. Mike Harris himself was a polarizing figure, and Lastman was seen at the time as being too close to him. (That changed later when Lastman publicly called Harris a "liar.") On the other hand, Lastman could appeal to suburban voters on the basis that he was one of them, unlike the downtown-living former mayor of the old City of Toronto. We countered that Hall would be more effective at bringing everyone together. In the end, Hall managed to win the wards in York and East York and in the southern parts of Etobicoke and Scarborough.

In the dying days of the campaign, we got a boost from a gaffe by Lastman, who declared that there were "no homeless in North York." (A day later, a homeless woman was found dead at a North York gas station.) We had momentum on our side, but it was not enough. Hall lost by barely five percentage points. If the race had been a week or two longer, she might have beaten him and Toronto might have been spared the embarrassment of a mayor who openly raised his fear of travelling to Africa because he thought his destiny might be a boiling pot. (Admittedly, afterward he did say sorry some fifty times in one sentence.)

* * *

After the 1997 municipal election, my dear friend Libby Burnham, a net-worked Conservative loyalist who hailed from New Brunswick and whom I had the good fortune to meet in the 1994 Hall campaign, invited me to lead the grassroots campaign to save the Wellesley Hospital, where she served as board chair. Located at Wellesley and Sherbourne, the hospital had been targeted for closing by Mike Harris's Health Services Restructuring Commission, with its services to be transferred south to St. Mike's. The Wellesley was not your ordinary hospital.

Though located south of Bloor Street, it had a north-of-Bloor pedigree that rose up to meet the challenge of attending to the diverse populations that surrounded it. It was a glimpse for me into the unique pleasure and challenge of effectively representing the richest and the poorest at the same time, a privilege I was to gain later as MPP for Toronto Centre–Rosedale. The hospital had sown deep connections with the surrounding community since it began operating in 1911 behind the stone fence that still partially stands on that corner. In 1996, it merged with the Central Hospital, just down Sherbourne. Together these hospitals were open to their neighbouring communities, including the gay population, marginalized street people, sex-trade workers, low-income tenants, and new immigrants. They were also in the forefront of the fight against AIDS. There was heartfelt fear that St. Mike's, as a Catholic hospital, would be less receptive to gay people, many of whom have a challenging relationship with the Catholic Church.

The Wellesley's openness to marginalized communities had built strong community loyalty, and the breadth of the health care offerings was impressive — ranging from the Ross Tilly Burn Unit to a mobile health bus for homeless care, a well-regarded birthing centre, and leading research into arthritis. The Wellesley had also been one of the primary teaching sites for nurses, and even today Wellesley nurses dot the landscape of Ontario health care. That said, not every hospital with those loyalties could leverage them. That's where I found the special sauce of the Wellesley Hospital: the ability of a very large organization to find strength from its community roots.

The writing was on the wall for the Wellesley. The well-regarded CEO had fled, and the Wellesley was being led on an interim basis by a practising physician who lacked sophistication in matters of politics and organizing communities. She was no match for Libby Burnham and her board, which included seasoned community veterans Dennis Magill, Aileen Meagher (a former Larry Grossman staffer), Tony DiPede, and Don Rickard. Together they crafted the campaign to save the hospital and the "Staying Alive" slogan. Rickard, a lawyer, made sure that the campaign did not go afoul in the use of public funds.

Among a variety of tactics, we got thousands of signatures on a petition and, in true downtown activist style, staged a spirited protest march to push the petitions on a gurney along Wellesley Street to the offices of the Health Services Restructuring Commission (HSRC), at the corner of Bay and Wellesley. The protest was a bit borderline, as we did not have a permit and there was a lot of anger among the hundreds of marchers. I recall at one point giving Dennis Magill a knowing look as if to say, "Let's keep our eye on things to make sure they don't get out of hand." It was in this heated environment that the HSRC's Ron Sapsford, my future deputy minister at the Ministry of Health, arrived to receive the petition in the lobby of the building. Sensing correctly that the protesters who had gathered were very angry, he was polite but, in my recollection, quite petrified.

In the end, we were not successful and the Wellesley Hospital was closed, but not before the board successfully championed the idea before the courts that the capital that was contributed to the hospital by the community should not be transferred to St. Mike's. We won that fight to the credit of Libby Burnham, who showed us all that you can fight city hall (so to speak). That created a legacy for the Wellesley that was used to create a long-term care home, a supportive housing facility, a park on the site (the latter two bearing the names of DiPede and Magill), and the Wellesley Health Institute, which continues to champion research focused on urban health.

As a minor concession to the neighbourhood, we were also promised an urgent care facility. This emerged over time as the Sherbourne Health Centre, located on the former Central Hospital site adjacent to Allan Gardens. Progress was slow, however, and in my first term as an opposition MPP at Queen's Park I spent lots of time speaking to Tony Clement, my predecessor as health minister, to move it forward. Today it houses critical services and programs for the same communities that the Wellesley strived to help.

Considering that tough things were said about the risks to the gay community faced by the loss of Wellesley, St. Mike's CEO Jeff Lauzon moved promptly to name Dr. Phil Berger, a highly regarded Wellesley physician leader, as the head of family health at St. Mike's. Further steps taken by Lauzon stand out as a great example of the surviving organization's openness to adapting its own culture in order to accommodate the needs of the perceived loser in the merger battle. Full credit to St. Mike's for taking advantage of the opportunity to make itself better by instilling the best of the Wellesley's very proud history and values. I even forgive Lauzon for making my closest friend Jason Grier the first person he fired at the Wellesley, where Jason, having left Ottawa, was serving as director of public affairs.

Many years later, when I was minister of health and Ron Sapsford was my deputy, I often invited people into my office to show them the Wellesley boardroom chair that I was granted for my service in the campaign to save the hospital. I was letting them know that, while I was very nice (good cop), Sapsford (bad cop) had even closed my local hospital.

* * *

After the Wellesley campaign, my mind returned to the upcoming provincial election in 1999. My riding, then known as Toronto Centre–Rosedale, was represented by a Conservative, Al Leach, the minister of municipal affairs. He had won a tight three-way race in 1995 against the Liberal incumbent (Tim Murphy) and NDP candidate Brent Hawkes. They were all within a thousand votes of each other. But by 1999, the Harris Conservatives were deeply unpopular in Toronto. This was an opportunity for me, and politics is all about opportunity. You have to pick your spots. And in my political career, I have picked some right and some wrong.

I had long ago concluded in my own mind that I would run. In 1995–96, I spent my days supporting Barbara Hall and trying to protect Toronto from Harris's cuts, especially those aimed at the poorest Ontarians. One day, while walking from city hall to my home in the Moss Park area, I came upon the depressing sight of a woman smoking crack in the stairwell of an old mansion turned rooming house at the corner of Sherbourne and Shuter. The Harris government had been pursuing an agenda of targeting marginalized street people and those on social assistance. Seeing this woman that night triggered something in me. "I'm going to run against Harris and work for that lady," I said to myself.

When it was time to revisit my decision and actually get to work I discovered (not entirely surprisingly) that I wasn't alone in my aspiration. James McPherson, a political unknown but the son of a doctor, was being advanced as a potential Liberal candidate by the Ontario Medical Association, the doctors union. The OMA had contracted a known Liberal organizer to help in McPherson's campaign. I was in Florida at my stepmother's home when I got wind that McPherson and his crowd were manoeuvering to take control of the Toronto Centre–Rosedale provincial riding association. I outmanoeuvered them by rallying my troops, beginning with a call to the unrivalled Wanda O'Hagan, yet another woman of distinction I had gotten to know through Barbara Hall's 1994 campaign. Wanda, along with her husband, Dick, a former aide to both Lester Pearson and Pierre Trudeau, and who died late last year, always stood by my side over my years in politics. On that day, she agreed to stand for president on our slate as we sought to take over the riding association. Friends Jason Grier, Tom Allison, Tom Jakobsh, and Guy Bethell also joined the team.

We aggressively knocked on fifteen thousand doors selling memberships and building my profile. "My name is George Smitherman," I would say. "I live and own a business in the riding. I worked for Barbara Hall at city hall and ran the campaign to save the Wellesley Hospital. Would you be willing to join the Liberal Party to help get rid of Mike Harris?" Over fourteen hundred people signed up and we submitted those memberships and the funds to go with them. My opponent didn't, so we had no real way to know how many memberships he was sitting on. In a riding executive meeting, we moved a motion to increase the annual membership fee from $10 to $25, which would make it much tougher for McPherson to function. He soon dropped out, never to be heard from again in the political arena. The Liberal Party later closed that loophole. Some people flattered me and Tom Allison by referring to it as the "Allison/Smitherman clause."

As a footnote, the best door I ever knocked on wasn't answered by a humpy naked dude, although that did happen occasionally. Rather, it was the door opened at 100 Wellesley Street East by a woman named Joyce Grigg, who traded in her NDP card for a Liberal one and until this very day serves as the heart and soul of Liberals in the east-downtown.

I had achieved a great deal of success in signing up members by knocking on all those doors, but I still couldn't count on winning the nomination. There was still one other potential opponent to be considered: Tim Murphy, the former Liberal MPP for the riding who had lost to Leach in 1995 after winning the riding in a by-election following Ian Scott's retirement. While Murphy no longer lived in the riding, he was rumoured to be considering the possibility of a comeback. (Such rumours persist in pretty much every election cycle.) Murphy and I had known each other for a long time and had campaigned together for Paul Martin in the federal leadership race in 1990. (Murphy later became chief of staff when Martin assumed the prime ministership.) Murphy had been one of just three Liberal MPPs to vote for Bill 167, the gay-rights bill, in 1994 and had taken it on the chin for the party's flip-flop in the subsequent general election. Luckily for me, Murphy chose to exercise his political skills by becoming president of the provincial party, and to the satisfaction of his family he continued to earn a serious living as a lawyer.

Now I had a clear run at the nomination, which I secured by acclamation in September of 1998 in the Betty Oliphant Theatre at the National Ballet School on Jarvis Street. Following a nominating speech by Dick O'Hagan, I delivered a rousing address, promising to take the fight to Al Leach in the coming campaign. That night, I posed for a photograph with

With Barbara Hall and the boxing gloves, at the nomination meeting for Toronto Centre–Rosedale, 1998. The beginning of my formal political career.

Barbara Hall, in what was a very early Liberal venture for her. I was wearing boxing gloves, showing my readiness to take Leach on.

But soon after that, Leach turned the campaign upside down by announcing he would not seek re-election. To replace him, the Tories recruited a star candidate, Durhane Wong-Rieger, a psychologist with a track record as an advocate for people who had contracted HIV and/or hepatitis C through tainted blood transfusions — a sad and terrible debacle in our history. A Chinese-Canadian woman with no baggage of her own from the Harris years, she was not nearly as easy a target as Leach. On the other hand, her complete lack of political experience made defending Mike Harris in downtown Toronto a little on the difficult side for her.

Further complicating matters was the entry of John Sewell into the race as an independent candidate. Sewell, the mayor of Toronto from 1978 to 1980, was a high-profile critic of the Harris government. (He had led the local campaign against amalgamation, along with Kathleen Wynne.) His candidacy threatened to split the anti-Harris vote. So did the running of NDP candidate Helen Breslauer, a university professor whose husband, Dr. Bob Frankford, had previously been an MPP and was highly regarded among his peers. But Sewell didn't have a party behind him. And Breslauer and the New Democrats still suffered from bad memories of the Rae regime.

Brent Hawkes's exit from partisan activities after the 1995 campaign further deflated them.

As the campaign unfolded, Wong-Rieger showed her inexperience with a disastrous decision to boycott all-candidates meetings other than those held in Rosedale. We rented a chicken costume (worn by John Zerucelli, later director of operations in Prime Minister Justin Trudeau's office) and showed up at an all-candidates meeting at All Saints Anglican Church at Dundas and Sherbourne to mock her. Sewell was outraged by this stunt, which is ironic because he had practised guerrilla theatre himself as a city councillor back in the early 1970s. I vividly recall seeing him go nose-to-nose in protest with Tom Allison, my campaign manager. Perhaps only All Saints could have hosted such a colourful exchange without a fuss. After the chicken's first appearance, the *National Post* ran a story and photo the next day. It is not often that local campaigns get noticed by the media, so I am still dining out on the story today, and by now Johnny Z is surely sick of me greeting him with an enthusiastic retelling.

As for Breslauer, the NDP candidate, she was not a forceful public speaker, so I contrasted well with her. The 519 Church Street Community, the physical heart of the gay community, has a history of hosting raucous all-candidates meetings, and I like raucous a lot. By 1999, I had attended several such meetings and had participated boisterously when provoked, such as any time the other party's candidate spoke. Coming one election after the same-sex benefits issue had dominated the local vote, there was still a political tension in the air that night at 519. In her opening remarks, Breslauer said: "Just six short weeks ago I was pleased to be nominated in this very room to be the NDP candidate." Following on her heels, I proclaimed: "Not six months ago in this very room, I was awarded the Tonya Harding Award by the Gay Hockey Association, and when I get to Queen's Park I promise not to be Miss Congeniality there, either."

The crowd loved the line, and Breslauer probably knew she was cooked at that moment.

Toronto Centre–Rosedale is an incredibly diverse riding in every way — ethnically, culturally, economically, and sexually. But I had a good story to tell that cut across these boundaries. I highlighted my work for Barbara Hall (who publicly endorsed me), my campaign to save Wellesley Hospital, my ties to the community (as both a resident and a business owner), and my strong opposition to the Harris government. That left no oxygen for the NDP or for Sewell.

I also took a new approach to campaigning, one that I profess until today is more realistic and effective when applied well. That is, voter *motivation* over voter *identification*. Campaign organizers have forever focused on the voter identification model, whereby political parties will hack and claw their way to each voter's attention and beg them to confess their loyalty (one way or the other). They use a few codes to capture what was derived from the encounter. Then on election day volunteers run to the doors (and phones, too) where the encounter led to the identification of a living, breathing Liberal. All fine and good, but minds change, people lie, volunteers mistake signals, and lists are terrible. So in many areas the stability of the data is so hit-and-miss that it is practically worthless. Instead, I concluded that, in areas where there were known to be lots of Liberals, the more achievable goal should be voter motivation.

Take a community like St. James Town, one of the densest in North America. Bounded by Wellesley, Howard, Sherbourne, and Parliament

As always, I'm chasing after Barbara Hall, who helped inspire me to run.

streets, it consists of nineteen high-rise buildings, including some public housing. It is ethnically diverse and working-class, with a high turnover in tenancies, and it is home to a lot of loyal Liberals. I used my resources to motivate them to get out and vote. That didn't mean we neglected to knock on doors and deliver pamphlets, but our practice was "knock and drop" rather than depend on hard voter identification.

To this end, I held multiple BBQs in the riding, using my stepfather's pickup truck to haul our BBQ kit. (One of these events, in Regent Park, attracted a young Somali refugee named Ahmed Hussen, who later became Canada's minister of citizenship and immigration.) We concentrated voter identification on neighbourhoods where the lists were better and the doors were close together. Fortunately, the largest enclave of closely bunched Victorian houses in North America is in Toronto Centre riding.

In the end, while Dalton McGuinty's Liberals lost province-wide in 1999, I won my riding quite handily with 39 percent of the vote to 30 percent for Wong-Rieger, 19 percent for Sewell, and 9 percent for Breslauer. (Interestingly, the headlines following the election focused not on me or my Tory opponent, but on Sewell. "Novice Liberal wins on renters' votes: Sewell surprised by defeat," said the *Globe*'s headline. "Sewell tries to swallow election defeat to Liberal," echoed the *Star*.) The only poll I noticeably lost (I lost others but didn't notice) was on Toronto Island, where I finished FOURTH, behind even the Tories. I decided then and there that the Islanders simply didn't know me, and I set out to improve my standing with them. With my team, we participated in the construction of housing on the Island, and I met my future executive assistant, Scott Lovell, while hanging drywall and shouldering enormous wheelbarrows full of building materials. (I was only thirty-five then!) In later elections, as the Islanders came to know me as a strong ally, my votes there improved a lot. One time, in trying to slight me for the compact size of my riding, a northerner scoffed: "You could walk from one end of your riding to the other in a day." Within a heartbeat, I replied: "You pay me a great compliment, sir, as the southern portion of my riding is an Island."

Everybody can recognize the complexity of representing giant swaths of territory in northern or rural ridings, but few acknowledge the complexity of representing neighbourhoods that have major language barriers and where issues can be dramatically different on opposite sides of the

A young Ahmed Hussen with my first Muslim supporter, Khadija Abdi.

same street, a contrast that can be seen in the Regent Park–Cabbagetown division on Gerrard Street, although I am proud to say it is much diminished today.

* * *

I was now, at age thirty-five and in my twentieth year in politics, an elected representative, the first-ever *openly* gay member of the Ontario Legislature (and, as I like to say, only the two-hundredth gay member in history!). And, as chance would have it, my maiden speech in the Legislature was on a gay-rights bill, which covered much of the same territory as the defeated 1994 legislation. What was different this time? In the intervening five years, the courts, citing the Charter of Rights, had instructed the provinces to change their laws to give same-sex partners the same benefits, rights, and obligations as their heterosexual counterparts. Jim Flaherty, the attorney general at the time, called it "the devil made me do it act," because the Conservative government of the day was clearly uncomfortable about bringing it forward. Jaime Watt, a friend of mine and Flaherty's, called me to ask if I could manage to bring the Liberals along to support the bill without complaint. I did, and I was given the honour of leading off the debate for

My first swearing-in as an MPP, 1999.

the Liberals. In so doing, I helped to close a lousy chapter for both gay people and my party. In the public galleries that day were many friends and supporters from my riding plus my mother, stepfather, sister, and nephew. In my mind were memories of the 1986 and 1994 votes. And some of those who had been shackled and removed by latex-gloved security officers in 1994, such as Rev. Brent Hawkes, were in attendance as I rose to speak:

> I've been in this place before, although recently elected, and the galleries have been important steps along the path in my own evolution as a gay man. In 1986, when the government of the day was debating Bill 7, I sat in that gallery on the east side — I must say, I much preferred the view — and watched the government deal at the end of a very, very difficult debate. But at the end of the day, Ontario legislators from all parties — not equally distributed perhaps, but from all parties — supported what was then entrenchment of sexual orientation in the prohibited grounds for discrimination of the Ontario Human Rights Code. I was proud of my government that day.
>
> On June 9, 1994, I stood or sat in that gallery, and I will not go on at length but I must say I don't think that

was the proudest day in the history of this place. Today, we have a chance to put that behind us.

I want to turn a little bit to the debate. What is this about? Well, these are not about special rights, these are about equal rights, and having gained them our community must now live up to them. I'm so convinced that we will because the indefatigable spirit of gays and lesbians has brought us this far. Today we set a new seat at the table.

And without further protest of any form from any party, Ontario swiftly and surely got caught up. A headline in the *Toronto Star* proclaimed, "Contentious bill voted into law quickly and quietly." An accompanying column, which noted that thirty-one Tory MPPs and nine Liberals were absent from the debate, observed, "The absence of a recorded vote provided cover for those who still opposed the legislation but didn't want to defy their party."

From that day forward, the Ontario Legislature ceased to be a bastion for homophobia from any quarter (at least until very recently, that is, with the election of Doug Ford as premier with support from social conservatives).

It is really remarkable what five years and a Charter can mean for the progress of LGBTQ people and other minorities. For the Liberal Party, the page was turned, and my Toronto Centre team shifted to attract tons of energy from the gay community to aid the party. We took it upon ourselves to join David Caplan and Dominic Agostino (two MPP colleagues) in making sure Liberal events were strong on hospitality and fun. I will never forget the stampede of people who wanted their picture taken with one-time Toronto mayoral candidate Enza Anderson, a trans woman, in our hospitality suite at a province-wide gathering of Liberals in London. It struck me that the farther one hailed from Church and Wellesley, the keener the desire to have a photo with Enza!

* * *

Beyond the cozy confines of Queen's Park, however, there was trouble in my riding: specifically, six murders in Regent Park in the first six weeks after I was elected. If there had been six murders (or even break-ins) in Rosedale, there would have been a community uproar. But because it happened in Regent Park, the post–Second World War era public housing project in downtown Toronto, there was little in the way of a community-organized backlash. No emergency meetings were called and no protest rallies were organized. Upon asking why, I was told that it was up to me and my dear friend Pam McConnell, the city councillor for the area, to call the meeting. It was an important moment of cultural awareness for me, and from that moment on I knew that building a dynamic community voice representing Regent Park's residents was to be a priority of mine.

At this time, I lived just steps north of Regent Park on Sword Street. I knew first-hand that it was a stigmatized neighbourhood because the youths I met from there always told me they lived down Parliament Street or across Gerrard Street or Dundas Street. They would not even admit to living in Regent Park.

The housing project was badly designed, with park-like settings that proved very convenient for drug dealers. By the turn of the century, its buildings were in declining condition. Everyone said it had to be redeveloped. But I came to realize that, as much as there might be an inclination to tear Regent Park down and build anew, the people living there needed to have a big say in whatever plans were made. When I look back on my accomplishments as an MPP, helping to create a distinct community voice at Regent Park ranks among my proudest. For months, we met every Saturday under the watchful guidance of community organizer and humanitarian Carmel Hilli at the Toronto Christian Resource Centre at 40 Oak Street, right in the neighbourhood. Gradually we developed a structure for a democratic organization — the Regent Park Neighbourhood Association — that would speak for the community, and we had it ratified by the community. Ahmed Hussen was one of the early leaders of the association. We used the Barbara Hall model of maximum participation and consultation at the front end.

At the same time, I learned from Carolyn Acker and Camille Orridge, respectively the executive director and chair of the Regent Park Community Health Centre, of their "community succession model." Simply put, they concluded that so long as all the good jobs in the community were going to people from outside the community, it would remain mired in poverty. Pathways to Education, now a national success, was born and immediately set out to promote high-school and post-secondary success in the community. I am so lucky that in the earliest days of Pathways I was able to leverage a financial contribution for the organization from the six biggest Canadian banks. I am prouder still that the kids of Regent Park now graduate from high school at rates equal to the wealthiest neighbourhoods in Toronto, thanks to comprehensive tutoring, mentoring, direct financial assistance, and merit-based scholarships and bursaries.

It's common in politics that some people are motivated by the perceived power of being in cabinet. It helped that I was an opposition MPP at the time. I wouldn't have had the time to devote to these tasks in Regent Park if I had been a cabinet minister. So you could say that the most powerful thing I did as an MPP was when I had no power. The subsequent redevelopment of Regent Park has not been perfect. Regrettably, the final two phases still haven't been built because of a lack of government funding, and some people who were uprooted with the promise they could return to the new housing have not seen that promise fulfilled.

*   *   *

One of the first things I did after being elected to the Legislature was to hire a woman I had met during the campaign: Doreen Winkler. She had come to lobby me on behalf of Ontarians with disabilities. I was impressed with her empathy and her clarity in presenting arguments in favour of legislative action to enhance the lives of people living with a disability. Doreen had a master's in social work, was blind, and read a computer only with the aid of sophisticated technology. When I sought to acquire that technology to help her, I was told that it wasn't covered by my legislative budget. Correctly sensing that I was going to make a stink about the issue, Claude DesRosiers, the Clerk of the Legislature, stepped in and bought the technology with his own budget.

On another occasion, I staged a scooter-and-wheelchair protest at a newly renovated Pizza Pizza store on Parliament Street in my riding. Despite spending $250,000 on the reno, the store still left lips of six to eight inches on all its various entrances — just enough to prevent access for many people with disabilities. Shortly after our rally, the store was made accessible, and I am sure that has been very good for its business.

A couple of years later, when MPPs were given the opportunity to present Queen's Golden Jubilee Medals to people in their ridings who had made a significant contribution to their communities, I declined to award them to the many constituents who had reached out to me and asked for them. Instead, I gave them to a wide array of neighbourhood heroes, including participants in the Pizza Pizza protest and pure community people just like them. We had a great ceremony for the recipients at the Legislature. I have found in life that, for every impressive person seeking an award or recognition, I knew an equally impressive unsung hero. I delighted in highlighting them and pride myself in my instinct to lift people and communities up.

Another issue I got involved in as an opposition MPP was the Marc Hall case. He was a gay kid who wanted to bring his boyfriend to the school prom. But it was a Catholic school, Monsignor John Pereyma in Oshawa, and the principal had vetoed the idea. Marc appealed to the Durham Catholic District School Board but was again rebuffed. My assistant, Todd Ross, who had suffered discrimination at the hands of the Canadian navy, and I reached out to Marc to let him know he wasn't alone in his battle.

Eventually, only the courts offered a remedy for Marc, and we rallied the best possible legal representation to his side: David Corbett, now a justice on the Ontario Superior Court, aided by intervenor Douglas Elliott, a legal legend in the gay community. Elliot called me one day and said: "You do realize that Marc is only seventeen and cannot be held accountable for costs that might be assessed by the court, and you will have to be his litigation guarantor?"

"Sure," I said, "so long as you realize if there is a judgment against us the first person I am asking for a donation is you."

Todd and I also got a thirty-minute meeting with Cardinal Ambrozic, then the Catholic archbishop of Toronto, at his Yonge Street office (in my riding!). He articulated the Church line, and I stuck to mine. There was no room for compromise. Many meetings drift on for longer than the allotted time, but this one ended on the dot with Ambrozic rising after thirty minutes. In the end, Hall won his case in court and went to the prom with his boyfriend. My team and I pitched in to help to pay for the limousine.

In the same time frame I was named Grand Marshall of the first Sarnia Gay Pride Parade and walked with the colourful Liberal MP Roger Galloway, but not Sarnia's mayor Mike Bradley. (I was surprised he was in hiding that day.) I also had a great time at the London Pride celebration, where I did a little MC job and mostly hung out with entertainers like the great drag king Deb "Dirk" Pearce. Halton, York, Hamilton, Kingston, and Ottawa were some of the other Pride festivals I participated in.

* * *

Back at Queen's Park, I was settling in as a rookie MPP. There were ten of us Liberals who had won our first elections in 1999. We provided something of an energy jolt to the caucus. To us, 1999 was a victory, not a defeat. Our leader, Dalton McGuinty, had withstood an onslaught of attack ads, our popular vote had increased, and Mike Harris's majority had been whittled down.

Initially, my seat was in the far back corner of the Legislature, something Ian Scott loved to torment me about. "You backbencher," he would say over and over with great hilarity. I soon got shifted to the middle of the back row, where my heckling skills could be better employed. One of my targets was NDP Leader Howard Hampton, who (along with other New Democrats) spent much of his time heckling McGuinty. (The New Democrats saw McGuinty as standing in the way of their path back to power, and like others they underestimated him.)

My principal target, however, was the premier himself, Mike Harris. I made an issue out of his frequent absences from the Legislature (even though, under arcane parliamentary rules, no member is allowed to refer to the absence of another). With the help of the legislative library and a day-by-day review of Hansard, I did some research that showed Harris had attended just one out of every three Question Periods, whereas Premier Peterson had attended 80 percent and Premier Rae more than 60 percent. It was the subject of my first question in the Legislature. Since it was tricky ground, it was a great start, and I hoped it would show my colleagues in the Liberal caucus that I had guts. The argument about Harris's absences gained some traction; people began really giving him the gears about his spotty attendance record. In the fall of 2001, Harris announced he was quitting. I personally take some credit for helping to push him out of provincial politics, but it always amazed me just how out of gas Harris seemed to be as early as the 1999 election. He morphed from reformist crusader to cigar-and-putter aficionado in very short order.

In the Ontario Legislature with Sandra Pupatello and Dalton McGuinty.

In this and other initiatives, I was really a deployable asset of the leader's office. I was never a candidate for the big critic roles, mostly taken by the class of 1995, like the Windsor twins, Dwight Duncan and Sandra Pupatello. Rather I got to do a host of things that were not only fun but also helped to hone my skills and knowledge. My first executive assistant at Queen's Park was Gerald Butts, former principal secretary to Prime Minister Justin Trudeau. By the time he came to work for me, Gerald and his equally impressive soon-to-be wife, Jodi, had a lot going for them. That made him an easy target for advancement. In the four months or so before Phil Dewan, then McGuinty's chief of staff, made the smart decision to poach him from me, Gerald and I travelled hither and yon to call upon every GTA mayor. (I was the GTA critic.) That meant zooming about in my neon yellow VW GTI, with me changing gears, cradling the phone, steering and typing on the second generation BlackBerry that had but one line of text, almost like a pager. In many cases, I knew the mayor we were meeting from my work for Barbara Hall and for the federal government.

Ironically, given my poor driving habits at the time, one of the other issues I took on was auto insurance, which was gaining public traction. The Liberals had no well-defined policy in the area, and I set out to harness it and make it a winner for us. I held hearings in municipalities across the province, many of them with future MPPs like Phil McNeely in Ottawa-Orleans and John Wilkinson in Perth-Middlesex. After fifteen or so hearings, I put together a package of recommendations that became part of the 2003 Liberal platform and largely informed government policy for years after the election. I always thought McGuinty made me health minister because he was impressed by the way I handled that sticky file.

I was also the lead critic on a pension reform bill that Finance Minister Janet Ecker had brought forward to the house. She backed down on the so-called reforms after I packed the Legislature's galleries with three-hundred-odd former National Trust employees who were about to see their pensions eviscerated by the bill. Even now people who benefited from my actions will stop me on the street to thank me.

Another role for me was being the lead party critic on the SARS crisis in 2003. I attended all the government's press conferences, which were held daily during the height of the crisis. As the epidemic originated in China, it hit the Chinese-Canadian community in the Toronto area particularly hard. I remember visiting the Pacific Mall in Markham with Dalton McGuinty at the time and finding it eerily empty, especially as I had seen that place in full flight so often. But the economic and social impacts were felt across the city. It was an important lesson for all of us in managing a public health crisis. And it gave me crucial insights into health communications, especially the knack possessed by some clinicians for taking clinical data and making it comprehensible for everyday folks.

My favourite assignment of all was triggered when Mike Harris called it quits. I proposed to my boss that I attend the campaign launches of all the Tory leadership candidates, a feat I achieved for all but one of them because of car trouble. I recall attending Elizabeth Witmer's launch at the Waterloo Inn. With a good hometown crowd, Witmer took time from her speech to call me out by name and tell me I was going to meet my Waterloo. In response, I got to call her a wolf in sheepskin clothing and reminded people of her role in the gutting of labour laws in the early Harris years. My aptitude for providing on-site commentary without too much collateral damage led to ever bigger stages and opportunities for me, culminating in my role shadowing Premier Ernie Eves in the run-up to the 2003 campaign. So familiar was I to the Tories that they began to expect me at their events.

Best photo op ever. "Ernie Eves Trough," at the Hog Barn, Riverdale Farm, where the pig literally took the prop.

At the Conservative platform launch on the eve of the 2003 campaign, Eves made a point of autographing a copy of the document for me.

I was a hard-charging ambitious person, but my ambition was for my boss (McGuinty) and my party, not for myself. I always figured the ends justified the means (bye, bye, Harris), and if my brashness ruffled feathers, then so be it. I played hard, but I was never a leaker or a back-stabber. My loyalty to my leader was unquestioned, although during McGuinty's leadership review period (after the 1999 election) some eyebrows were raised when I supported Alvin Curling for party president. Curling, a fellow MPP and someone who swept into politics with David Peterson, was seen as a stalking horse for the anti-McGuinty faction in the party. But that was never my motive; I supported Alvin (or "ambassador," as I now call him, because he later became our envoy to the Dominican Republic) with a pure heart. I just didn't want to see him isolated. The entire Toronto Centre delegation voluntarily joined me in supporting Alvin, fully aware of the risk. In the end, Curling lost the presidential race to Greg Sorbara, and McGuinty easily won his leadership review vote.

* * *

The culmination of my time in opposition was, of course, the 2003 election campaign. Some elections are more fun than others, and this one was fun, because we could see we were winning. I was on the road a lot during that campaign, helping out in other ridings because mine was seen as safe. Most enjoyably, I stalked Ernie Eves at many of his campaign events. I remember one day driving to an event with Andrew Steele, a young gun who was working with Bob Lopinski in the opposition leader's office. I hope I never forget the very moment I was driving us along Highway 403 just past Wayne Gretzky Parkway when Steele looked up from his BlackBerry and over at me and told me sternly: "You are not allowed to crash the car when I tell you this, but you should know that a Tory operative has just called McGuinty an 'evil reptilian kitten-eater from another planet.'" I was laughing so hard that I had to pull over the car. We finished the drive to London but never made it to the Eves event that day. The campaign head office quite rightly told us to turn back because there was nothing we could say that would top that.

Besides his campaign staffers' gaffes, Eves was also hurt by his own drab performances, notwithstanding his natty appearance. (I once compared him to an aging Sea King helicopter: "For every hour of serviceable duty, he needs four hours of primping.") But the real key to the Liberal victory in the 2003 election is that we presented ourselves as a party that was ready to govern. Unlike in 1999, we had a hefty platform that comprised seven booklets and was fully costed out. The ideas in it were (almost) all backed up by expert opinions. Much of the credit for this goes to McGuinty's policy guy, Gerald Butts. (I have to take double or triple credit because I sometimes get left out of the stories about Butts's ascent.) I had some input in the writing of the platform, especially in the sections on auto insurance, health care, and GTA gridlock. But I was not heavily involved in platform-making. My strengths were applied more on the political and operational side.

A few days before the October 2 vote, I hosted the wrap-up leader's rally at Jarvis Collegiate in my riding. (McGuinty's campaign team had confidence in me to fill the hall with a supportive crowd in addition to the throngs of supporters who travelled in from across the GTA, and the location was handy for the press.) It was a very loud event, with lots of cheering and placard-waving. I introduced the leader and said: "It won't be long now." Meaning, we were going to win it. Indeed, we did — resoundingly, with seventy-two seats to just twenty-four for the Conservatives and seven for the NDP. My victory party was in an old warehouse space off Yonge Street, just behind the Sutton Place Hotel. I also spoke at a GTA-wide Liberal victory party at the Masonic Temple a few blocks away on Yonge (also in my riding). I don't remember much of what I said. I was pretty amped up. My life was about to change, dramatically. Was it a good or bad omen that two men wanted to sleep with me that night?

CHAPTER FOUR

Health

On October 23, 2013, I was sworn in as minister of health in the first Liberal government in Ontario for thirteen years. As I said at the beginning of this book, it was heady territory for the son of a trucker from Etobicoke with no post-secondary degree and no experience in cabinet. But I didn't arrive at the Ministry of Health with a blank slate. Far from it. I had a detailed mandate in the form of the Liberal platform. I had my values informed by the fight for the Wellesley Hospital. And I had deep exposure through Carolyn Acker to the Regent Park Community Health Centre's model, which brilliantly proclaims that no community is going to prosper so long as all the best jobs in the community are going to people from outside.

Luckily for me, the Liberal platform relied heavily on the 2002 report of the federally appointed Royal Commission on the Future of Health Care in Canada. I had accompanied Premier McGuinty when he made a presentation to the commission, chaired by former Saskatchewan premier Roy Romanow. Both the party platform and the commission report contained full-throated endorsements of a single-tier, universally accessible, publicly funded health care system. The goal was to modernize medicare and address its glaring shortcomings without resorting to privatization or a two-tier

October 2003, the first McGuinty cabinet swearing-in. Full deer-in-headlights in effect, according to the look on my face (top row, third from left).

format as panaceas for the access and quality citizens desired. The platform included promises to shorten wait times for several critical areas — cardiac care, cancer treatment, diagnostics, and joint replacements. Shortening wait times had been a key Romanow recommendation. We also promised to establish "family health teams" with interdisciplinary groupings of doctors and other health professionals collaborating to deliver enhanced care and better access hours for patients. And we pledged to expand home care, invest in mental health, and increase the supply of nurses and doctors. The doctor shortage was to be addressed, in part, by removing barriers to foreign-trained physicians and so put to rest those nagging stories about doctors driving taxis.

We managed to do most of this, notwithstanding the budgetary constraints on us. The McGuinty government inherited a massive $5.6 billion deficit from the previous Conservative regime (under Premier Ernie Eves) — a shortfall that had been covered up in the budget immediately preceding the election. And that $5.6 billion was a low-ball figure, for it overlooked the $1 billion in accumulated hospital "working capital deficits," which were off the government's books but guaranteed by the province.

So I approached David MacNaughton, McGuinty's principal secretary (and now Canada's ambassador to the United States). I knew MacNaughton well and enjoyed working with him. We had a chat about the hospital deficits outside the Legislative Building. I recall him turning back over his shoulder as he walked away and saying, "We will find a way." But I think he and I both knew that it was going to be very tough. I do not know whether he shared my sense of lost opportunity, but those hospital deficits loomed large every one of the 1,702 days I served as health minister. But if every big issue at the health ministry were labelled a crisis, that would not engender public confidence, and restoring confidence in the system was at the heart of my mission.

People use the expression "drinking from a fire hose" to describe the information overload involved in taking on a new challenge. That may have been an apt description for ministers in other portfolios. At Health, where spending is measured in billions, not hundreds of millions, I was drinking from a river with a lot of powerful tributaries. The flow of information was remarkable. Just for example, nearly four hundred thousand pieces of correspondence get addressed to the minister annually.

But before grappling with substantive issues, I faced another challenge: filling some thirty-odd positions on the minister's staff. As head of the largest operating government department in Canada with eight thousand direct employees, four hundred thousand indirect employees, a $30 billion budget (at that time), and about half of all the government appointments to agencies, boards, commissions, and regulatory bodies, Ontario's minister of health has one of the largest political staffs in the country.

Within one minute of stepping off the elevator and before I even set foot in my own office, I looked down the long hallway of empty offices and got a sinking feeling. I called over to someone in the Premier's Office and said: "If you have any adults around, please send them over." Lo and behold, soon afterward I was connected to Charles Beer, then sitting on a dock and drinking a beer. Beer was a veteran of the provincial Liberal Party. He had been minister of community and social services in the Peterson government, and he had run for the party leadership in 1992 (losing out to Lyn McLeod). Besides being experienced, he had the advantage of being widely liked and wise. A phone call that started out as a link to an informal adviser progressed quickly and I wisely named him my executive assistant.

He was an enormous help to me because he was familiar with the rhythm of government as well as being a calming presence. He helped me survive in my early days in the ministry.

Working with Hugh O'Neil had taught me that the number-one key to a minister's survival is effective management of relations with the government caucus. For caucus liaison, I chose Scott Lovell, who had been my campaign manager in Toronto Centre and my executive assistant in opposition. Lovell had been trained in attending to local matters by his mother, Ruth, then mayor of Owen Sound.

He became known as the go-to guy for MPPs of all parties. (Partisan as we were, our effort to aid MPPs was not.) They came to know that, if they wanted to talk to me about an issue or a scheduling matter, they had best start with Lovell. We had great fun keeping the map in Scott's office up to date as we celebrated every new hospital visit or other event, such as a fundraiser, that took us to a riding that was new to us.

As director of policy, I chose my long-time friend Jason Grier, who had been director of public affairs at Wellesley hospital and then McGuinty's chief health policy adviser in opposition. At Health, he and I assembled the finest starting line of political policy advisers I have ever seen. Proof positive is how their careers evolved after they left my office: Grier became a noted health strategist at Santis, a boutique health consultancy where he works with Dan Carbin and Janine Hopkins; Ali Samian is a global pharma executive; Rita McGrath continues to run health care systems in the Middle East; and Ken Chan was recently named an assistant deputy minister in the Ontario government.

Grier had written most of the health sections in the Liberal platform. In effect, he was my living mandate letter. There were also a couple of notable health policy experts in the Premier's Office with whom we worked closely and co-operatively: Karli Farrow and Jamison Steeve, each of whom later became my chief of staff. My office sought to be in alignment with them on the issues of the day, because in a Westminster-style government progress is made much easier when one enjoys the support of the so-called centre (the Premier's Office).

Changes were also afoot among the senior civil servants in the health ministry even before I arrived. For, in the transition period, the premier-elect comes into contact with the senior bureaucrats BEFORE the not-yet-appointed ministers see them. And suffice it to say that premier-elect Dalton McGuinty did not see eye-to-eye with the deputy minister of health, Phil Hassen, who had just been recruited from a Vancouver hospital by the previous Conservative government. So McGuinty fired Hassen and replaced him with an acting deputy, Marguerite Rappolt. She was a career bureaucrat who was very skilled at holding the fort and had a tremendous institutional memory. Fortunately for me, another Conservative recruit from British Columbia, Hugh MacLeod, was already at the ministry and was named associate deputy minister. His agile mind and Rappolt's steady-as-she-goes approach made for good progress.

Rappolt was there only on an acting basis, however. To replace her, Tony Dean, the cabinet secretary (the province's chief bureaucrat, and one of the best public servants I have ever known) allowed me to interview the final two candidates for the position: Ron Sapsford, who had worked for the Tory-appointed Health Services Restructuring Commission and then became COO at Hamilton Health Sciences, and Kevin Smith, CEO of St. Joseph's Healthcare, also in Hamilton. I liked them both and felt good chemistry with them. When Sapsford emerged as my deputy, the health community was very pleased. He had a rich history in Ontario health care, beginning at the District Health Council in Owen Sound, and was well placed to help lead the transformation of the ministry.

While I understood how important the bureaucrats were, my first instinct in my earliest days was to reach out beyond them to key players in the health sector on my own. (This established a pattern that I would carry on throughout my tenure.) I took to the road to meet doctors and nurses. Nearly immediately, I drove to an outdated strip mall in Scarborough to see Dr. Larry Erlick, a family physician who was then president of the Ontario Medical Association. I made sure he knew that I had my own priorities. In particular, we discussed the always-sensitive issue of compensation adjustments among doctors influenced by new technology. Erlick gave me a hint at some of his early priorities, including compensation for general surgeons and psychiatrists.

Another early contact was with Doris Grinspun, executive director (later CEO) of the Registered Nurses Association of Ontario. She took me on a tour of Mount Sinai and North York general hospitals. The theme of our visit was unsung heroes. This was the first of a multitude of steps I took to acknowledge the role of nursing and, especially, the risks. That day at North York General, I paid my respects at the memorial to Nelia Laroza, the nurse who died there during the 2003 SARS epidemic. (Later in my time as minister, I was faced with a recommendation that there be different levels of protective masks for different health care professionals in case of a pandemic. I overruled the ministry advisers and insisted on the highest protection standard for all who were risking their lives for all of us, despite the higher cost.)

SARS was still fresh in everyone's mind when I became minister and had a big impact — financial, emotional, and regulatory — on my early days in office. The Conservatives had appointed Justice Archie Campbell to inquire into the province's response to the crisis, and I inherited his excellent report. His recommendations became my marching orders for fixing the public health system in Ontario, which had shockingly been allowed to deteriorate under the Tories. I didn't need Campbell to tell me everything that needed doing, however.

One of my first actions was to remove Dr. Colin D'Cunha, the province's chief medical officer of health. (The office handles communicable disease management, health promotion, chronic disease, injury prevention, and emergency preparedness.) D'Cunha had presided over the province's response to the SARS outbreak, which killed forty-four Ontarians. He was, to be frank, not a confidence-inspiring individual. A blue-ribbon panel blamed the crisis, in part, on the infighting between the federal government and D'Cunha's office. "The lack of collaboration between the federal and provincial governments [during the SARS outbreak] was an international embarrassment," said David Naylor, the University of Toronto's dean of medicine and head of the panel. So D'Cunha was encouraged to pursue new challenges, and I replaced him with Dr. Sheela Basrur. Looking back, I think it was the single most impactful thing I did as minister of health.

Basrur was Toronto's medical officer of health during SARS and was hailed for her work in handling the crisis. Especially evident were her clear-headed communication skills. She had also distinguished herself in other areas, including implementing a city-wide ban on public smoking and requiring restaurants to post the results of health inspections of their premises.

I had to sell Basrur on making the switch from the city to the province. Rather than go through the usual channels, I contacted her directly and told her we were willing to pour resources into public health (including a huge upload of costs from municipalities to the province) to put wind back in the sails of the people in the sector, who had felt like outcasts under Mike Harris. What astonished me was that she was surprised to be asked, which tells you a lot about her lack of ego. She was leading the largest public health organization in the province, and she was a great communicator — a key skill in the public health field. In other words, she was the obvious choice. "You have to do this for the sake of the province," I told her. "You're a hard man to say no to," she replied. At her city hall exit party, Mayor David Miller griped to me: "Thanks a lot for stealing my prize talent." I retorted: "With all due respect, your worship, her talents are needed for a higher purpose."

Basrur and I did some great work together as we rebuilt the capacity of the public health sector across the province. Among other things, we created the regulatory environment for food carts and trucks to expand their offerings beyond their traditional fare of hot dogs and sausages. And we introduced the Smoke-Free Ontario Act, which replaced a ragtag collection of municipal bylaws with one strong ban on smoking in public places across the whole province. Another feature of the act that I am proud of was requiring hidden displays for cigarettes in stores.

The legislation prompted an internal debate as some argued that the government-owned casinos should be exempt from the smoking ban. Apparently the incidence of smoking is higher among gamblers than in the general public, and the casinos foresaw a rapid decline in attendance — and, by extension, government revenues — if smoking was banned on their premises. But, with Premier McGuinty's support, we stuck to our guns. "You can't ask people to support a government policy if the government is exempting itself," said McGuinty.

(An aside: Except for a bad stint in Grade 3, I have not been a smoker myself, although between my mother, grandmother, and many nights in smoky gay bars — hello Eartha Kitt, Key West, 1993 New Year's! — I have consumed a lot of second-hand smoke. During one rare evening session of the Legislature, Conservative MPP John O'Toole accused me of being a smoker. He said he and I had smoked together by the Legislative Building's east door. I thought he was mistaking me for another cabinet minister from Toronto and asked him to correct the record. When he refused, I called him a liar and got thrown out of the Legislature for using unparliamentary language. It was worth it to make a point.)

Basrur and I were not always in agreement, and those moments were especially fun. By necessity, there is a streak of independence in the public health sector. One dispute was over implementation of a public health regulation requiring raw fish to be frozen before it was served. Sushi chefs and consumers were outraged, and we quickly backed down. I remember her at my office door with a fresh regulation in hand. "Sorry, boss," she said. Luckily, we moved fast enough that most people don't remember the frozen sushi "scandal."

Another dust-up involved the growing determination on the part of public health officials to make sure farmers' markets and other outdoor food-serving events were safe for consumers. Overzealous prosecution led to a real backlash. It was brought to a head when public health officials poured bleach on egg salad sandwiches to prevent their sale at an outdoor event in Windsor. The sandwiches, made by volunteers, were to be sold in support of an important Windsor heritage property. Notwithstanding the risk of food poisoning from egg salad left in the hot sun, the bleach attack sparked a reaction. That led to a new regulatory framework that has contributed to a wonderful expansion of the popularity of farmers' markets. Heritage advocate that I am, I sent a personal cheque to the organizers in Windsor to let them know that I hadn't missed the story.

Overall, Basrur and I worked well as a team and accomplished a lot. Unfortunately, she had to step down for health reasons in December 2006, less than two years into her job. We named the Public Health Agency after her, and the naming ceremony at MaRS (the Toronto Discovery District project) was among the most touching I have ever experienced. I was lucky to get to know Sheela's daughter, sister, and parents, who were so welcoming to me. When she succumbed to cancer in 2008, a friend of Sheela's lashed out at me out of sorrow and said Sheela died because I worked her too hard. Maybe, but I don't think she would have had it any other way. Nevertheless, the comment continues to sting.

* * *

One of my first pieces of legislative business as minister was to introduce the Commitment to the Future of Medicare Act, a promise from the campaign platform binding the government to "universal, public medicare." Somewhat symbolic, at one point it was under consideration to be the first bill introduced by the new government. (It lost out to a bill cancelling the private-school tax credit and increasing corporate taxes.) In connection with my bill, a departmental briefing was scheduled. When the bureaucrats assembled, I was surprised to see one Thomas O'Shaughnessy, a senior policy adviser in the ministry, in the lead. Ironically, he had taken a leave of absence to be the campaign manager for John Adams, my Conservative opponent in the provincial election just concluded, an election during which O'Shaughnessy had heckled me at an all-candidates meeting. Luckily for him, I don't hold grudges.

It was one of many examples where I saw no threat in having people of different political stripes working for me. Another was Gail Paech, assistant deputy minister of health under me. In 1999, she had lost the Conservative nomination in my riding to Durhane Wong-Rieger by one vote. (Yes, there were accusations of ballot-stuffing.) The deputy minister's office also had two key staffers who supported me and my team so well. One, Lana Sheinbaum, I had known as a Peterson staffer, while the other, David Sachow, had previously served on Tony Clement's staff. Fact is, working on the political side made these folks very aware and perhaps sympathetic to the challenges facing a politician. Accordingly, they served me loyally and with great effect.

Another early issue for me was the reversal of some of the previous government's privatization schemes, including the outsourcing of diagnostics (MRIs and CT scans, etc.) to for-profit clinics. In our platform, we had promised to "end the Harris-Eves agenda of creeping privatization," which we did going forward. However, when we got into office, we soon realized that a complete reversal would be prohibitively expensive in both time and money. So we allowed the private clinics to stay in business if they repositioned themselves as non-profits. Earnings for employees were acceptable, but not profits for the operation.

Renegotiating the P3 (private-public partnership) hospitals that were already in the works in Brampton and Ottawa was incredibly difficult. These new hospitals, both very badly needed in their communities, would have been delayed for years by cancellation, so we insisted on fundamental changes to the contracts that ensured long-term control remained in the name of the public hospital corporation. In the case of Brampton, the contract, nearly six thousand pages long, was made available for public viewing. That also was a first.

Upon arrival, I became familiar with the ministry's traditional manner of building new hospitals. The hospital in Thunder Bay, with a three-storey atrium, was just being completed. Its cost had spiralled from an initial estimate of $140 million to a final price of $284 million, an overrun of more than 100 percent, with all of the risk borne by the province. It was in response to Thunder Bay that I coined the phrase "tajmahospital with glass atriums in the sky," and for every day since I have had architects tell me how efficient atriums are. "Fair point," I tell them, "but when a new hospital design forces employees to travel 50 percent farther in a shift, then maybe we weren't focusing on the right things."

In short, the traditional model had left plenty of room for improvement, including the annoying and expensive habit of allowing "change orders." These are better described as blank cheques for construction companies asked to make changes while construction is already under way. Possibly because the plans weren't studied in fine enough detail at the outset? To move a wall in the CEO's office after construction has begun is costly, but nobody was exercising constraint on behalf of the province.

The media were always attracted to events that involved Ontario's hospitals.

The Conservative response had been to hand the responsibility for hospital construction over to P3s. In opposition, we had been against them. But once in office, various forces combined to force us to rethink the issue. The problem was that the P3 label had become toxic. So we invented a new one — "alternative financing and procurement" (AFP) — and stipulated that, at the end of each agreement, ownership of the hospitals and the hospitals themselves must revert to the public domain in excellent working condition.

While the AFP model has its critics, particularly in the labour movement, it has been widely heralded. Without AFPs, it is very doubtful that the remarkable rebuilding of Ontario's hospitals in the past decade could have been achieved, even if we had had the fiscal capacity to pay the price under the old model (which we didn't). David Caplan, who was minister of public infrastructure before we switched positions in 2008, deserves much of the credit for this. Under his leadership, the government became much more sophisticated in asset management than it had been. And it was a necessary change in direction because so much of our public infrastructure — not just hospitals — had been built in the 1950s and was badly in need of replacement by the early twenty-first century. Unfortunately, many people still have the misconception that P3s (or AFPs) are free. They aren't. At the end of the day, the government still has to foot the bill. But, like a mortgage, it is paid off over a lengthy period of time.

My biggest headache at Health was not capital spending, however; it was operational expenditures. The ministry was chronically over-budget and so was imperiling the government's overall fiscal situation and badly undermining the ministry's regard within the government. By the time I got there, the central agencies of government (cabinet office, finance ministry, Treasury Board) had lost all confidence in the ability of the health ministry to stay within budget. And the biggest culprit was the hospital sector, which customarily ran over-budget by hundreds of millions annually and then demanded bailouts from the government. Convenient as it might have been to let the hospitals off the hook because they have a tough and vital job to do, I instead drew a very firm line in the sand, with the premier's backing. First, I had to make the hospitals believe that I meant what I said.

The showdown came at a meeting at the Microsoft headquarters on Mississauga's "Pill Hill" (as it is known, because it is home to many pharmaceutical companies). Tony Dagnone, CEO of London Health Sciences, chair of the Ontario Hospital Association, and thought to be no friend of Liberals, took centre stage to tell me the facts of life in the sector. I told him and his expensive suit that there was a new sheriff in town who was packing a concealed weapon ("accountability agreements," as they came to be known). Word of the dramatic encounter spread. Soon after, Lawrence Bloomberg, the prominent financier who was then chair of Mount Sinai Hospital, gave me a sheriff's badge, which I placed in the middle of my desk as the most precious among my many keepsakes. I have had to fight off advances from both my children, Kayla and Michael, to claim it as their own.

This event reinforced my view that the hospital CEOs had to be put squarely on the hook. Accordingly, I shaped legislation that would require their hospitals to sign accountability agreements committing them to balance their budgets within a two-year time frame. If they failed to balance, the CEOs' salaries would be docked. This was an attention-getting device. It was all about reversing the onus, and it worked. But like a good tennis match, onus can pass back and forth. The hospitals now had to tell us how they would get back to balance. It was a trade-off. On the one hand, we could have just told them to arrive at a balanced budget however they wished, and they would have immediately exacted a heavy toll on the government with hurtful cuts to patient services. On the other hand, signing off on proposed cuts meant we owned them.

A more particular problem was the limited capacity of the ministry to evaluate 154 proposals covering $13 billion in spending within a period of weeks or short months. There simply wasn't the in-house expertise to evaluate all that detail. Hence I called in reinforcements in the best form I knew: consultants Michael Guerriere and John Ronson. Guerriere, a medical doctor and former executive vice-president at Toronto General Hospital, was managing partner of the Courtyard Group, a health care consulting firm. Ronson, a lawyer with Liberal ties, was co-founder of Courtyard. I had known these two guys for decades and appreciated their depth of knowledge in the field. I was convinced that, if we were going to analyze the hospital's budgetary proposals properly, I needed somebody on our side with real-world experience — that is, somebody who knew where the bodies were buried in the numbers. So I instructed the deputy minister of health, Ron Sapsford, to get these guys into our stable. Why no tender? I had three days, not three months, to get the job done. This decision proved to be one of the most consequential during my time as minister of health. While the controversial matter of a sole-source contract later drew all the attention, I haven't any doubt that the move saved billions of dollars for the province.

That said, the hospitals now had the upper hand in how cuts would be characterized. And they knew we were vulnerable when it came to nurses. One of the features of nursing contracts is that if there is a change in role, the nurse is laid off and then rehired, resulting in many "layoffs" where no job was actually lost. This phenomenon created a tremendous communications challenge for us, because the budgetary proposals from the hospitals included a total of 857 layoffs of nurses. Since we had campaigned on a promise to INCREASE the number of nurses, this was, to say the least, awkward for me and the government. Even though I knew the number was largely an illusion, it was nearly impossible to communicate that fact. The *Star* ran with the "857 layoffs" story, and Elizabeth Witmer, my Conservative critic and a former health minister herself, latched onto it. This was richly ironic, given the way nurses were demeaned by the Harris government. (As premier, Mike Harris had compared nurses to workers in a hula hoop factory.)

To fight back, I brought together Doris Grinspun of the Registered Nurses Association (the professional body) and Linda Haslam-Stroud of the

With Doris Grinspun, a key stakeholder as leader of Ontario nurses.

Ontario Nurses' Association (the union) and created a $25 million nursing retention program, a safety net of sorts for any laid off in the budgeting process. Grinspun and Haslam-Stroud were named as trustees of the fund. Quite recently, the press reported that none of the money was actually spent. The good news is that this fact proves the spate of predicted layoffs didn't occur. The bad news is that, because the funds were made available on an emergency basis, we used a year-end funding mechanism that left little capacity to claw the money back once distributed. The trustees were left in control.

There was another financial runaway train when I arrived at the ministry: prescription drugs. The cost of providing these drugs under various government programs was rising at a double-digit annual rate — an increase of 140 percent since 1997. I slowed the pace down dramatically through an ambitious piece of legislation called Bill 102, "Transparent Drug System for Patients Act," which reshaped the pharmaceutical landscape in Ontario. Introduced on April 13, 2006, and passed into law on June 19, the bill was more than just a pricing mechanism. Rather, it was a highly complicated balancing of interests in the pharmaceutical system, which has a lot of moving parts: pharmacies (independents and chains), pharmaceutical companies (brand-name and generic), prescribers, and patients.

To get the pharmacists onside, I increased their compensation for using their expertise to advise patients. In effect, what I did was force a change in their business models. As a former shop-owner myself, I knew that retailers normally face their customers. But customers mostly saw the backs of pharmacists as they prepared prescriptions. I wanted to get higher value from pharmacists by turning them around to talk to their customers and to counsel them on the appropriate use of their medications. After all, a pharmacist has six years of education, the same as many practising doctors. We needed to make better use of their training.

The pharmacists welcomed this change. However, they did not appreciate the quid pro quo: limitations on the promotional rebates (I called them "kickbacks") they were getting from generic drug firms for favouring their products. Many pharmacists said Bill 102 would drive them out of business. This was a concern for me. I did not want be remembered as the health minister who caused the death of the community drug store. I applied the "Tweed test" to our policies to make sure that didn't happen. (Tweed is a bucolic town in eastern Ontario with a population of six thousand. The policy was designed to ensure that towns like Tweed, with only one non-chain pharmacy, did not lose their drug stores.) As a result, only one pharmacy actually closed, and it operated only a few days a week anyway.

As for the pharmaceutical manufacturers, we proposed to use the government's bargaining power as a major buyer of prescription drugs to force down their prices significantly. Not surprisingly, they reacted negatively. I was lobbied heavily on the issue by both the brand-name companies and the generics. The generic firms, in particular, hated Bill 102, even though it proposed greater interchangeability of their products with the brand-name drugs. The generics were afraid we would hold down their prices but not their expenditures (the rebates). The most heated intervention I recall was from Barry Sherman, founder and CEO of Apotex, the generic giant. (A decade later, he and his wife were found brutally murdered in their Toronto home; the case is still unsolved.) Sherman was a very smart man with many admirable qualities, but he was far from reserved in advancing his point of view. At a meeting in my office, I held my ground, but Sherman warned me: "Minister, this won't be the last time you hear from me on this matter." Indeed, it wasn't, but the policy prevailed and the players have adapted.

The brand-name companies, most of them foreign-owned, also had their grievances. I remember meeting with the CEO of one Big Pharma company in the lobby of a Toronto hotel. His firm had developed a drug to treat schizophrenia, and he was offering it to me at a discount (nudge nudge, wink wink). I was tempted by the proposition, but I was also struck by how isolated I was in making a decision like this. Why should a politician be the direct arbiter of such medical issues? So, under Bill 102, I shifted the decision-making structure around drugs in Ontario to limit the political input and expedite decisions.

I believe that the decision to delegate my powers to an executive officer who was then empowered to enter into competitive agreements has been one of the most transformative initiatives influencing public drug pricing across Canada.

Many of the brand-name pharma companies were more perturbed by the proposed constraints on their prices. They felt the Ministry of Health was motivated by cost savings (it was) and had ignored their investments in Ontario, where several of them had branch plants involved in both research and manufacturing. They went over my head to Premier McGuinty, who at that time was also serving as his own minister of research and innovation. In that role, he would attend the annual American Pharma conference, where representatives of Big Pharma lobbied him and threatened to pull their investments out of Ontario. But I never felt undue pressure from the premier — the kind of pressure exerted unhelpfully when you are asked to make a win-win out of opposing principles or objectives. This was a test of his backbone, and he had plenty of it.

The pushback against Bill 102 also caused some turbulence for my colleagues in cabinet and caucus, particularly the threat of rural and remote pharmacy closures. But the reforms were projected to shave costs of $200 million in the first year, and the finance ministry had already taken that amount into account in its calculations for my ministry's budget. So if my colleagues were opposed to the adjustments in Bill 102, they knew the $200 million would have to be found elsewhere. That's the rub in politics. It is often appealing to give in to the demands from interest groups, but if you do it too often you soon bump up against fiscal reality. Government is all about the allocation of scarce resources. For ministers and senior bureaucrats, that tension is part of their daily routine.

One last word on prescription drugs: the system would work far more efficiently if there were a national pharmacare plan instead of ten provincial ones, which sometimes work at cross-purposes. I was constantly mystified by the lack of interest in this idea in Ottawa. Given the federal role in the regulation both of drugs and of international trade, it would seem to be a natural shift of responsibility. But the federal government, under both Liberal and Conservative leadership, always shied away from it, seemingly because of the potential cost pressures. I had given up hope that it would ever happen. However, just recently the federal government, under Prime Minister Justin Trudeau, has signalled its intention to launch a national plan. I hope it comes to fruition. But if it doesn't, I think we should consider three or four regional prescription drug plans, with Ontario teaming up with the Atlantic provinces both to exercise our purchasing power and to agree on a common drug formulary. That would likely both save money and expand coverage.

The latter — which drugs are to be covered by government plans — is a tricky issue. I was repeatedly hammered, often on totally unscientific grounds, about the lack of coverage for new cancer drugs. Because cancer touches almost every family, an emotional argument can be made in favour of covering any and every new drug. People see us at war, with cancer as the enemy. "We must defeat it, at all costs," they say. So there was enormous pressure on me to make decisions that would cost the government tens of millions of dollars to pay for products that, at best, would add weeks to a cancer victim's life. Andre Marin, the provincial ombudsman, was the source of much of this pressure. He went well beyond his mandate to articulate the idea that EVERY cancer drug should be funded, regardless of its efficacy. There were also numerous newspaper stories — notably by Lisa Priest of the *Globe and Mail* — about cancer victims desperate for a new drug that was financially beyond their reach. These stories cut me to the bone; I took them very personally. But emotion and hope cannot be our only guides in health care decisions.

* * *

My term as health minister was not all about spending restraints. Far from it. There were also major investments in the sector, notably in mental health, an area that had been underfunded for too long. My first announcement as minister came at St. Joseph's Healthcare in Hamilton. It was also the occasion of my first unburdening. "We are all touched by mental health problems, and the people who say they aren't are liars," I said.

For a roadmap to reform, I turned in part to a report that had been prepared for the previous government by Michael Wilson, the former federal minister of finance under Brian Mulroney. Having lost a son to depression and suicide, Wilson had become a strong mental health advocate. But after asking for his advice, the Tories never formally received his report. That's an even worse fate than having your report shelved. I received the report and made it public, against the advice of many. (I was told it would increase pressure on me to spend more. I said: "Who cares? It would be about time, and why shouldn't mental health get to call out for resources since everyone else does?") The Wilson report recommended a pivot away from the acute-care model for mental health to a community-care model. I increased annual spending in the area by $185 million. It still wasn't enough, but it was more than my predecessors had accomplished in the sector, which was the square root of zero over ten years.

We also made significant new investments in primary care, notably in the establishment of the aforementioned family health teams (FHTs). Because of underfunding of primary care by the previous Conservative regime and the deliberate restriction of new doctors by the NDP government in the early 1990s, we faced a dire situation when we took office: the looming prospect that millions of Ontarians would have no family physician. We dramatically increased the supply of physicians: there are 15 percent more today than in 2003, and family practice has flourished with the introduction of new practice models.

We did this both by increasing enrolment in Ontario's medical schools and by speeding up certification for foreign-trained doctors. (The cliché fifteen years ago was that foreign-trained doctors were driving cabs in Ontario. That is no longer the case.) And one in four Ontarians is now attached to an FHT. The combined effect of these measures was to improve service for Ontarians and reduce pressure on emergency wards, the most expensive form of medical intervention.

To accomplish this, we aligned our financial resources behind FHTs. There was no increase in the budget for sole practitioners charging fee-for-service, but there was $1 billion more for FHTs. This required buy-in from the doctors. So I spent my first year in office negotiating a new contract with the Ontario Medical Association (OMA), the union for the province's twenty-thousand-plus doctors. We managed to strike a deal with the OMA bargaining committee. If you sign a deal in good faith, you really ought to try to sell it to your membership. Unfortunately, the OMA executive did not do that, and the deal was voted down by the members. The new OMA president, John Rapin, an ER doctor from Kingston who had replaced Erlick, then appealed to me to return to the bargaining table. "We don't have additional resources to put on the table," I told him. So we were at loggerheads.

After a speech at a hospital convention, I had a massive "scrum" with the media on the OMA negotiations, where I said we would have to consider unilaterally legislating an agreement. The OMA went bananas.

"We've been somewhat shanghaied," griped Rapin.

"When I looked the definition of 'shanghaied' up in the dictionary, it wasn't usually associated with $1 billion in new pay," I retorted.

Nonetheless, we resumed talking with the OMA and achieved a deal, after some modest tweaking of the details. And as a quid pro quo in the subsequent provincial budget, Finance Minister Greg Sorbara gave doctors the right to incorporate, which was a huge benefit for them.

Another investment was directed at reducing wait times for medical procedures in several critical areas (cardiac treatment, cancer care, joint replacements, and diagnostics [MRIs and CT scans]). The long wait for these procedures had become a major source of public complaints about the health care system. To tackle the problem, I hired Alan Hudson, a world-renowned neurosurgeon and former CEO of the giant University Health Network in Toronto. He had the wherewithal and the gravitas to tell surgeons and hospital administrators the things they needed to hear. Surgeons, stuck in their silos, had been keeping their own private lists of patients waiting for treatment. That practice had to end. So we created a provincial wait times registry, which was so successful that the model was adopted in the rest of the country. Wait times were significantly reduced as a result. Hudson and Sarah Kramer, whom he recruited for the job from Cancer Care Ontario, deserve enormous credit for this. Ironically, it was the success they achieved in the development of the registry that led David Caplan, my successor at Health, to elevate them to the two key roles at the newly formed eHealth agency. Unfortunately, their early steps at that agency further inflamed the already badly scorched electronic health landscape and led to their demise, as well as that of Caplan and Deputy Minister Ron Sapsford. More about that in a later chapter.

*   *   *

As I have mentioned, some of the funding for these investments came from the federal government as a result of the health accord with the provinces in September 2004. By that time, Ottawa was flush with cash, and the provinces demanded their fair share of it. After all, the provinces reasoned, the federal government (with Jean Chrétien as prime minister and Paul Martin as finance minister) had balanced its budget in the 1990s partly at their expense by cutting back on medicare transfers. When Martin became prime minister early in 2004, he set out to make amends by offering the provinces $41 billion in new medicare funding over the next decade. He said the money would provide medicare with "a fix for a generation." But Martin, egged on by the Romanow Report, attached strings to the additional funding: the provinces would have to spend it on reducing wait times, reforming primary care, expanding home care, and improving long-term care. And there would have to be accountability: monitoring and reporting of the results. Ontario had no problem with any of this; we had already begun aligning every new dollar behind Ottawa's targeted areas. And we were completely open to more transparency to make sure the money was spent as directed. But other provinces, notably Quebec, objected to federal interference in an area of provincial jurisdiction (health care). Martin, with a big assist from Premier McGuinty, had to stickhandle his way around that dilemma to get a deal.

The result was "asymmetrical federalism," a frank admission that Quebec is a province unlike the others. In fact, of course, all the provinces are different from each other when it comes to the delivery of health care. Anyone who thinks health care systems are the same across the country hasn't travelled enough. For our part, we in Ontario sought to lead in accountability. We need to thank Peter Glenn from Kingston for helping drive the wait times information system forward.

When Stephen Harper became prime minister just over a year later, many people lamented his hands-off approach to health care funding. He preferred to leave it to the provinces to decide how to spend federal funding while he fulfilled the terms of Martin's accord with annualized increases. I saw it as more of a resignation on Harper's part that the overarching values of medicare — public funding and universal access, laid down by Monique Bégin's Canada Health Act in the early 1980s — could not be altered by his political philosophy. But Ottawa's financial participation has diminished sharply from the original fifty-fifty cost-sharing arrangement for medicare. Now it is the provinces that pay the lion's share of the cost and have all the responsibility for actually delivering health care to Canadians. But the average Canadian still sees Ottawa as being in the driver's seat because medicare has become a core value for the country. There's a public literacy problem here that works very well in Ottawa's favour.

While I want Ottawa to play an activist role in promoting good health, I have always found it cruelly ironic that the only group for which Health Canada has direct responsibility for the delivery of care is our Indigenous Peoples, who have far and away the most terrible health outcomes in the country. And for all those who think that reserves are teeming with money, consider that while federal health transfers to the provinces were growing at a very healthy 6 percent annually for a decade, Harper and his government decided to cap growth in spending on Indigenous Peoples at 2 percent a year. This history has led me to believe that we need to put more responsibility for health care spending directly in the hands of Indigenous Peoples.

In Sioux Lookout, Meno Ya Win Hospital stands as a model for Indigenous Peoples taking the lead in health care delivery for their people. The Ontario Government and Nishnawbe Aski Nation (NAN) signed an agreement in 2017 that moves in a good direction, so long as we don't create new silos of Indigenous health care organized narrowly across nations. Nor can we forget that very large numbers of Indigenous people live in urban centres, and many of them suffer from inequitable access to health care and the poor health outcomes that follow.

* * *

Another major reform on my watch was the creation of Local Health Integration Networks, or LHINs. This was an attempt to decentralize decision-making in the ministry by empowering the regions, in recognition of the principle that not all parts of Ontario have the same demographics or circumstances and we should allow for customization of program delivery at the local level. Other provinces had previously embarked on regionalization of their health care systems in one way or the other, but Ontario had long resisted the move before I took office. My feeling was that the people on the ground would have a better perspective of what worked in their regions, and I really hoped to create a culture where people could actually absorb what was happening in their area. Plus the sheer size of the health ministry when I arrived — over eight thousand employees and a budget of over $30 billion — made a heavily centralized operation difficult to manage. Since the scarcest resource is always time, I was determined to spend less of it mired in day-to-day issues like whether a local ER was going to stay open for the weekend.

I concluded that the ministry was missing a fundamental element necessary to any large organization in the public or private sector: definable regional areas within which service providers could be held accountable for service outcomes. Unfortunately, there was no regionalization plan on the shelf waiting for me when I became minister. But there was entrenched opposition from the hospitals, which saw regionalization as a threat to their independence. (Ontario's hospitals are fiercely protective of their independent board governance.) I also soon discovered that all the other provinces' regionalization models were flawed; there was nothing we could simply copy. As for anyone (Elizabeth Witmer, hello!) who thought regionalization would somehow shield me from political accountability, the evidence in other provinces on that point was also clear: shit still runs uphill to the minister's office and will as long as there is a Question Period in the Legislature.

Boundary-drawing for the LHINs was a particularly thorny issue. I learned that there is always going to be an unhappy faction somewhere and that we just had to accept a little imperfection here and there. People want all their hospital services to be close to home, but that is not always possible. Plus we planned to make the boundaries porous — that is, we did not want the LHINs to turn their backs on people from neighbouring jurisdictions. We have a lot of concentrated health specialties and services in Ontario. Accordingly, not all the LHINs could be self-sufficient and able to cover every single health service. Also, my mother lived in Collingwood while her doctor was in Etobicoke, and I wasn't going to mess with my mom.

Although many critics proposed we simply adopt municipal boundaries for the LHINs, this wouldn't work because health care delivery often extends well beyond municipal jurisdictions. And then there was the snobbery factor. Burlington, for example, sees an affinity with affluent Oakville, not working-class Hamilton. But when it comes to health care, Burlington residents usually turn to Hamilton's first-rate hospitals. It was my good fortune that Rob MacIsaac, then mayor of Burlington and now CEO of Hamilton Health Sciences, used hospital referral data to help bring reason to the debate.

Finally, the opposition parties chose to attack the LHINs for allegedly adding another layer of bureaucracy to the health care system, But this argument flopped because I made sure the LHINs were created through the reallocation of staff from the closure of the ministry's regional offices, the District Health Councils, and reductions in Community Care Access Centres (CCACs). That meant that LHINs began with no net new employees.

The Ontario health care system is one of the most administratively efficient in the world. But the system cannot be run without at least some people managing the money. Considering that LHINs are responsible for the accountability agreements with the hospitals, their role is now pivotal to maintaining fiscal discipline as well as health care planning and delivery.

Also overlooked in the opposition criticism is the 50 percent reduction in the size of the Ministry of Health, which declined from eight thousand employees when I arrived to less than four thousand today, as we strove to change the ministry's focus from day-to-day operations and crisis management to overall stewardship.

My critics also suggested LHINs would introduce inequities into the delivery of health care, given that they were allowed some flexibility in tailoring local delivery of provincial priorities. Again, this criticism is wrong-headed. We already had built-in inequities in the system, and for once we were moving toward quantifying and addressing them. To a certain extent, our model of concentrating high-cost services builds in inequities. But that can't be an excuse to refrain from doing our utmost to meet patient needs locally. Someone living in Timmins does not have the same immediate access to world-class hospitals as someone living in downtown Toronto. That, in turn, explains our heavy reliance on Ornge, the air ambulance service. But with LHINs, we could pursue excellence everywhere, either through the sharing of best practices or just sheer jealousy. I called it virtuous competition, the idea that uncorking fourteen vats of creativity would raise all boats with citizens in one area clamouring for services offered in another. Unfortunately, as soon as I left the ministry, my successors started to roll back the autonomy of LHINs. In my opinion, we should be liberating them and letting them be more innovative as we continue to grapple with the systemic challenges. I think it is far more likely that local communities are going to be the first to identify that some of the resources they need are perpetually being wasted, as 20 percent of their hospital beds are clogged with patients who would be better accommodated elsewhere. Today in Ontario, we are actually debating adding new acute-bed capacity to address pressure largely from an aging population. Instead, we should be discussing measures to stop ambulances from rolling to hospital emergency rooms in the first place.

In order to make local needs and wants a priority, I also pushed the ministry to locate the LHINs' offices in less logical locations. I say "less logical," because outside of the GTA a lot of public services might tend to concentrate in a region's largest municipality. I wanted to make sure that the beaten path for health care didn't cause us to lose sight of the vastness of Ontario. My time spent looking up at the map of Ontario in our family trucking business office had driven this point home to me. So for LHIN offices (and the jobs that went with them), I chose Orillia not Barrie, Grimsby not Hamilton, Belleville not Kingston, and North Bay not Sudbury. In some cases, these decisions were greeted with slacked jaws. But I stuck to my guns and enjoyed the response.

The premier cut me a lot of slack on these issues. So did the Liberal caucus — I hope because individually they knew I had their backs. I learned my lessons from Hugh O'Neil well. With Scott Lovell's help, I tended to the needs of MPPs and tried never to leave a smouldering wreck behind when I left town. It did not hurt that I was the biggest good-news provider in the government, with almost weekly announcements of new health care initiatives.

The future of LHINs is now up in the air, with a new Conservative government at Queen's Park under Doug Ford. It is unclear what Ford intends to do in this area. He could choose to tinker with LHINs by changing the name and shifting the boundaries. Or he could decide to abolish them. If the latter, he will find that their core functions cannot be fulfilled unless he brings responsibility for overseeing all those hospital accountability agreements back to head office. Then perhaps Toronto will be the beneficiary as hundreds of new staff are hired at the centralized Ministry of Health while hundreds of others are being laid off in smaller municipalities across Ontario.

Personally, I would devolve more authority to LHINs, not less, and I would create an Indigenous LHIN that covers all of Ontario. The 2005 Kelowna Accord — agreed to by the federal government, all the provinces, and the Indigenous Peoples themselves — would have transferred more responsibility to the provinces for delivering health care to Indigenous Peoples. Unfortunately, it was a casualty of the NDP decision to bring down the Martin government. That resulted in the election of a Conservative government under Stephen Harper, who promptly killed the Kelowna Accord.

* * *

In the midst of all this activity at the health ministry, which included answering more than half the daily questions in the Legislature, I added a new title to my job description: deputy premier. The *Star* reported at the time that I was given the title because I had threatened to quit cabinet and the Legislature to run federally. This was not true. It is a fact that in the summer of 2006 I had breakfast with my federal counterpart and friend, Bill Graham, and he told me he was leaving politics. Previously, he and I had an understanding that I would be interested in succeeding him. But by then I had a great job at Queen's Park and a pending marriage to boot, and the federal Liberals were in opposition. Maybe someone in McGuinty's office was worried I would decamp, but it was a groundless fear. I was a very happy camper, although my temperament might not have adequately conveyed my happiness at all times.

The deputy premiership came about because I raised the idea with Peter Wilkinson, then McGuinty's chief of staff. At that time, there was no one with the title of deputy premier. Instead, the government relied on a rotation of ministers filling in for McGuinty when he was unable to be in the Legislature. That was less than ideal from a messaging standpoint. Because I was a target of so many opposition questions in the Legislature, I was pretty much forced to be in attendance. Otherwise, all those answers would have to be foisted on the premier or another minister. "So," I said to Wilkinson,

Dalton McGuinty and me with my stepdad D'Arcy Kelley, my mom, Christopher, and my sister Joanne, on the occasion of my being made deputy premier of Ontario.

"if I am going to be there anyway, why not make me the deputy?" The logic of my position evidently appealed to the premier.

Of course, being deputy premier involved not just subbing in for McGuinty in the Legislature but also delivering some speeches around the province on his behalf and doing more fundraising duties for the party. Fundraising can be a real drain on politicians' time and energy in a way that is utterly out of proportion to the actual dollars being raised. Before Kathleen Wynne's move to ban corporate and union donations and enhance public funding, political parties were raising $10 million to $20 million annually. And I was a big draw at fundraising events.

Unfortunately, these events exposed ministers to heavy lobbying from people who had bought tickets (typically, for $500 to $1,000 each). In fact, it wasn't uncommon to see the same lobbyists over and over again. In order to survive, I deliberately failed to recall which pharma company produced what therapy, lest I be expected to speak specifically about their issue.

There is, of course, another way for political parties to raise money: direct mail or, in the internet age, email. We have all heard about the mastery of direct mail and email by Obama. Well, here in Canada the federal Conservatives raise tons of money this way. But the Ontario Liberals were far too slow to adopt that approach. I recall this internal debate vividly from the time I worked at the Ontario Liberal Party office in the 1980s. Don Smith (of Ellis Don, the giant construction company) was party president at the time. He sneered at anyone who proposed using direct mail to raise money. "What you can raise in a month or a year that way I can get in an afternoon of phone calls," he would say (and do). Meanwhile, the Conservatives and the New Democrats jumped eagerly into the direct-mail pool. The Liberals are still playing catch-up.

* * *

Back to the health ministry: everyone thinks the thing in shortest supply in government is money. It isn't. Rather, it is ministerial time and talent. In our system, the decision-making apparatus in government is rooted in cabinet. It is a narrow portal that opens only every once in a while, and all the ministers are competing to jam stuff through it. As minister of health, I spent at least one-third of my time trying to justify my ministry's initiatives to the central agencies — the Premier's Office, finance ministry, and Treasury Board. That's called accountability. But it is also an excruciatingly inefficient use of leadership time and talent. And it can be exhausting. So I strived to align the health ministry with the priorities of the central agencies rather than be seen as working against them. Other ministers had a decidedly different approach and were constantly fighting the centre. I was fortunate in that health was an area in which there was already an alignment of both government resources and the will to get things done. Still, it was not as easy as it may have looked from the outside.

One of the things that you often hear is that people have been told that their "file is on the minster's desk." This is a ploy to redirect the onus. I delighted in showing people my desk, which was bare of their file or any other. The other pile of malarkey spread by everybody — opposition critics, media commentators, patients and their system advocates — is that the required resources are "only a rounding error" in such a big budget and that the minister has all the power. There is this naive idea that, because the minister has the power of his signature, this is the same as having the power to get things done instantaneously. One thing I think that the media likes to ignore — because it makes their work easier — is that complex issues take time to address. The *Toronto Star* can run three days of headlines and force a policy change and then move onto the next issue while the minister is still bogged down trying to write the terms of reference for an advisory panel to address the first problem the newspaper raised. While the eHealth issue was brewing, for instance, I was elbows-deep in trying to fix the problems at Smart Systems for Health, highlighted in a prior auditor general's report. More about that later.

Nonetheless, the drive to implement our agenda was unrelenting, and the premier was keeping a very close eye on progress in fulfilling health care commitments. As the son of a trucker, I was always asking: "Where's my drive gear?" To push our agenda ahead, we created a "health results team" attached to the ministry but with a mandate to break a few eggs in order to make omelettes. My deputy (Ron Sapsford), my associate deputy (Hugh MacLeod), and the cabinet secretary (Tony Dean) were all instrumental in the creation of the team, and it worked to advance unprecedented reforms in health care. Thanks to pressure from the health results team, we were able to move on different tracks simultaneously. But we discovered that maintaining the pace of reform was difficult when everything emanated from the head office. That is one reason I favoured empowering the LHINs to transform the system.

For some ministers confronted with sticky issues, the path of least resistance is to launch pilot projects. I inherited a ton of them at the health ministry. One or the other of my predecessors had funded a program in this or that hospital to quell protests in the community. Of course, these pilots came at the expense of equity across the whole system. Ottawa and London, for example, had much better funded cardiac after-care than the rest of the province, and there were countless other examples of unequal treatment. I tried very hard not to be the guy that launched pilot projects here and there to solve local problems only to have them reappear later as hot potatoes when the special funding agreement ran out. In other cases, though, I had to fight the ministry to recognize and fund projects that addressed inequity caused by distance. Programs like angioplasty in Thunder Bay or the cancer bunker in Sault Ste. Marie never would have come about if I didn't know how ridiculous it was to drive from Wawa to Sudbury for a treatment or to fly from Thunder Bay to Hamilton (alone) for a cardiac procedure.

* * *

I worked incredibly hard at the health ministry, especially in my first two years there. Just getting my head around all the billions wasn't easy. Most ministers' offices operate on the idea that all decisions first have to go through the chief of staff. I decided this was too restrictive because I didn't expect anyone to work as hard as I was prepared to. But at the beginning, I made myself too available. Packages and letters to be signed were coming at me from all quarters and at all hours, including drops at my residence. Sign this, sign that. Because I refused to delegate my signature, I signed tens of thousands of letters — to hospitals, long-term care homes, CCACs, and so on. I stubbornly rejected the signature machine as an alternative because I was struggling to align the language in the letters with the government's priorities.

The problem was that the ministry received some four hundred thousand communications a year. So people would approach me at a public event and say: "I wrote you six months ago and you never replied." At my cynical best, I would tell them: "Don't worry. They are working on it." ("They" may very well have been doing so, but I couldn't be sure.) The cost, in staff time, to draft an independent response to all these letters was in the hundreds, if not thousands, of dollars each.

I also pushed my staff very hard, in the early days especially. I made it a badge of courage for them to try to outwork me, and I was working up to a hundred hours a week. To say I was driven is an understatement, and sometimes my passion alone wasn't enough to excuse my excesses. About 20 percent of the time, I went beyond what could be described as just "passionate" and resorted to yelling at staff or just generally. And I'm loud even when I am not yelling. Not surprisingly, then, my nickname inside the ministry was "old yeller." I joked that I should have a T-shirt printed up with the slogan "The beatings will continue until morale improves." Abid Malik, the high-school student who introduced Barbara Hall at a mayoral campaign event in 1997 and was now one of my most loyal staffers, kept on working right through his cancer treatments. That was a wake-up call for me, and I began to aim for a little more balance, especially as my 2007 wedding approached. But mixed in with the yelling were frequent expressions of gratitude from me toward my staff. I was a terrible boss at times and an inspirational one at others. I tried hard to let people know where we were going. As a result, my staff, while large, never appeared to lack harmony. It was a team environment, and we knew we were doing important stuff. We paused, if only briefly, to celebrate our victories, even if they didn't look like victories to others. And I adopted the David Peterson approach of regularly putting my excess swag up for grabs.

* * *

I also have to give much of the credit for my successes at Health to Dalton McGuinty. Early in his time as premier, he had the courage to say Yes to a health premium (for which he paid a steep political price) in order to invest more in the sector. (The premium wasn't my idea. I heard about it just two days before it was announced in the government's first budget.) McGuinty wants to be seen as the "education premier," and he certainly can be proud of his many accomplishments in that area. But in my opinion, he should be remembered as the "health care premier." The actions of his government

At the 2007 swearing-in as MPP with (from left) my uncle Doug Wood, my sister Christine, my niece Tamara Clancy, my mom, Christopher, and my stepdad.

saved medicare in Ontario and provided a fine example to the rest of the country. How so? OHIP is, in its essence, an insurance plan. The measure of any insurance policy is confidence. But by the time we attained office, doctors were abandoning family practice, public health was in disrepair, and patients were waiting interminably for vital surgery. McGuinty restored that confidence. As a result, our health care reforms proved to be a positive contributor to the outcome of the 2007 election.

* * *

One last word: earlier in this chapter, I described the importance of insulating yourself in the health portfolio. I tried hard not to let any one heartbreaking story hit me or to make decisions motivated by the situation of a single person. The only real exception to this rule was Brandon Gibson. He and I were pictured striking a pose on the front page of the *Toronto Star*. Brandon was a SickKids patient suffering from cystic fibrosis. After he underwent a double lung transplant, my political association and the

SickKids Foundation helped Brandon and his family travel to the world transplant games in Australia, where he competed. He later resumed playing hockey. When I heard later from Brandon's incredible mother, Muriel, that his transplanted lungs were failing and his life was going to end, I took it very hard. Writing about it even now brings me to tears.

CHAPTER FIVE

So-Called Scandals

No history of my time as health minister would be complete without a chapter on the so-called scandals on my watch, eHealth and Ornge. I stand indirectly accused by the province's auditor general of wasting $1.64 billion in taxpayers' money on the two agencies — $1 billion on eHealth and $640 million on Ornge. Neither figure — repeated endlessly in the media — is anywhere near the truth. Rather, what the whole episode shows is that, if you expose over a billion dollars in spending to a team of accountants with a snarly disposition and a jaundiced way of thinking, you could make anything look like a pile of cow dung. Frankly, I think the real scandal is that an officer of the Legislature, the auditor general, deprived Ontarians of an accurate accounting of value for money, which was his sworn duty. By contributing to a misleading and self-serving narrative, he permanently weakened public confidence in two vital agencies. Here are the facts, first on eHealth, then on Ornge.

* * *

When I became the minister in the fall of 2003, I inherited a mess around the digitalization of medical records, a goal that everyone supports for both health and efficiency reasons. The previous Conservative government had created an agency called Smart Systems for Health to handle the assignment. The agency had been criticized by the auditor general even before I got there.

My big first leadership action in the area was to appoint a new board for Smart Systems, including Michael Lauber, former head of the Toronto Board of Trade; David Johnston, then president of the University of Waterloo (later governor general); and Marc Kealey, head of the Ontario Pharmacists Association. The new board set out to address the auditor's concerns about things like high staff turnover rates and the organization's near complete reliance on consultants.

But even as we addressed those problems proactively a bigger problem lurked: in order to protect patient privacy, Smart Systems had decided to install its own fibre optics network rather than share one with other users. This was a big mistake, and it drove up the cost of the project exponentially, because of both higher capital expenditures and the cost of bringing a platform to life very slowly. After much soul-searching, I have concluded that my mistake was not reversing my predecessors' mistake. And I cannot plead complete ignorance. I had a breakfast meeting with Jean Monty, chair of BCE Emergis, the network solutions company. "I already have fibre optic cable operating to every pharmacy in Ontario," he told me. "And it is perfectly secure. You don't have to build your own network." Did I miss my cue? Perhaps.

In my defence, by then the Conservative government had already spent hundreds of millions of dollars on building its own network. Walking away from that investment would have been seen as a scandal in its own right. Still, I wish that I had sparked a more lively debate about the sanity of following our predecessors' approach. The problem was compounded because we tried to begin operations before the cable was laid. Server space was reserved. We were paying for it. And it wasn't required for users who would only join the platform years later. Furthermore, the bureaucrats in the health ministry never accepted Smart Systems as a legitimate offshoot. They were second-guessing it all the time. I inherited all those tensions. The file was so complicated that it ran the risk of becoming an orphan. No one could get a full grasp on it.

* * *

Among my most significant final acts as minister of health was to gain cabinet approval for the creation of a new agency, eHealth, which was set up as a Crown corporation. We were counting on this new model to build greater momentum toward digitization of health records.

Ironically enough, the scandal I am associated with involves an organization that had exactly zero employees when I left the ministry. It was my successor, David Caplan, who put Dr. Alan Hudson and Sarah Kramer in charge of eHealth, although I probably would have done the same. Those two individuals had contributed greatly to the successful reduction of health care wait times and to the launch of the complicated wait times information system. Their appointments seemed like a no-brainer, given the confidence that Premier McGuinty placed in them as well as the centre's general familiarity with them, especially Hudson. When David Caplan consulted me, I entirely endorsed his decision to hire them. Unfortunately, in order to expedite change, eHealth cut corners under the leadership of Hudson and Kramer and awarded some untendered contracts. There were also expense claims by eHealth staffers for expensive furniture and limos and for trivial stuff like cookies and muffins, all of which became fodder for the auditor general and, subsequently, the media and the opposition.

In the absence of a government strategy to aggressively undermine the political spin from the auditor, opposition, and media, the crisis over eHealth deepened in the Legislature. The premier gave me a heads-up that he was going to fire Caplan after just fifteen months on the job. I felt bad for Caplan. It's rarely ever fair that any minister be forced to resign for a government's collective mistakes, but that is how the parliamentary system works.

While regretful that Caplan had to go, I did not feel personally responsible for his firing. Yes, Caplan inherited a mess (as did I), but it was identified to him as he took over, and he could have taken steps to address the problem. Instead, upon his exit, his press secretary forcefully advanced the storyline that I was to blame for anything and everything that went wrong at eHealth.

What really finished Caplan was NOT any dereliction of duty on my part. Rather, it was a consequence of the Premier's Office's instinct to follow the path of least resistance and accept everything the auditor general said at face value. (Was this issues management by Catholic guilt?) Easier to have a one-day message track that says we accept all of the auditor's findings, even if upon hard-headed examination the findings themselves are wrong or misguided. And, by the way, while I was supposedly complicit in the gritty details of the auditor's report, I was never given the courtesy of challenging the findings.

The alternative path — to fight back and challenge the auditor's findings — would have been much harder politically, but I believe it would have ultimately been more persuasive. After all, it could hardly have gone worse than it did. And I think it could be said that the McGuinty government lost its innocence on the eHealth file. Me, too. (It is worth noting that under Premier Kathleen Wynne, the government followed this more combative path in other areas addressed by the auditor.)

Despite the initial setbacks and slow progress, digitized medical records have begun to emerge and to provide a return on the province's investment. Nevertheless, the eHealth issue stuck with me long after I had left the health ministry and the government — all during my run for the Toronto mayoralty, for example. On election night after I lost to Rob Ford, I went back home to a small family gathering, where a young campaign worker borrowed one of Ford's favourite expressions and asked me, jokingly: "So where's the billion dollars, George?" That sums it all up.

* * *

As for the air ambulance service, it was also in disarray when I arrived at the ministry. The service had eight helicopters, all of which were based at different hospitals and funded by those hospitals. Their supply and maintenance was contracted out to a company called Canadian Helicopters, which was holding us to ransom. (This was an arrangement that the auditor general had previously criticized.) The bureaucrats in charge were the least confidence-inspiring people I ever encountered in my time at the ministry.

In response, we created an arm's-length, non-profit corporation with a mandate to provide a coordinated air ambulance service that covered the whole province. It was subsequently called Ornge. (The name is not an acronym. Rather, it is the colour of the helicopters, with the "a" dropped for trademark reasons.) To run it, I picked Dr. Chris Mazza, who had been hired by the Conservatives before I got there. Mazza is a physician with an MBA and a very engaging and passionate man. He had a vision to use Ornge's

Air ambulance announcement at Sunnybrook, with crew members and Dr. Chris Mazza.

expertise as leverage to pursue for-profit activities elsewhere in Canada and in other countries. This was to become an issue.

Looking back, I don't see Ornge as a mistake. And it was certainly not a scandal. The story of the progress in the air ambulance service has been lost in all the foofaraw about Mazza and Ornge. Ontario now has one of the best-evolved models for air medical transportation in the world. Why not leverage it? As for the criticism from the left (notably CUPE) that we "privatized" the service, the opposite is true: we took it back from the hands of a private company (Canadian Helicopters). I did agree to allow Ornge to take on debt in order to purchase new helicopters and planes. That was not a radical step; hospitals have the same authority. The model was a good one. But Mazza took that model and manipulated it to his own benefit.

Subsequently, after I had left the government, Mazza set up a web of for-profit spinoff companies, and the trouble began. What followed was a dubious deal with an Anglo-Italian helicopter manufacturer and a question-able payment to a Brazilian law firm, along with an allegation that Mazza had promoted his girlfriend to the position of associate vice-president at Ornge. All this ended up in the media, especially the *Toronto Star*, which made it into a crusade.

A major point of contention was Mazza's overall salary, which he had managed to keep a secret thanks to Ornge's complicated public/private hybrid status. The government was hammered on this point day after day in the Legislature. Deb Matthews, by then minister of health, said she was unable to obtain the salary information because Ornge was "stonewalling" her. If I had been minister, I would have just called in the chair of Ornge and demanded an answer, or else I would have darkened the doorway of Mazza's office unannounced until a satisfactory response was forthcoming.

I was just a private citizen by this time, but I was so exasperated by Matthews's response that I picked up the phone and called Mazza myself to ask him how much he was making. When he gave me the answer ($1.4 million), I was gobsmacked. That was roughly DOUBLE what the CEOs of the province's largest hospitals were making. "That's crazy," I said. "I'm never talking to you again." And I haven't.

There has been lots of speculation about why Mazza went off the rails like this. My theory is that he was deeply shaken by the death of his fourteen-year-old son in a skiing accident and, quite simply, lost his perspective. Indeed, after he was fired by the government, he checked into Guelph's Homewood Health Centre to be treated for post-traumatic stress disorder. Looking back, I think perhaps I should have paid more attention to Mazza's personal issues. I could get angry, but mostly I just get sad.

But the management responsibility did not rest with Mazza alone. Ornge had a board of directors that included some distinguished Ontarians. The chair was Rainer Beltzner, also chair of Humber College. He signed off on Mazza's salary and he knew how it dwarfed the salary that the president of a large community college was pulling down. I contend that Beltzner and his fellow directors were asleep at the switch and failed at their fiduciary responsibilities. They would have been the target of much more criticism if accountability had been doled out in an impartial rather than political setting.

Where were the minister's political staff and the ministry staff during those hundreds of days of stonewalling over Mazza's salary? Did it not come to any of their minds that swift changes to the regulations or a hiccup in transfer payments to Ornge could have shifted the balance of power in the relationship?

I accepted responsibility for not taking into account every eventuality when I handed Mazza the reins of Ornge. "I didn't see it coming," I told reporters after speaking to the all-party legislative committee probing the Ornge affair in 2012. "For the rest of my life, I will regret that." Perhaps I gave Mazza too much licence. But most of the bad stuff happened long after I left the ministry. The critics said the excesses were made possible because of deficiencies in the legislation creating Ornge. But had I remained as health minister and the deficiencies had become apparent, I would have acted. Does anyone seriously think Chris Mazza would pull in $1.4 million a year while I was minister and get away with telling me to fuck off if I asked him about it?

Still, my former colleagues in the government were all too happy to shift the blame to me. Their collaboration in the Boxing Day (2011) massacre column by Martin Regg Cohn of the *Star* was breathtaking. Citing government sources, Cohn wrote of me: "It's not that everything he touched turned to dross; he merely left a mess behind for others to clean up." That was my first real visit under a bus, although as the son of a truck driver I have been under many a truck in my day.

Today, Ornge is just a brand, used as a sort of drive-by political slur in Ontario politics. A failed symbol of some kind. Screw that, I say. When I see a modern rotor- or fixed-wing Ornge aircraft above, I know it is on a flight of mercy, carving precious minutes on the way to saving lives. I know, too, that the service we have now in Ontario is more public, more integrated, and more capable than the fragmented, privately manipulated one I inherited in 2003.

* * *

What are the lessons here? First of all, arm's-length agencies can cause trouble for governments because they are free from the usual oversight mechanisms for public spending. They are launched with good intentions as vehicles to get things done at a faster pace than the ponderous machinery of government normally operates. But the salaries they pay and expenses they file and contracts they let often become ingredients for the opposition and the media to cry "scandal." There is no easier story to tell than one where people apparently take advantage of a situation to enrich themselves or their friends. Does that mean we should never create such agencies? No. They can be essential to progress in the public sector. But governments should always keep in mind the potential for them to backfire.

Secondly, we have a problem with the various bodies that report directly to the Legislature, not the government — the auditor general, ombudsman, privacy commissioner, and so on. They have become sort of a cottage industry, competing with each other for headlines. And the quickest way to a headline is to throw out a number like $1 billion, no matter how far back one has to reach to get there. In both the eHealth and Ornge cases, the auditor general let stand, even if he didn't utter it in the first place, the notion that $1 billion and $640 million, respectively, were either unaccounted for or simply wasted. This despite the fact that in both cases almost every penny of the allocated money was spent in the intended way, if imperfectly. To say it was all wasted is a gross exaggeration. But that was the impression left by the auditor general. Ironically the very officer paid to provide a sense of value for money to Ontarians ripped them off.

I think governments are partly to blame for this, given their institutional instinct to keep everything confidential even where this is no material risk in its transparent release. That gives power to others who work in secret. I remain convinced that much more value-for-money analysis could come from eagle-eyed researchers and intrepid citizens if they were given greater access to government data. Instead, we have legislative officers duelling for headlines and reverting to tactics like leaking to get them. It is fair to treat their reports with far greater skepticism than before. Of course the media and opposition make much hay in the telling of scandal and anyone being criticized is naively advised if they think it's all going to come out impartially.

* * *

Of late I have gotten a bit tired trying to educate people about what really happened with eHealth and Ornge, so I just say: "If you really think I blew $1.64 billion, then at least give me credit for the $3 billion–plus I saved the government in drug-purchasing expenses and the untold billions more in savings from diminishing annual hospital bailouts."

If you ask me, the real scandal of my time as minister of health was my delay in making rates of *C. difficile* in hospitals publicly reportable. Despite moving sooner on this than most jurisdictions, I wonder until today whether lives at Joseph Brant Hospital in Burlington might have been saved had I been less politically defensive.

CHAPTER SIX

Health Reform

During my time as minister of health, I prominently displayed a picture of Tommy Douglas in my Hepburn Block office. I was paying homage to Douglas's role as the father of medicare in our country. But I was also acknowledging his local presence, for there is a housing co-op named after him on River Street in my riding. And Tommy's daughter, Shirley, was also living in my riding, practically across the street from Queen's Park. Each served as local reminders of his incredible legacy in our country.

The fact remains, however, that the model of public health care that we adopted fifty years ago fell far short of the model that was originally advocated by Douglas. Specifically, there was inadequate support for community care. Today, medicare (what we call OHIP in Ontario) is badly in need of a remake that saves us from the "doctors and hospitals" funding preference. The truth is that, for all the talk about the transition to community care, it is being funded by incremental table scraps while the legacy health care system (doctors and hospitals) gobbles up most of the available dough.

In a constrained environment with various demographic pressures threatening quality health care, I believe we must reset our priorities. We must stop encouraging patients to begin or renew their health care journeys with gatekeepers in the most expensive settings with the most costly providers. I call this a move away from "catch and release" toward "catch and care."

Late in 2017, Ontario announced $140 million in new funding as a so-called surge, but most of the new money was allocated to old solutions. Faced with 20 percent of regular hospital beds being occupied by patients who did not require that level (and cost) of care, Ontario announced plans to open more of the same. One wonders how many hours it will take to have all of that surge capacity eaten up before calls begin for the next surge? Did anyone other than hospital administrators get asked what they could do with $140 million to relieve the pressure of seniors seeking care?

I have been told I was the most transformative health minister in a generation. As much as I believe that to be true, I have come to recognize that the forces against change (represented by the citizenry, society, press, and health care providers alike) make incrementalism *feel* like a transformation. Players inside the system celebrate increments that are unrecognizable to the untrained eye. And one thousand increments do not a *transformation* make, no matter how many times you use the word.

If we really want to survive the twin statistical tsunamis of chronic disease and aging with some semblance of quality, then health care must be completely retooled and a new operating system installed. Only a monumental makeover will give us the system that the patients deserve and that our values and pride already project. After all, what is the purpose of living longer if we cannot also live better?

Have no doubt, we are paying a price for our continued over-reliance — established at the outset of medicare — on hospitals and doctors. In the process, we have ignored solutions that could fundamentally reorient the gravitational pull of the Emergency Room, that 24/7 window to the most expensive care possible. Most damning is that those same high costs are often on a path toward the release of a high volume of at-risk patients back into the community. Meanwhile, we all remain smugly content that, if something goes awry, Mrs. Jones can always call 9-1-1.

By being far more proactive in support of the needs of about 10 percent of the population, we could increase the mobility of health care professionals and replace $700 ambulance rides with $15 taxi fares.

I am talking not just about more home care but also about a new kind of medicine to be practised in the hallways of Canadians' homes. How about a system that recognizes the frail elderly and people with chronic disease or serious mental illness as our best customers and reduces their need and instinct to head to the ER? We could do that by allowing them to remain as "admitted" patients of the hospital even after they go home. Then they can enjoy the confidence that comes with having someone to call who knows their name. A number as convenient as 9-1-1. I have seen this hospital-in-the-home model at work in Sweden.

In Ontario, St. Joseph's Healthcare in Hamilton is the closest thing I have seen to a genuinely integrated system. That's because St. Joe's took an active interest in delivering care across all verticals of delivery, including community and home care. I don't favour gutting the role of hospitals. Rather, I favour freeing up our hospital capacity and resources to deploy them more proactively as we look to reward providers for outcomes rather than for inputs.

Canadians love their health care system, and rightly so; yet access issues, whether due to lack of resources or habit, create problems that are manifest when our health care outcomes are compared to those of our peers globally. According to report after report, there are two quality-crushing problems with our system, and both of those relate to wait times: namely, the wait to access primary care even if you have it, and the wait to have various specialty consultations and surgical procedures completed.

I propose the following five reforms, which would improve quality within the current fiscal profile. They are audacious, ambitious, and revolutionary. But the change we need can only be accomplished if everybody recognizes his or her own power to contribute something to a universal benefit that has become a Canadian value. Revolutionary reforms, by their nature, ask a lot of everyone, not just some.

Don't get me wrong. Since serving as minister of health, I have been on the receiving end of health care, just like other Ontario families. And in respect of myself, my kids, my spouse, and my two aged parents, I have seen a range of exemplary care in a wide array of settings and in lots of hospitals.

I have also experienced primary care in a family health team environment, and two things are clear to me: if I need minor care, I can go unannounced and see a nurse who will, if necessary, immediately consult with others in the team, including nurse practitioners and doctors. And if my kids and I need care, we know the clinic hours and locations for each evening and weekend. All shots are administered by nurses. I rarely see my

122 Unconventional Candour

own doctor, who has known me well for some time. When I do see him, we review entries in my electronic health record and address new business. My son, who has ADHD and a learning disability, is a patient of a hospital that runs clinics with a precision that is both graceful and efficient. Continuous quality improvement seems to be the approach. And my mother, who suffered a brain aneurysm and a three-month decline, rapidly transitioned down the health care food chain from brain surgery at a University of Toronto–affiliated hospital to a restful death at home. Her death came just hours after coming home, where she was showered with love and supported with a lot of helpful facilitation by government-funded home-care providers (dare I say, they were profit oriented) organized seamlessly with the hospital discharge plan.

Our family teamed up with those same home-care providers to keep my aging stepfather out of long-term care despite his eligibility. His final brief stay in hospital was facilitated by compassionate and skilled palliative care professionals as well as by bedside love from his family, and he passed two years and one day after my mother.

So I have those personal stories and reflections. But I also know that the hardest thing for the Ontario health care system to get was that my mother and stepfather did not "go by" the stated names on their health cards. In a move down the hall from the ICU at one hospital, my mother Margaret's identity was reset to Irene, her actual first name. I can't get the picture out of my head of staff trying to get a rise out of my mother as her brain got foggier and foggier. "Irene! Irene! Irene!" And at another hospital, D'Arcy, the name my stepfather has been called since around the time of the Great Depression, was reset to Terrence, a name I'm not sure he would have recognized even in his prime.

With the personal experiences noted here and my lengthy tenure running the largest government department in Canada, I want to offer my best ideas for reform. I should add the caveat that many people much smarter than me have proposed solutions for health care, usually to accolades. But their proposals often lack common sense because they depend on impossible new political or constitutional deals. My solutions are smart insofar as they don't play "nudge nudge, wink wink" with two-tier and other assaults on universality and the Canada Health Act. In fact, I see the Canada Health Act as helpful insofar as it prevents reforms that would threaten medicare's underpinnings.

Here are several things that people need to know if they are going to honestly appraise the solutions that I am proposing: 1) I believe in health care as a core service and a value of Canada that should be offered equitably and universally; 2) I believe that the framework of insured services should be as broad as possible; 3) I do not support models where preferential access to insured health care services is available to those who pay or use undue influence or live closer; 4) I believe that private health care is neither a natural-born threat nor a panacea for the delivery of health care; 5) I believe that an appropriate regulatory environment can be created to protect core values and expectations like quality; and 6) I think we should more openly acknowledge that much of what we cherish is already delivered privately, at the cost of billions annually, including long-term care, home care, laboratory and diagnostic services, and many physician services.

Finally, I think it's time to turn things upside down and leverage all of our community capacity before building more bricks-and-mortar institutional facilities. That is, we need to interrupt the cheery continuum that imagines everyone staying in a long-term care home for a time before their death. Also, hospitals are too big and too expensive to build and too costly to operate. We need to look for ways to shrink the building envelope and better leverage and develop other community infrastructure, starting with long-term care homes.

What follows are my Big 5 ideas.

1. WAIT TIMES GUARANTEE

A patient that fails to receive a procedure within the established medically appropriate time frame shall have the right to a voucher covering the service at an accredited community-based, not-for-profit facility.

- We need to establish, collect, and report ALL surgical wait times using the existing platform. This is a long overdue step toward transparency and accountability. Even if some of the data are troubling, we all need and deserve to know.
- We need to create a regulatory framework to enable the formation of not-for-profit clinics offering services to non-OHIP-insured individuals (non-resident expats,

professional athletes, and medical tourism patients), taking all steps to protect against threat of two-tiers (real or perceived).

- We have to broaden the health care connect role, empowering real live health care professionals to connect individual patients, who are sometimes stragglers, to timely care. The voucher should be co-funded by the health ministry and the non-performing LHIN or hospital, thereby ensuring accountability and an incentive for performance improvement at the health system level.

While the primary thrust here is to address the chronic quality question facing too many Canadians as they wait for care, the approach differs from prior wait times strategies, where almost all the action was dependent on new spending. In my proposal, new funding would be allocated based on real patient experience. This would shift the power. In particular, poor-performing LHINs or hospitals or surgical teams would feel the pain and gain a greater motivation to care for their captive patients proactively rather than suffer high rates of voucher cases in their captive territory.

There are also two tremendously important benefits that would go along with the emerging not-for-profit facility capacity envisioned here: 1) leveraging our substantial public health care knowledge for more jobs and for the generation of foreign revenues through the promotion of medical tourism; and 2) enhancing our critical event or epidemic surge capacity, as not-for-profit clinics would be legislatively obligated to shift their resources for public health emergencies when prescribed circumstances warrant (such as SARS).

2. CHOICE IN PRIMARY CARE

Create competition in primary care by allowing alternative providers and teams of providers to roster patients and provide care.

- We should modernize primary care by providing real choice for patients to designate and roster with a provider or team of providers of their choice rather than just doctors, as is now the case. That would immediately improve access to timely care for people in under-serviced areas.

- Why not compensate alternative primary care providers or teams of providers when they can fulfill a similar scope of practice as family physicians? This would provide the benefit of timely care to patients while accentuating team models of care.
- A rostering model prevents a patient from having a whole fleet of different providers, ensuring cost effectiveness. Case in point: My local pharmacy helps to advertise a physician home-call service. I needed a timely response to my daughter's need for a medicated cream for eczema. Simple enough. The health care system was willing to pay a doctor to come to my home for this ailment. Meanwhile we were at the pharmacy, and it was very obvious that this ailment could have been diagnosed and treatment initiated immediately at huge savings while greatly enhancing the patient experience.

The premise of our current primary care model is that OHIP would pay for a physician for anyone that wants one. Since we have established how much we are willing to pay (physician compensation) and what we can get for that money (scope of practice), this pool of funding should be open to a broader array of providers. We should start first by getting care to patients living in rural and remote areas who have been teased for too long with the promise of every sort of program and incentive possible to address their physician shortages. Meanwhile, models of teams meeting service need already abound, including the stand-alone nurse-practitioner model I initiated in Sudbury. But rostering patients and the compensation for doing that is not currently allowed.

Downstream we could see a model where regulated practitioners of traditional Chinese medicine work alongside practitioners of Western medical philosophy to meet the patient's needs holistically. Or pharmacists and nurse practitioners could consult with a physician as needed to allow their team to meet patient needs.

Extended hours of operation that push health care delivery into real-life hours and beyond nine-to-five would be a condition for participating in the Primary Care Choice Program.

3. RIGHTS, OBLIGATIONS, AND REWARDS

Look at the words behind the OHIP acronym: Ontario Health Insurance Plan. Why don't those people ever talk to me as a plan member and engage me in the way I use the health care system? Some critics have proposed patients get an invoice showing the cost of the services they have used. I bemoan the lack of any sophisticated system user guide that outlines rights, expectations, and services for the insurance program's members, the residents of Ontario. If we ever want to engage as a society in the goal of trying to make our health care system more sustainable (think quality, not just money), then the power is in our own hands. That's because so many of the highest costs the system is asked to deal with are influenced by the personal choices we all make. Not just lifestyle choices, which are important, but choices like when is the right time to go to the ER?

With timely access as the cornerstone, I think we need to reimagine the patient's experience and develop a Patients' Bill of Rights that balances expectations of timeliness with the fulfillment of obligations. For instance, I would have preferred to introduce "presumed consent" for organ and tissue donations, but the panel I appointed to advise me on increased organ and tissue donation didn't recommend it. That would have meant anyone could "opt out," but no "opt in" would be required, as consent to offer valuable organs and tissues would be presumed.

More importantly, I believe it should be the mandatory obligation of plan members to have executed a binding power of attorney or care direction by the time they reach age fifty-five. Such an obligation would reduce our costly reliance on usually pointless and always expensive end-of-life heroics, thereby saving both anguish and hundreds of millions of dollars annually. At the same time, it would ensure that your end-of-life wishes are not trumped by family members who can't stand to lose you.

Furthermore, it is time to encourage and reward our plan members for doing their best to help achieve good outcomes in the same way that an insurance company rewards good drivers. Now don't allow yourself to get worked up in a lather pretending that I just endorsed fat-shaming, or a ban on horseback riding for OHIP members because of the inherent risks. Rather, I am saying that in this day and age, personalized health care is becoming the new normal; yet our health care system refuses to recognize the power shift.

I think we should develop a reward system, funded by health premiums, that provides a refund to Ontarians who actively help to achieve the best measurable outcomes particular to their status, be that healthy or with underlying challenges. It makes a material difference, for instance, if a person with type 2 diabetes, no matter how obtained, takes a very active interest in his or her blood sugar levels. Compliance is sometimes hard, but we human beings are known to respond well to incentives. So why not reward people for their efforts at best possible outcomes even if their baseline isn't and will never be perfect or even great? Compliance rewards for the person with schizophrenia who stays on his or her drug regime could prevent untold trauma. Payback for that approach would be nearly immediate, and in the secure app world we can achieve that faster than ever while encouraging innovation. A well-developed model would equitably reward Ontarians for doing their upmost to protect and improve their health regardless of their starting point. Such incentives would of course restore rewards to people of all ages for enrolment in sports, exercise, or gym activities.

4. INDIGENOUS HEALTH LHIN

Eyes glaze over when one brings constitutional issues into the discussion of health care — or most public policies, for that matter. But when it comes to Ontario's Indigenous population, I would say it's high time we ditched the paternalism and hand over autonomy for the provision of health care to Indigenous Peoples themselves for the entirety of their traditional lands in the province.

The shocking irony is that we see medicare as a core national value while the federal government has always had primary responsibility for Indigenous health care, and Indigenous Peoples suffer from the worst (by far) health outcomes. Count me as cautiously optimistic as I recognize that some big steps are being made by the national and provincial governments (here in Ontario for instance) in recognizing that autonomy on the part of Indigenous people in organizing and running their health care is essential in achieving first-world health outcomes.

However, there are attendant risks if funding and program delivery are allowed to narrowly revolve around reserves or individual nations. I believe that a province-wide Indigenous LHIN would be an effective model. As in the case of Regent Park, where the concept of community succession (local people getting the good jobs) drove expectations of better educational performance and attainment, so, too, can the promise of economic opportunity in health care delivery and administration be a motivation to enhance the socio-economic situation for Indigenous people in Ontario. Let's face it. There are big dollars to be made in health care and pensions to be earned. We need to turn these into opportunities for today's Indigenous youth and put the pressure on us all to produce better educational attainment.

5. HOSPITAL-TO-HOME BUDGET SHIFT

If health care really is the big deal that Canadians seem to think it is, then maybe it is time for a little straight talk about how we need to adjust our expectations and use of the system. We have a very serious maldistribution of resources, much of it due to our aging population. This problem is only going to get worse, and we are no doubt headed toward a permanent state of crisis in the system where the needs of seniors run the risk of diminishing the chance for a quality outcome for them and for everyone else, too.

Everyone wants improvements in health care, and most people asking for them are largely hoping more money will be invested in the system. The truth is we are pretty much spending as much as we can. So what's going to give? There are two related areas that I believe need to be treated with urgency: one would put the onus for change on the patient; the other would put the onus on the system. In both cases, we need to enhance health care literacy to better arm our society to survive aging with as much grace and dignity as possible. Why live longer if you can't also live better?

There isn't much in the way of low-hanging fruit in health care that can be achieved by pursuing more "efficiencies." But there is unnecessary care being provided, and there is a lot of care being provided in settings that are far too costly. Reprofiling these several billions of dollars of current hospital operations is the most promising area for reform to create more care in the right place. I said in Big 5 idea number three that I believe that, as a condition of good citizenship, every Ontarian reaching age fifty-five should have designated a power of attorney and given direction about their care expectations. These steps should be mandatory before someone gains access to the Ontario Drug Benefit program at age sixty-five. This task can be completed thoughtfully and with assistance from community support agencies and entities like legal aid clinics. These are things that the patient can do.

The second matter is that 20 percent of Ontario's hospital beds are housing "alternate level of care" patients, sometimes called "bed blockers." Rather than add beds, as Ontario is mostly doing, I believe we need to cash out all those high-priced hospital beds and the costly ambulance rides that deliver patients there. Instead, we should buy more beds in the community, including the novel idea (for us) that an admitted patient of a hospital can remain in his or her own home.

The hospital waits all night long for the $700 ambulance ride to offload the needy cargo. It's high time that we set a goal of sharply reducing the number of ambulance deliveries and transition ourselves from the reactive to the proactive. In my model, the long-term care home would reverse its role. Rather than sending patients to the hospital, the long-term institution would deliver greater care and serve as an added resource for others, keeping aged loved ones in their own home.

Arguing that insecurity and social isolation are sometimes the source of 9-1-1 calls, I would deploy a small army of trained social assistance beneficiaries (the disabled and those on welfare) in a friendly home-calling program that would consistently check in on the isolated and would send any concerns about their situation up the food chain. The incremental wages for these home callers would provide a secondary benefit by reducing their underlying poverty and health status. A third benefit would be the ability to develop a vulnerable-persons database as a resource for emergency planning and civil defence, which is sorely lacking in Canada.

Recently many physicians have expressed frustration with the practice of hallway medicine, whereby a hospital patient is stationed in a hallway, not a room. In trying to fashion a response, I was reminded of an opportunity I was given to rethink capacity and save lives. A lot of adverse patient outcomes can occur in hospitals when an admitted patient's deteriorating health runs up against the sheer limits of critical-care or intensive-care capacity in a hospital. Dr. Tom Stewart led the development of a critical-care plan, where we created mobile capacity within the hospital that assembles en route to the patient, rather than the old model where we tried to move the patient to the often non-existent capacity.

I believe it's time to rethink the ER and its magnetic appeal. Rather than sit there and wait for the inevitable return of frail Mrs. Jones, we would check in on her proactively and organize our resources to suit her, including delivering more care right in her hallway at home.

CHAPTER SEVEN

Energy

After the 2007 election, I wasn't moved out of the health portfolio, at least not immediately. I was grateful for that because I had some unfinished business to deal with, including sex reassignment surgery, which the Harris government had delisted from OHIP funding. Earlier in 2007, I had met with the premier and won his commitment to move forward on the issue AFTER the election. (He didn't want the hassle of dealing with a social conservative backlash during the campaign.) McGuinty kept his word. He actually called me and told me to set the wheels in motion to restore funding for the surgery.

In support of my position, I noted that even Ralph Klein's Alberta was funding it. "If they are doing it, how can we not?" I asked. It wasn't a cost issue: fewer than two dozen sex reassignment surgeries had been performed annually in the early 1990s, when the Rae government had funded the procedure. In announcing the decision to restore funding in early 2008, I estimated the cost to taxpayers at just $200,000 (out of an overall health budget of $40 billion) and added: "It's a very serious medical condition that affects a very small number of people."

Of course, soon after that Alberta delisted sex reassignment surgery. And the number of people seeking the operation has climbed significantly as "trans" identification has emerged to an extent no one could have foreseen back then. Caitlyn (formerly Bruce) Jenner has something to do with that. But maybe she found the courage to come out because the world view of transgendered people changed. It is a chicken and egg question. Personally, I have great admiration for the trans community, which has been marginalized and abused for so long. Now they have a chance to match their body parts with their brains. I am proud of the role I played in making that happen and recall signing name change forms for constituents transitioning as one of the most emotional experiences ever.

* * *

My days were numbered in the health portfolio, however. One can never grow bored there, but there are declining rewards for initiative as one bears more of the institutional history. As time marches on, the incumbent minister becomes a symbol of inertia rather than a force for change, even though you are still trying to bring about change. I began to realize this in dealing with the issue of the perceived quality of care in our long-term care homes. Early on in my days at Health, I was exposed to images on the front page of the *Toronto Star* of a patient named Natalie Babineau. They are not images I will soon forget. She had gangrenous bed sores on her back as big as an adult hand. Wiping away tears at a press conference, I promised a "revolution" in long-term care. "We will fix this," I said. "We will." To address understaffing in nursing homes, I managed to secure more than $1 billion in additional funding that provided for nearly three thousand new employees. But because I had promised a revolution, nobody was inclined to offer up much credit for that improvement.

Looking back, I think long-term care was one of the files I handled most poorly, in terms of giving people confidence about performance. I rate myself poorly most especially because I set expectations so high. Pointedly, though, I came to realize as well that because the clientele is so vulnerable, they can appear neglected even if perfectly well supported.

After the 2007 election, long-term care remained an issue for me. The question then was whether to implement a new type of adult diaper that was more absorbent and, accordingly, would require fewer changes. In a scrum with reporters, I let down my guard. Despite ample warning from my staff, I candidly said I was seriously considering putting myself in the place of nursing home residents by wearing an adult diaper for a time. This exposed me to ridicule, from both the media and the opposition. Despite my having approached the issue with the seriousness it warranted, others couldn't help playing political games with it. (NDP critic Peter Tabuns called me "a damned embarrassment," and Conservative Leader John Tory said I was "a disgrace.")

It was my lowest moment. I was so depressed that I ducked out of sight for a few days. I even skipped the big annual Liberal fundraising dinner, where my friend Lawrence Bloomberg was chair. You see, I was the son of a proud man who had lain in a hospital bed for seven months with only the ability to move his eyes, and yet those eyes told me a lot about the loss of dignity he experienced at diaper-changing time. That taught me a lot, but it also left me unguarded and vulnerable. I was victimized by my own ill-advised openness.

A few months after this episode, Gerry Butts, the premier's top aide, asked me if I would like to move to another portfolio. I hadn't thought of that, asked for it, or hinted I wanted to move. Given that the health ministry accounts for 45 cents of every dollar the provincial government spends, and given that I was an unlikely candidate for the finance portfolio, anything else might seem to be a demotion. But Butts came to me with some intriguing ideas, including the merger of two important portfolios to create a super-ministry: energy and infrastructure OR energy and the environment. I knew I didn't want to be environment minister because I viewed it as a regulatory department laden with files. I had seen Jim Bradley's office when he was the environment minister in the 1980s. Bradley is an aficionado of paper collection (that's a euphemism for a hoarder), and his office was overwhelmed with files. That was etched in my mind as I opted for "energy and infrastructure."

The important point is that I was given the opportunity to decide what I wanted to do. That was a courtesy not often extended to a cabinet minister. I also got a heads-up that I was soon going to be leaving a place where I still had many irons in the fire. So I sat down with Jamison Steeve, by then my chief of staff, and, taking him into my confidence about the impending move, said: "Take a list of things we want to get done." It was a long list, because I was intent on pushing as many things over the line as I possibly could. The bureaucracy in the health ministry must have wondered what the hell had gotten into me during my final weeks there. When you have spent five years in a portfolio, you really don't want to leave a lot of undone stuff with your successor. He or she might not invest the same energy, interest, and motivation toward getting it done.

* * *

I was appointed minister of energy and infrastructure in a mini-shuffle in June, 2008. To understand my time in the new portfolio, one has to recognize that I took over in the midst of the Great Recession of 2008–9. The energy and infrastructure ministry quickly emerged as the focal point of the government's proactive response to that crisis.

There were two dynamics at play: 1) the government already had in place a plan to eliminate coal-fired power plants, both to cut down on pollution (and smog days) and to reduce our greenhouse gas emissions (the cause of global warming); 2) as a subnational jurisdiction, Ontario was extremely vulnerable to the recession because its economy was so reliant on one sector — the auto industry. The Green Energy Act, which I brought to fruition, was an attempt to leverage one to aid the other.

The project created in Windsor is an example of what was planned. At the height of the recession in 2008, the city was dependent on the auto industry, which was flailing at the time, and had one of the highest unemployment rates in the country. But Windsor became the home for as many as eight manufacturing plants supplying equipment for solar projects and wind turbines. And Windsor's unemployment rate fell below the national average as a result.

As I was taking over the energy portfolio, I had a verbal mandate from the premier to move in the direction of green energy. "I like what we are doing on energy," he told me, "but we need to do more on renewables." To underscore the point, the day after I was sworn in he invited me to a meeting with environmentalist David Suzuki and Hermann Scheer, the father of Germany's green energy transformation. Suzuki and Scheer both pushed us to pass a green energy act. "Use Germany as your example," Scheer told us. "We have a strong manufacturing base, productive relations with labour, and progressive green policies. Ontario has a lot in common with us." (Ever the heckler, I needled Scheer a little about Germany's continued reliance on domestic coal.)

Soon after that, I went on the road to Europe and California to examine what other jurisdictions were doing. More than anything, I came away with the California example in mind. There, since their well-documented energy crisis, they have managed to cap per capita growth in energy use, whereas pretty much every other jurisdiction in the West has seen dramatic increases. That informed my mantra, quickly forgotten after I left, that the Green Energy Act was about the ability to make more green energy on the one hand and, on the other hand, for Ontarians to be able to use less electricity (in recognition of the fact that the unit price was going to rise).

In Spain, I learned that green energy funded by fiscal subsidy from the state was a poor idea. But in Germany, I realized that all states find a way to subsidize the emergence of green industry. This reinforced my view that, in moving toward more green energy in Ontario, we should also pursue domestic content to create jobs.

I also got a huge boost from an active Green Energy Act working group, led by Deb Doncaster, a noted environmentalist. She chaired a group that was a coalition that included representatives of First Nations and Ontario's farmers as well as environmentalists and global leaders in various forms of renewables. Part of the group — and also an attendee at the Scheer/Suzuki meeting — was an irrepressible environment professor at York University named Jose Etcheverry. He joined my trip to Europe and provided instant pushback in our many meetings. Also aboard was Saad Rafi, my incoming deputy minister at energy, who negotiated early leave from his private-sector job to tag along on the European tour. Rafi, with prior experience as deputy at other tough ministries like community safety and transportation, was returning to the public sector after a senior stint at Deloitte.

I also benefited from the appointment of Colin Andersen, former deputy minister of finance, to be CEO of the Ontario Power Authority (OPA), the agency that contracts with electricity suppliers on behalf of the government. Andersen was someone I had known socially for decades, and he was well regarded in the Premier's Office, which choreographed our career moves. Unfortunately, for some odd reason Andersen's predecessor, Jan Carr, had been given quarters elsewhere on the OPA's executive floor to ease his transition from his $500,000-plus job. Carr used the platform to critique our green energy policies.

Carr wasn't alone. As people saw the scale and scope of the proposed legislation, a variety of interests lined up against it. Energy is a multi-stakeholder area. First off, there is competition by fuel source for market share: nuclear versus wind, or hydroelectric versus natural gas. On top of that, there is a blend of Crown corporations (Ontario Power Generation [OPG] and Hydro One) working alongside (or against) the private sector. To boot, my predecessors had further entrenched the influence of the Power Workers Union by installing its leader on the board of Hydro One. Notwithstanding all this turbulence, I had wind at my back, so to speak, and I benefited from the earlier efforts of my predecessors, Dwight Duncan and Donna Cansfield, in the development of the Renewable Energy Standard Offer Program (RESOP) to make it easier for small renewable generating facilities to participate in the electricity system.

I gradually developed a sense that we needed legislation with two pillars: 1) incentives to make it easier to bring renewables online, and 2) incentives to encourage consumers to use less electricity. The latter involved, among other things, the implementation of time-of-use pricing, a key rationale for the earlier costly decision to install "smart meters" in people's homes. This meant higher prices during peak hours, which drove up hydro bills for those too stubborn to adjust their air conditioning usage in the hot summer months.

(I acknowledge the rate hike has also caused hardship for low-income people. Indeed, the move away from coal was to have a consequence for low-income earners trying to pay for sky-rocketing energy bills, and I think the Wynne government made a mistake in addressing the issue with across-the-board subsidies rather than targeting relief to those most in need: low-income people, whether residing in rural and remote Ontario or in cold basement apartments in cities. In some cases, the installation of solar panels or other distributed electricity generation at demand source to reduce reliance on grid supply would have been the most cost-effective means of delivering real relief and enhancing grid reliability. This would also have been a great generator of employment.)

I introduced the Green Energy Act in February of 2009 and it was passed into law by the Legislature in May. It mandated a "feed-in tariff" for wind, solar, and other renewables, a "right to connect" to the electricity grid, and a streamlined approval process for green projects. On the conservation side, it required North American–leading efficiency standards for household appliances, energy audits before homes were resold, energy efficiency as a central tenet of the Ontario Building Code, and greening of government-owned buildings. Items like energy audits and enhanced efficiency within the building code were immediately subject to intense lobbying by the real estate and development industry, which delayed progress on these fronts. That was unfortunate. My former colleague in the Legislature, Phil McNeely, an engineer, was right to say that if a home should have a "walk score" telling us how easy it is to get along without a car, then it simply follows that a home should have a score that tells us how efficient it is in the use of energy.

There was also opposition from some unexpected sources, including the Toronto elite. That's because the shorelines of our Great Lakes are the nexus of wind resource and wealth, in the form of cottages and other recreational properties. The property-owners, most of them well-off Torontonians, turned against wind power. I got it right in the neck from various friends — including my former cabinet colleague Greg Sorbara — who argued that they were appalled that the wind turbines ruined their views. And they found a sympathetic partner in the CBC.

Others believed the turbines would adversely affect their health and wasted untold millions of public dollars trying to shore up their arguments. I was somewhat sympathetic to these health concerns, so I used an abundance of caution in recommending the setbacks for wind turbines. I pushed for a distance beyond what the ministry of the environment had already approved for an earlier wave of wind farms, including Wolf Island.

Even solar farms — noiseless and, to my eye, as aesthetically pleasing as a field of corn — had their opponents. Now we all bear the cost for forcing solar farms to be set back from roads and hidden behind berms or rows of trees. Meanwhile, the same critics neither seem to care where nuclear waste goes nor acknowledge that green energy has no waste and no residual costs beyond its operational years.

Another target for the critics was an offshoot of the Green Energy Act: the Samsung deal. It actually emanated from the Premier's Office, but I won't say that it was foisted on me. I was an economic nationalist before

Trump, and I had concluded that, if we were to make a big play in green energy, it needed to have an element of industrial policy. However, in order to force domestic content you need confidence that the suppliers would be here to meet market demand. And Samsung, the Korean-based conglomerate best known for its consumer products, was proposing to use its financial might to invest $7 billion in Ontario and develop the largest renewable cluster of green energy in the world: 2,500 megawatts, with a corresponding industrial supply chain. This included manufacturing plants producing wind towers and blades, solar panels, and transformers.

The deal was called a "disaster" by the opposition parties. It was, in fact, a calculated risk. Without the impetus from Samsung, there would not have been an ambitious green power initiative that attracted billions in foreign and local investment and enlivened a sector. Under the Green Energy Act, 60 percent of the overall content of green projects, consisting of both hard and soft costs, had to be sourced from companies based in Ontario. You could choose to bring in your panels from offshore, but that would mean engineering, financing, accounting, legal advice, and construction management would have to be local. It was a flexible framework that recognized the need for industrial jobs and the need to support white-collar professional businesses as well. Toronto, for instance, now has a global presence in renewable financing, fostered by the Green Energy Act.

I left the government before the Samsung deal was formally signed. But looking back, I have to say that Samsung more than fulfilled its commitments regarding investment and job creation despite significant reduction in the scope of their project by the government and a lot of harm to the company's reputation. But one example of Samsung's impact can be found on the Six Nations Reserve near Brantford, where a massive solar farm has provided huge economic benefits to the area.

However, the biggest criticism of the Green Energy Act was that it threatened Ontario's economy and overburdened consumers by driving up the price of electricity. Much of this criticism was based on invidious comparisons between electricity rates in Ontario and in other provinces, as if we were all imbued with the same natural gifts of falling water. Our immediate neighbours, Quebec and Manitoba, are blessed with these gifts. Ontario is not, except for Niagara Falls, which supplies about one-quarter of our power.

Furthermore, every rate increase in Ontario gets attributed to renewables, which is crazy. Part of the reason for this is that the feed-in-tariff pricing of renewables is transparent, whereas in other sectors producers get to obfuscate about their all-in costs. The province's electricity market supply is provided by a wide variety of sources — nuclear, hydroelectric, natural gas, and renewables — and each of these has an impact on prices, as have long overdue investments in transmission and distribution.

In defence of green energy, I ask you to consider the comparative cost of nuclear power. First off, while green energy has been panned as expensive and unnecessary due to the fact that we now have an electricity glut, we should be blaming the Pickering nuclear plant. That tired old plant (it opened in 1971) continues to churn out expensive electricity at prices (and risks) we can ill afford. As the Green Energy Act was envisioned, the corresponding Ontario Long-Term Electricity Plan had Pickering long since closed. But for reasons unbeknownst to me the government decided to keep it going, probably under pressure from OPG, the government-owned operator. Hundreds of millions of dollars are being spent to keep Pickering sputtering along while producing electricity we can't use or store. Nuclear power has many tremendous attributes and it has been a pillar of power in Ontario for half a century, but lost in all that is the tremendous challenge presented when you have too much of it.

This is not to mention just how expensive nuclear power really is when you consider capital and long-term waste costs, not just operating expenses. We are still paying a big price for cost overruns on past nuclear plants, notably Darlington. (Initially estimated at $3.9 billion, it finally came in at $14.4 billion.)

I had the prescience to stop the province from buying two new nuclear reactors by refusing to sign any pending contract. I had inherited a request for proposals (RFP) for the new reactors, but in my view we already relied too much on nuclear power, which now supplies more than half our electricity. Beyond this issue of proportionality, the biggest drawback for nuclear power is its sheer cost: the reactors are so expensive that previous governments have had to take them off book to be able to pay down their huge capital costs. And Darlington has made every government since nervous about the potential for cost overruns.

To try to limit the government's exposure to future cost overruns on new nuclear reactors, the RFP required the applicants to take on the risk themselves. And, as might have been expected, the applicants built any potential cost overruns into the pricing of their bids, with staggering results. The situation was exacerbated because Atomic Energy of Canada Ltd. (AECL), with its CANDU technology, had always been Ontario's sole supplier of reactors. That led to skepticism among AECL's foreign competitors (the few that remained in the field) about whether they would get a fair shake. Put another way, an RFP without much competitive tension is a bad omen when you are trying to make the province's single biggest purchase in a generation.

The winning bid came in at $30 billion, or more than double the cost of Darlington for a plant half the size.

My mind was made up: the price was just too high to proceed. But I still had to convince the premier, who had seemed determined to install new reactors. I am not sure who first put the idea in his head. There are a lot of old white guys in the energy sector, and they love nuclear power. As a province, we also seem to be locked into the idea that nuclear power is cheap. (It is only if you discount the capital expenditure and the cost of waste disposal.) Plus we are proud that the CANDU reactors in operation in Ontario are Canadian-designed and engineered. However, the next generation of CANDUs was still on the drawing board and unproven, and the federal regulator had signalled it would not approve any more of the old CANDUs. (Opinions on that have since changed, I am told.)

To my eyes, there was no political upside in building new reactors, whether CANDU or a foreign design. I would have been happy to put a spike right through the project. But I took it as far as was politically possible at that time and recommended it be shelved indefinitely. McGuinty replied: "Show me that won't impact the reliability of electricity supply or the phasing-out of the coal-fired plants or impair Ontario's economic future." I had good answers to all those questions, and I got the sense the premier had already reached some similar conclusions. History has proven us correct.

A reasonable consensus against buying new reactors had also formed at cabinet. There was no backlash from other ministers, including Dwight Duncan, who had initiated the RFP process. But there was some unrest in the eastern GTA (around the Pickering and Darlington plants), where there is an extraordinarily intense network (including municipalities, unions, media, and suppliers) in favour of nuclear power. That is understandable.

Any decision NOT to build new reactors was going to have some negative impact on their local economy. This caused some angst for the regional MPPs in the Liberal caucus. As it happens, however, the decision (made after my departure) to spend $12.8 billion refurbishing the Darlington plant will soften the blow for those looking for economic benefit from the spending and ongoing operations.

Meanwhile, the opposition Conservatives kept peddling the same old lie: that electricity from every new renewable project costs 80 cents a kilowatt hour and nuclear is cheap. The fact is that new nuclear and offshore wind were each projected to cost about 17 cents per kilowatt hour.

* * *

Another thing I often get blamed for is the cancellation of the gas-fired power plants in Mississauga and Oakville. I didn't do it; indeed, I was out of government by then. But many of my critics and a few of my "friends" have suggested that I was complicit in their cancellation. Here are the facts.

When I arrived at the energy ministry, a contract had already been awarded to a private company, Greenfield South, to build a smallish (280 megawatts) gas-powered plant in southern Mississauga, near the Sherway Gardens shopping mall. But the plant had not been built; indeed, the proponents seemed to be dragging their feet and there were rumours that they were struggling to get their project financed. As time passed, opposition to the power plant grew. The local MPP, Peter Fonseca, was adamantly opposed to it. He was not prone to exaggeration, so I took his intensity very seriously. Accordingly, I asked the Ontario Power Authority (OPA), which had awarded the contract, if there was any way we could get out of it. I was told, in unequivocal terms, that the contract had NOT been breached by the proponents and, therefore, we could NOT pull the plug on the project without an enormous penalty. So I did not cancel the project.

Beyond that site, however, the OPA was still intent on addressing perceived electricity supply inadequacies in the southwestern GTA by contracting for another, larger gas plant. Whether to use the site of the closed Lakeview coal-fired plant was an intense local issue. I knew the site well: my father had hauled coal to the plant there, our family frequented adjacent Marie Curtis Park, and for years I had a nearby newspaper delivery route.

Ontario Power Generation (OPG), the government utility that owned the site, and Enersource, the profit-oriented City of Mississauga electricity distribution company, both saw dollar signs and sought to put a gas plant there. Mississauga mayor Hazel McCallion was also behind the idea. And, to be frank, there was a lot of logic in continuing the historic use of the site for a power plant.

There was another vocal school of thought, however, one with support on Mississauga City Council and among citizens I knew from having worked that turf in the 1987 provincial election campaign. Charles Sousa, our MPP for the area (later to be finance minister), reached out and, perhaps to his surprise, found me intensely sympathetic to the idea that this site had a higher purpose over the long term. Just weeks after I took over at energy, I announced that the Lakeview site — two hundred hectares in all, more than double the size of Exhibition Place — would NOT be used for a new power plant. Instead, it would be the site for a major waterfront redevelopment project, including residential, commercial, educational, and recreational facilities and a parkland trail. Because developable waterfront sites like this are so rare, I stand by the decision. I am confident that, given time, Mississauga will have a glorious waterfront opportunity realized with a tangible value of greater than $1 billion and an even greater intangible value.

However, I acknowledge that the decision to take Lakeview out of play helped tip the balance in favour of the eventual decision to locate a gas plant beside the Ford plant in Oakville, although there were multiple sites in Mississauga and Oakville that were part of the competitive process run by the Ontario Power Authority. I was not directly involved in the selection process. When the OPA selected the Ford/Oakville site in the fall of 2009, I was a little surprised because I had heard about a competing site in the Southdown Road area of Mississauga that had already undergone an environmental assessment. But I wasn't concerned with the Ford site selection at first blush, given that Oakville had already zoned the lands for industrial use and that the laws governing emissions from such plants are quite strict.

So, a decision was made, but I made sure the Premier's Office signed off on it before going ahead.

I was mindful that just a few years earlier, while I was minister of health, our government had decided to install a 650 megawatt gas plant on the waterfront in my riding: the Portlands Energy Centre. (Ironically, in my first event as minister of energy, I attended its formal opening.) I was very dissatisfied with the lack of a heads-up on that decision for me and my community. I was especially displeased that my relationship with the Toronto Island and waterfront communities wasn't considered. But instead of griping from the sidelines, I undertook my largest single effort to inform my constituents about a local public policy development. I spearheaded a public meeting at the historic Enoch Turner schoolhouse in Corktown, where I forced the senior executives from proponent partners OPG and TransCanada to make their case and take questions from the community. I remember that two New Democrats from the neighbouring riding, MPP Peter Tabuns and City Councillor Paula Fletcher, also attended. But rather than making a big fuss as anticipated, they absorbed the information and left. This might be another example of Barbara Hall–style public engagement.

Taking a cue from this previous experience, I brought Colin Andersen of the OPA with me to a public meeting at the Mississauga Performing Arts Centre, and in front of a hostile crowd numbering hundreds we made our case for the southwestern GTA power plant procurement to move forward. That night I earned one of several below-the-belt Hazel McCallion scars, but I knew what I was getting myself into.

The Oakville site was announced in September 2009. At that time, I was seriously considering a run for the Toronto mayoralty. Over the next few months, energy matters influenced my decision to quit provincial politics, but I don't remember this being one of them. That is to say that the pressure to cancel the Oakville plant grew over time, and the shit didn't hit the fan until after I had gone. The timing of my departure fed the narrative that I made a controversial policy decision and then didn't stick around for its implementation, but I take that slur as a compliment. By which I mean that the government lacked the stomach for governing after I left. My mistake was that I imagined my successors would be as active and involved on files as I was. They weren't. They lacked the backbone to defend the initial decision and bowed to public pressure. Shorter-term political calculations came much more into the fore — "ignore the headlines" gave way to "reverse the headlines." That attitude fueled the notion that every policy position, stance, and value was up for grabs or somehow malleable.

The government became conflict-averse and sought appeasement instead. So the controversial gas plants were cancelled — first, Oakville in 2010 and then Mississauga in 2011, at the outset of the provincial election campaign. In their place, plants would be built in Sarnia and Napanee, two "willing hosts." The saddest bit about this for me is that the principle of local generation, which should be central to a smart and safe electricity grid for the future, was thrown overboard. Instead, we are going to burn a fossil fuel to make an electron and then ship it hundreds of kilometres because the GTA couldn't meet its own requirements. It's a proper concession to import hydroelectric power from Quebec or even to get more renewable energy out of Ontario's north, but transporting energy from a distant fossil-fueled generator is a step back to the 1950s.

The cost of the cancellations soon became an issue. The government, on the advice of the OPA, initially pegged it at $40 million. The price tag then began creeping upward, with a new figure seemingly every month. What that tells us is that the decision was made hastily in an over-heated political climate. I feel confident that, having been involved in all the contracts myself, I could have quickly indicated the high-end risk and discounted the ridiculously low first number, which was eventually inflated by the auditor general's office's preferred scandal plateau of $1 billion. I think that a more honest early assessment on the actual cost risk would have slowed enthusiasm for cancellation.

Liberals like to tell themselves that the cancellations, however costly, at least served the purpose of saving the seats of four government MPPs. But I believe they would have won their seats anyway, and reliance on this seat-saver rationale enhances public cynicism.

In defence of the gas-plants decision, McGuinty said: "It is never too late to do the right thing." It is nice to land on the same side as Erin Brockovich, even if it was a tortuous path getting there. But I think the arguments on the other side are more compelling. The cancellations pushed Ontario backward, rewarded crass politics, and emboldened local selfishness about energy generation.

There is always an upside to bad news, however. The good news in the gas-plants saga is that in the coming years I am going to be able to go with my kids and enjoy the Mississauga waterfront because the political leaders of the day decided the Lakeview site didn't have to be used for generating electricity. Pickering deserves the same fate. By closing the aging Pickering nuclear plant, we could begin using that site to create another gem on the GTA waterfront.

* * *

The other half of my portfolio was infrastructure. And here, after criticizing McGuinty on gas plants, I have to give him credit. He realized that the government needed to get its infrastructure act together, and he moved forcefully on this front. The government was responsible for 154 hospital corporations, 22 universities, 24 community colleges, almost 5,000 schools, 16,900 kilometres of highways, 2,800 bridges, more than 6,000 government buildings, and so on. And it was flying blind, without a clue where it stood with respect to the state of repair of all this infrastructure.

In his first term, McGuinty put David Caplan in charge of infrastructure renewal, and Caplan did three big things: 1) he implemented a "smart growth" plan for the GTA, favouring "intensification" of already built-up areas as opposed to urban sprawl; 2) he adopted a pan-government view of infrastructure as opposed to the "siloed" thinking of the past; and 3) he significantly reworked the Tory P3 model, replacing it with "alternative financing and procurement" (AFP). Critics — especially in the labour movement — say P3s and AFPs are one and the same. There is some truth to that. We essentially relabelled P3s, which we had fought in opposition. But unlike P3s, the AFP model does ensure ultimate public ownership of new facilities, and some unions have even invested their members' pension funds in these projects.

As I noted in chapter 5, P3s (or AFPs) are not "free," contrary to widespread public belief. They still require significant spending by government, which in turn increases the public debt. I am not insensitive to debt. But spending on capital, as opposed to operations, is an *investment* that will pay off for many years in the future. And we invested far more than previous governments in the province's infrastructure. The Rae government, for example, built one new hospital (in Wawa); the McGuinty government built or rebuilt forty-two across the province.

Unfortunately, because the capital planning process is stretched out over years, projects are too often celebrated by politicians well in advance of their actual construction. As a politician myself, I am quite familiar with the attraction of announcements. But the trap set by early announcement is cost projection. Because politicians cannot resist the temptation to make announcements, they set themselves up for "gotcha" moments years later when the costs come in way beyond the projection. An excellent case in point is the Thunder Bay hospital, which, as I mentioned in chapter 4, had a cost overrun of more than 100 percent.

The problem is that individual ministries, such as Health, can handle only a small number of capital projects at the same time. The ministry does not have the capacity to oversee, say, the construction and significant renewal of forty-two hospitals. So the McGuinty government established Infrastructure Ontario (IO) as an agency to handle all the government's big capital projects. IO was equipped with the skills and resources to handle multiple projects simultaneously and to attract outside funding (including foreign investment) for them. The cost of raising money was higher for the private sector. But for the government that cost was offset by the private sector taking on the risk of cost overruns, not to mention the ability to undertake many more projects simultaneously.

During the financial crisis, I was the front person in dealing with the federal government on infrastructure funding. (As a response to the recession, Ottawa set up a $4 billion "stimulus" fund for capital projects that could be brought on-stream quickly. The money was supposed to be matched by the provinces and municipalities to maximize the impact on the economy.)

My role brought me in contact with three former members of the Harris government — Jim Flaherty, John Baird, and Tony Clement — who had migrated to Ottawa under Stephen Harper's banner. You might think that our partisan differences would make for a difficult relationship, but we actually got along very well for the most part and we understood each other's needs fairly well. Some 2,600 different projects were approved by the two governments in a short time span. It was the ultimate in political horse-trading. They wanted, say, to initiate construction of a four-lane highway in Kenora to help their local MP, Greg Rickford, whereas I sought federal investment in the Sheppard LRT in Toronto. We both got what we wanted. These were win/win deals.

One area of potential conflict was over Toronto's demand that its proposed $1.2 billion purchase of new street cars from Bombardier to replace its aging fleet be eligible for federal funding. (Yes, people, this is the same contract that has caused the city so much grief in recent years.) The proposal did not meet federal criteria for stimulus funding because Toronto had already decided to buy the streetcars *and* the delivery date fell beyond the stipulated time frame. But Mayor David Miller was adamant, desperate, really, that the project should be supported. At one point, Baird was caught in an unguarded moment telling Toronto to "fuck off."

During this standoff, I got word that Miller wanted to speak to me, and he reached me at the University of Guelph. Despite my lack of sympathy for Miller's position (it was not "stimulative"), I supported him, and Ontario showed flexibility on the project. I did this for only one reason: if I hadn't, Miller would have called the premier, and McGuinty's instinct would have been to placate the mayor. Not being stupid, I concluded that if we were going to end up there anyway we might as well look nice doing it. By then McGuinty was well established as a pro-Toronto premier, and I played this one to brand. In the end, Toronto still didn't get federal funding for its streetcars. But as a result of a carefully calibrated compromise, it did get some $200 million for other projects. And by the end of 2018, most of the streetcars still had not been delivered.

Whatever goodwill I generated with Miller wasn't too apparent in his response to the arbitrary selection of the West Don Lands as the Pan Am Games Village site. I take full responsibility for this one. Ironically, David Peterson's government had designated the site beside the Don River for a housing development, to be called Ataratiri, and expropriated hundreds of brownfield sites for the project. That was in the late 1980s, when Liberals were aggressively pursuing housing policies. But the project was cancelled by the Rae government.

Two decades later, after massive spending on soil decontamination and flood control, a new neighbourhood had been extensively planned for the site. Peterson, by then chair of the Pan Am Games bid committee, came to me with a serious dilemma: PASO, the governing body for the games, had just adopted the Olympic accommodation standard for athletes, and that ruled out the planned use of York University student residences. "I want to build a village at Ontario Place," said Peterson.

Without skipping a beat I said, "No." Ontario Place had insufficient infrastructure and had not been planned for residential use, and installing the athletes' village there would be very complicated, in both a political and a planning sense. "As an alternative," I said, "we have a community that is already fully planned, and ironically it's part of your legacy as premier." Thus, the Pan Am Village at West Don Lands was born. When PASO representatives visited the site and saw what we planned, they were impressed. The athletes' village was both a prime selling feature and a prime legacy of the games.

Years later, however, I continued to hear that Mayor Miller was pissed because the city wasn't given the chance to decide on the site. But there was no time for that, and we sensibly leveraged work that was already approved by the city with local efforts from community veterans like Councillor Pam McConnell.

A few months after that decision, I was to leave my job and run for Miller's. He quit. I lost.

CHAPTER EIGHT

Christopher

Christopher Peloso and I liked to joke that we first met when I picked him up at the Toronto bus terminal upon his arrival from Sudbury in 1994. While not the case, it wasn't long after his arrival that we met. It was easy to strike up a conversation because, in the dead of winter (okay, a Toronto winter), he was walking about with his coat undone. I soon learned that was the norm for the claustrophobic Christopher.

He was nine years younger than me, but by then Christopher and I already had a lot in common. I hadn't even tried the university route, and he had bailed after one semester at Laurentian. A man not without his own obligations, he was drawn to Toronto by the prospect of liberation. Leaving Sudbury was bittersweet for Christopher because, while his sexual orientation was proving a tough fit in his home community, he was a new father. For every day that he lived, Christopher was steadfast in fulfilling all the obligations that fatherhood entails. I witnessed Christopher's sacrifices in Toronto to make sure his daughter had what she needed, both materially and emotionally.

* * *

For his entire professional career, Christopher worked in progressively more responsible management roles in retail chocolate. So Christopher and I shared a similar commitment and passion for our work. We lived the adage, "work hard, play hard." I can recall driving in the early morning from downtown to Scarborough Town Centre, where Christopher was managing a store, and arriving just in the nick of time.

Christopher and I had an unmistakable sexual connection, which often overruled other signals, even if we were not together. I am sure it was a point of frustration for Christopher's friends, as it was for mine, that anytime we were to find ourselves partying in the same environment, we were more often than not leaving together. The bloom was off the rose though as the 1990s progressed. Aside from a brief interlude in the late 1990s, Christopher and I drifted apart as my attention turned to elected politics. But by the time Dalton McGuinty's Liberals were swept into power in 2003 and I was nearing age forty, I found myself deeply fulfilled on the one hand and terribly empty on the other. I turned my mind to settling down and surveyed some pathways that were open to me at that time. Truth is, all pathways led to Christopher.

By then, Christopher was living near the Ontario Science Centre in Don Mills and had progressed within the Laura Secord family, which was constantly experiencing new owners. He had a maturing daughter and a coterie of friends. Whether he was dating when I called him was immaterial to me, and it never came up between us. Our reconciliation came full circle when Christopher joined me and a few friends in New York City, where we took in several days of the U.S. Open tennis tournament while staying in the other-world surroundings of the residence of Canada's ambassador to the United Nations, Allan Rock.

We flew separately. I met Christopher at the airport in Newark, and we took the train together back to Manhattan. It's so easy for me to remember how he looked because he had dressed in Lacoste from head to toe. From that moment on, Lacoste became his house brand. Sadly, though, I could never get Christopher to take up tennis, which had by then emerged as my sport of choice. (I had joined the Queen's Club on Dupont Street, Toronto's oldest indoor tennis club.) Christopher was content to dress the part while encouraging me to play and delighting in receiving tennis towels that I ordered from the Australian Open every year.

The towels came in handy because the secret to Christopher's happiness as a true northern Ontario boy could be found in lake swimming. No matter the darkness, temperature, or other perceived dangers (my greatest fear is death in cold water), Christopher was always ready for a swim. And I was always on the lookout for the next best place. Our car always had a suit and towel on hand, but, truth be known, he would have preferred swimming without the suit. Christopher's depravity was put to the test when, at the end of a canoe trip, he and one other from our group of ten braved the freezing waters of the Sutton River at its mouth on Hudson Bay. "Good enough for the polar bears, good enough for me," Christopher thought.

Several other swimming escapades of his terrified me. I hope never again to sense the fear I felt when he took to cliff-diving into the turbulent Atlantic Ocean at Crane Beach on the east coast of Barbados. Daredevils had to time their jumps into the height of the swells and then swim vigorously so as not to be smashed into the rocks. Ironically, Christopher survived but I was stung by a jellyfish and experienced a terrible allergic reaction as our plane took us home. Ever since, I have been forced to carry an EpiPen anytime I want to venture into the sea.

Soon after our reconciliation, an exciting opportunity came Christopher's way. After a brief hesitation due to his loyalty to Laura Secord, he leapt at the opportunity to begin building a retail chain for Lindt Chocolate. In very short order, he established a strong regional presence for Lindt and built a team of managers, some poached from Laura Secord, who brought his level of dedication to the job. Christopher was revered by his employees, and my sisters, Joanne and Christine, were at times part of his employee mix.

At Christmas 2006, I gave Christopher a white tuxedo. In the pocket, I tucked a letter asking him to marry me. He said yes, and we told the press it was a Stephen Harper Shotgun Wedding, triggered by the prime minister's threat to bring an end to legally sanctioned same-sex marriage. Planning for the wedding was such a happy time for us. During my many snowmobile trips throughout the Algoma District with the help of Mike Brown, the local MPP who rightly figured it was a good way to get politicians out to see the vastness of his riding, I came across a wilderness oasis that remains my favourite place in Canada (outside of Toronto): Laurentian Lodge, on Flack Lake, thirty-two kilometres north of Elliot Lake. It comes complete with a waterfall made for swimming. I had previously taken Christopher and some of his family to see Laurentian Lodge, and I told him we should get married there. The genius of our decision was that we got to pay respect to Christopher's northern roots while securing a venue that would limit our guest list to two hundred. Christopher and I, both very operationally and logistically prone, set about organizing the wedding weekend ourselves, despite our very busy day jobs. (I was minister of health at the time.)

We chose the August long weekend of 2007 for our wedding and set out to design a range of activities over three days. The central decision that we made was that our wedding would pay respect to the tradition of two-spirited people in First Nations culture. Though diminished through modernization and the presence of Christianity, there was still considerable history that informed the idea that in past times two-spirited people were given greater status. This proved tougher than we might have thought. Were it not for the fact that Chief Charles Fox personally cajoled a legitimate community mystic named Indian Ron Mandaman to make the trek from Shoal Lake on the Manitoba border to Laurentian Lodge, our wedding would have been very different with respect to all those past traditions.

We had all first met Fox and his partner, Melinda Hardy, when Christopher's daughter visited Toronto and we travelled together to the powwow at the Mississaugas of the New Credit Reserve. Fox and Hardy stood for us at our First Nations–inspired wedding, as we later had the privilege to do for them at their wedding in Thunder Bay, which triggered our son Michael's first airplane ride.

The "legal" part of the wedding was conducted by Justice of the Peace Gerry Solursh, yet another great person I met through Barbara Hall. Solursh had been Hall's accountant when she was in private law practice, and he also had a lot of experience as a campaign CFO for various Liberals like Jim Peterson (brother of David and former federal cabinet minister). As the 1997 megacity mayoral campaign was getting organized, Hall and I had reached out to Solursh to take on the same role for her campaign. To our good fortune, he said yes. Solursh, never one to let formality get in the way of hilarity, altered the wedding vows slightly to say, "By the powers invested in me by George" rather than "by Ontario."

Because Elliot Lake is a small community and our numerous guests overmatched the capacity of Laurentian Lodge, we took advantage of several other venues. On the Saturday, we organized several different outings, including golf, hiking, croquet, and pontoon boat rides. All the guests met at the Lester B. Pearson Civic Centre in Elliot Lake, where we sent them off with a Tim Hortons box lunch. It was fun to see Dick O'Hagan reminisce about being in Elliot Lake with Pearson, who, while a Torontonian, was parachuted into the Algoma East riding in the late 1940s. The pictures in the lobby of the centre were these great black and whites shot at a BBQ, and you do know how I like a political BBQ. Later that same night, we threw a big party at Denison House, where many of our guests were staying. It was built years earlier, at the cost of millions, by mining titan Stephen Roman (principal owner of Denison Mines). I had stayed there while travelling with Mines minister Hugh O'Neil back in the late 1980s.

The weather on that weekend was spectacular beyond belief — part of a lengthy heat wave that had hammered Toronto. The swimmable lakes in the region eased the heat and made the drive worthwhile. But our wedding ceremony had fire and blankets as part of First Nations tradition. I won't soon forget when Christopher and I stood up to be walked around the fire, bearing a Hudson's Bay blanket. We had been seated on a bench with our backs to the crowd. Only then did we realize that, aside from a stoic handful of guests, including my sister Joanne, almost everyone else had moved into the shade. Meantime, claustrophobic Christopher was wearing a tuxedo, albeit with an open shirt, and was being marched around a fire wearing a scratchy wool blanket, yet another aversion of his. Heat aside, it was all magical.

Among a very interesting array of guests were Tony Toldo Sr., his wife Josie, his son Tony Jr., and his wife Michelle. They had made the trek from Windsor. The Toldo name is synonymous with success, and their philanthropic commitment to Windsor is how I came to know them. Dalton McGuinty invited me to a meeting in his office very early in our days in office. McGuinty told me that this guy, Tony Toldo Sr., had been very helpful in Windsor and wanted resources for a local hospice. Luckily for me, our priorities included an expansion of residential hospices, and Windsor had a very evolved model with tons of community support, led by Toldo.

Achieving success in the plastics industry in the 1950s, Toldo had long since given up long drives in cars for short rides in airplanes. His aircraft grew in sophistication over time, and Elliot Lake Airport's runway couldn't accommodate his latest private jet. So he had to drive in from Sudbury, two hours away. Tony made it clear that wasn't a sacrifice he was accustomed to making for just anybody at that stage in his life.

Christopher and I both love carrot cake, and among Barbara Hall's many talents is baking. Her contribution to our wedding was two hundred mini-cakes, each carefully decorated on the day of the event by a team that included my mother and aunt Sylvia. The heroic aspect of all this is the fact that only twenty-four hours before, Hall had dismounted her bicycle in Montreal, having ridden for six days in a fundraiser for the Toronto AIDS service organization, PWA. I had done half the ride and left Hall a few days earlier in Kingston to head directly for Elliot Lake (by car). She slept in the back seat as her husband, the fantastic Max Beck, made the very long drive north. Fortunately, Beck is a North Bay native, so many of the roads were familiar to him.

Mike Brown, the local MPP, and Monique Smith, MPP from nearby Nipissing, also attended the wedding. Smith brought along well wishes from the premier, then gearing up for the coming election campaign. Molly Johnson sang and DJ TigerStyle kept the place jumping. Our honeymoon, beyond a few days on Manitoulin Island, was at a timeshare in Rio de Janeiro, provided by my mother and stepfather. But it was delayed until after the 2007 election.

Christopher and I were both keen to expand our family unit, so it wasn't too long before we started to talk about the prospect of adoption. Around this time, our home on Rose Avenue in Toronto's Cabbagetown was subjected to an OPP security audit (because of some harassment of me) and found to be severely lacking. Accordingly, in 2008 we moved into a spacious condo just a few short steps from Maple Leaf Gardens. We delighted in bringing our own tastes to this great apartment and experiencing a good quality of life with a combined income of $300,000. But by 2008, Christopher started to feel a lot of apprehension about my role in politics and had what he felt was a bruising experience with the spouse of an ambitious colleague of mine. Nothing was ever really the same afterward, and Christopher's insecurities outside of his own domain became more and more prominent.

*   *   *

Still, despite these problems, our lives continued. Christopher and I still both went about our day jobs with dedication. We also registered with the

Children's Aid Society and spent many days completing the CAS course for prospective parents. We spent days more filling out paperwork. And then we waited, but with no clear outlook about whether a match would be found, much less when.

As 2009 rolled along, the idea of running for mayor the following year remained an option; yet, as I have commented in chapter 7, it was never a subject I raised with many people, given the sensitivity of my position at Queen's Park. I set the trap for myself in September by admitting that I was considering a run, and several of my cabinet colleagues, seemingly anxious to see me go, sought to further their own prospects by generating turbulence around me. That deeply soured my cabinet experience. Brash and outspoken as I might have been, I never used power at the cabinet table to upset the apple carts of others. I later regretted that the same professional courtesy wasn't extended to me.

The gamesmanship, some of which was apologized for later, soured Christopher, too. He struggled as he saw me being backstabbed after so much work and loyalty to our party, the premier, and his government. I recall one night when I wandered home at 10 p.m., dessert in hand for Christopher but tired after another night of fundraising and still with hours of paperwork to attend to. "Fuck them, George," Christopher said. "Let them figure out for themselves what real work feels like when you're gone."

The year-end offered a brief respite, and as soon as chocolate season and Christmas passed, we took to the road and did our customary post-Christmas drive south to deliver my stepmother, her dog, and her car to her winter home near Ft. Lauderdale. Shortly after that, we crossed "Alligator Alley" to Tampa to spend a few days with the Toldos and with my own mother, who had a mobile home there. It was so cold there that we high-tailed it to Key West, but we found no reprieve. An omen, perhaps.

Just a few days after New Year's, I received an email from Don Guy (McGuinty's campaign manager) asking if I could resign my seat soon so that the government might move along with the anointment of Glen Murray as my successor. I was pleased that the party was able to replace me with a person of stature and values. Soon after this, I penned my letter of resignation from cabinet to the premier.

This major change in my political career was accompanied by an even more significant one in my personal life.

CHAPTER NINE

Mayoral Race

first began thinking seriously about running for mayor of Toronto in the summer of 2009. I was disgusted by Mayor David Miller's handling of the thirty-nine-day outside workers' strike, which turned various city parks into garbage dumps without extracting any public benefit whatsoever at the bargaining table. During that strike, I used my provincial political organization as a base to organize community cleanups of street corners across Toronto that were overflowing with garbage. That experience really got me thinking about moving from Queen's Park to city hall and back closer to my community roots.

Because of my Queen's Park job, I didn't have the luxury of consulting with many people about the possible move. One or more of them might leak to the media that I was thinking of exiting provincial politics, which would undermine me. But one person I did approach was former mayor Barbara Hall, my long-time friend and "big sister." She was supportive of my running, but warned me that provincial politics are very different from the municipal variety, where there is no party-line voting. "You might find that frustrating," Barbara told me.

I thought I was well aware of the differences, and despite my reputation as a partisan was actually excited about the prospect of spreading my wings into an arena that was not dominated by party politics. I had worked at city hall in the 1990s as Barbara's chief of staff when she was mayor. My office was right beside the mayor's, with a view of Nathan Phillips Square. Back then, I used to dream about being mayor myself. Of course, at that point in time I wasn't anticipating being a senior provincial cabinet minister and deputy premier. In 2009, it would take a leap of faith for me to leave my position and power at Queen's Park and attempt a risky run for the Toronto mayoralty against a powerful incumbent.

But there were other influences pushing me in that direction. While there was nothing to indicate that my position as a senior minister in Dalton McGuinty's government was in jeopardy, I was getting a little bit restless at Queen's Park. In ten years there, I had given a lot of myself. I was doing things in Dalton's name and in my party's name. I yearned to be the person in charge rather than a number two. The silos that dominate in the ministerial model limit one's relevance, as I was reminded on the day of the Sunrise propane explosion in Downsview when nobody called me, despite my supposed importance and status as the region's most senior minister. And with Dalton firmly ensconced as premier, I was looking at years of hard time in the trenches. Finally, while I don't have a bad word to say about Dalton, by 2009 the decision-making process inside the government was elevating some of those staffers I liked least. Increasingly, decisions were being made on the basis of how to pacify backbenchers. (This phenomenon presented itself most clearly in the decision to cancel the gas plants after I left.) Also, my fiscally conservative mindset was frustrated by the lack of discipline on the expenditure side, where I spent a lot of political capital in confronting spending on hospitals and prescription drugs. Despite the government being in deficit, full-day kindergarten was launched with only a sketchy understanding of the costs involved, especially on the infrastructure side. I was also frustrated that Ontario's approach to managing public-sector labour costs was dull, half-hearted, and often incoherent.

I could, of course, have waited for Dalton to step down (which he did three years later) and then run for premier. The reality I faced was that, when I looked at the man in the mirror, I had to admit my taste for partisan battle never applied within the Liberal Party. Whatever my reputation, I didn't have the stomach for battle with current colleagues. My ambition was to perform well on behalf of my leader. My sexual orientation was also a concern. Although my own openness about it had in a sense normalized the gay reality inside the Ontario government, I remained aware that haters always lurk out there. I felt that my sexual orientation would be a net benefit in Toronto and a mixed blessing provincially. Kathleen Wynne proved me wrong on the latter, and running as a gay man in Toronto didn't turn out so well for me. But more about that later.

There was also the fact that, for all my admiration of Pierre Trudeau, I never learned to speak French fluently. It is my number-one regret, and at times a point of insecurity. In a province with a million French-speakers and following in the footsteps of a bilingual premier (McGuinty), it was more than a nagging concern of mine as I considered my future.

Finally, there was a personal issue. My relationship with Christopher was under strain. Don't get me wrong; our reunification in 2005 and our wedding in 2007 made these among the happiest and most fulfilling days of my life. But the pressures of government put a strain on all families of politicians. In our case, Christopher had to fight his way against the established routines of a committed politician who was a long-time bachelor to boot. And I found it difficult for my ministerial staff to adapt to my married reality as they had come to know me when virtually no times on the calendar were off limits. Communication with Christopher, especially about my schedule and the events we were to attend together, was constantly mishandled. That left me treading too often on Christopher's legendary goodwill. During that period, I was also running a large government department. That kept me on the road two or three nights a week. While Christopher never complained about that and always deferred to my political career, we both felt our relationship would be better served by a job that kept me closer to home. Even though the mayoralty is also an all-consuming job, at least you get to spend most nights sleeping in your own bed. We called the strategy "up or out."

Tackling a well-entrenched incumbent like David Miller was a daunting challenge. Of greatest concern was whether I would be the only serious challenger or others would crowd the field and split the anti-Miller vote. Specifically, would John Tory — a former provincial Conservative leader, a prior candidate for mayor, and an oft-rumoured mayoral candidate in seemingly every election cycle — get into the race? He had the same concerns about me.

While Tory was no longer in the Legislature, he and I had stayed in touch, encouraged in part by veteran Toronto PC activist Justin Van Dette, a mutual friend. Tory tagged along on a couple of my community cleanups during the garbage strike. We competed vigorously, sweeping up as many cigarette butts and assorted bits of debris as we possibly could. And we chatted, in a wary sort of way. At my invitation, the two of us got together for a cup of coffee at a café on Church Street. Contrary to media reports at the time, no formal agreement emerged from this meeting, but there was a clear understanding that, if one of us ran, the other would stay out of the race. "Well, John, at least we know we both can't run," I said as we got up from our meeting.

In effect, this understanding put the two of us in a race against each other to get to the starting line first. This was in the back of my mind when, during a press scrum at Queen's Park on September 9, 2009, I was asked if I was thinking of running for mayor. The safe response would have been to duck the question by saying I was focused on my current duties in the provincial government (as I most certainly was). But I did not choose the safe route. "The status quo is not getting the job done [at city hall]," I said. "And it's counterproductive to have a race [for mayor] that doesn't have clear choices available to people." This was an unmistakable signal to the public (and to John Tory) that I was seriously considering running for mayor. It also immediately labelled me as the leading potential challenger to David Miller. (In this respect, Tory got the last laugh on me. Not only did I end up sacrificing my political career to Rob Ford, but also Tory got to watch and even contribute to my self-immolation over eHealth.)

There were other serious negative consequences for me from my premature announcement. At that time, I was in the midst of steering implementation of the Green Energy Act through cabinet. This was something to which I had devoted a lot of my political life and credibility, at the behest of the premier and in the face of uncertain economic times (the 2008–9 recession). And it became much more difficult to see it through to conclusion once my cabinet colleagues realized I had my eye on leaving. I had become a wounded, if not lame, duck. And that made everyone at Queen's Park much less deferential to me. Most of my colleagues were reluctant to raise the subject directly with me (although I do recall Greg Sorbara asking me, rhetorically: "Are you out of your mind?"). But I could tell that some were excited about my departure, and the actions of a few "colleagues" in consort forced my hand and hastened my exit. They were trying to pull the rug out from under me by interfering with my stakeholders. Later, one of them directly apologized for his conduct.

* * *

Then, on September 25, the political landscape changed dramatically with Mayor Miller's surprise announcement that he would not seek re-election in 2010. Suddenly the mayoral race was wide open. And even though neither of us had formally declared our intentions to run, John Tory and I were immediately deemed the front-runners to replace Miller. Ford was not on anyone's radar screen.

A few days after Miller's announcement, I was asked again at Queen's Park about my intentions during a joint press scrum with McGuinty on the way into the weekly cabinet meeting. I was more circumspect in my response this time. While acknowledging that I was "thinking about" running for mayor, I stressed "my obligation to show that I'm focused on my [provincial] job day-to-day." The premier was more to the point. He said some flattering things about me and then added: "George is not going anywhere. You heard it here first." Afterward, as we both walked into cabinet, Dalton said to me: "I meant all of those things."

It was the last face-to-face conversation we would have on this topic before I handed in my resignation six weeks later. While I was still sitting beside Dalton in the Legislature and we continued to work together on provincial matters, we did not discuss my future. That may seem strange, but there is no particular guidebook for how one goes about these things. We just sort of muddled through it. At this point in our relationship, Dalton McGuinty had already said through his actions how he valued my service.

I wanted to wait until Christmas to leave the government, but my diminished status left me hopelessly undermined at the cabinet table, with a few of my "colleagues" working directly against me. This was new to me. Rather than risk humiliation, I penned my letter of resignation and arranged to meet Dalton at his mid-Toronto home on November 8, a Sunday. Afterward, the premier issued a statement praising me for my stewardship in both the health and energy portfolios and adding: "As an MPP,

George has consistently stood up for the underdog, championed the rights and the needs of his constituents and used his considerable gifts and talents serving the people of his community." Oddly, I have no clear recollection of that day. My dear friend Erika Mozes, who saw me immediately after I met McGuinty, said I looked shell-shocked.

With all pretenses gone, I could now be completely frank with the media about seeking the mayoralty. I told reporters that my campaign would encompass people from all parties and I would be "a candidate of the broad centre," with an emphasis on fiscal reality. "It's time for post-ideological solutions," I said.

* * *

I kept my seat in the Legislature while I was getting my campaign up and running. But rather than risk being a distraction for my soon-to-be former colleagues, I stayed away from the Queen's Park precinct. And lest I be accused of using provincial resources to subsidize my municipal campaign, I never once set foot in my "new" office in the Legislative Building, although my name was emblazoned on the door. On December 10, the last day before the Christmas recess, I delivered my farewell speech on the floor of the Legislature after a decade as the MPP for Toronto Centre. "When I first arrived in this place ten years ago," I said, "I set out on a mission to serve this diverse riding with passion and dedication. Much progress has been made, and thanks especially to the confidence of my leader Dalton McGuinty, I have been provided with an extraordinary opportunity to serve my province, and in so doing, I have had my life deeply enriched by the people I have met and the remarkable places I have visited. Each of us privileged to serve in this place benefits from the companionship of members on all sides. My experience has not been any different. As much as I am enthusiastic about the new pursuit I am to undertake in the new year, I'm saddened that the relationships I have made here will be renewed somewhat less frequently. Yet I have noted that the mayor of Toronto does frequently attend here, sometimes even without cap in hand."

Then it was the turn of the opposition to speak about me. First up was Elizabeth Witmer, a Conservative MPP who, like me, had been minister of health. "I just want to extend to the honourable member, on behalf of our caucus, our sincere appreciation for his dedication and commitment," she said. "I don't think there was any time that I wasn't well aware of the fact that he personally had a sincere commitment to the people of this province and of his riding, and I want to thank him very much." Michael Prue, a New Democrat MPP and former East York mayor himself, addressed my future plans. "I wish him the best of luck going into municipal politics," he said. "Many of us have come from that sphere. I know he was involved with Barbara Hall in the past, but not as an elected politician. I think he will find, over time, that it's a very difficult job to which he aspires. All I can say is that the lessons you have learned here and the passion you have shown here will stand the people of Toronto in good stead, should they decide upon your candidacy."

* * *

With these words still ringing in my ears, the following day (December 11) I delivered an informal campaign kick-off speech to the Toronto Board of Trade. I said job creation and fiscal responsibility would be my top priorities as mayor. And I indicated I was open to the idea of selling city-owned assets to make ends meet and invest in other areas, such as transit. "It is our obligation to be open to some solutions that perhaps so far haven't been adopted by city council," I said. "The city should be strategic about what it owns."

It was a small-C conservative message that may have jarred people who saw me as a progressive politician. A question from the audience regarding funding for the arts produced a response on my part that had some thinking I was a little hawkish fiscally. It should have been an early message for me that constituencies were going to be taking a what-have-you-done-for-me-lately approach to my campaign. I only ever had this Barbara Hall construct in mind because I was so frustrated that city hall operated on some perceived left-right axis where those in the middle were somehow called mushy. As Barbara had, I wanted to run a "big tent" campaign that attracted people from across our political spectrum — Liberals, Conservatives, and New Democrats. For the New Democrats, I thought my progressive bona fides would speak for themselves. And for the Conservatives, particularly the Red Tories, I thought that there were aspects of my record in managing hospital budgets and reining in spending on prescription drugs that would attract them. I even did an event at the Albany Club, a Conservative bastion, with John Baird, a former member of Mike Harris's cabinet who by then was federal minister of transport in Stephen Harper's government. I told the Albany Club audience I was unabashedly progressive but not a spendthrift. I supported the narrative that David Miller had been a terrible manager who had contributed to Scarborough's sense of alienation.

But I discovered that what worked for Barbara Hall didn't really work for me, because my style and partisan identification were stronger than hers. While I was downplaying my deep Liberal credentials and abandoning red signs, Rocco Rossi quit his job as national director of the federal Liberal Party to steal the Liberal Party flag from my hands unexpectedly. And Michael Ignatieff (then the federal Liberal leader) and his crew — Pat Sorbara and Peter Donolo — stayed neutral. These were my friends, or so I thought. Donolo's father-in-law, the late and wonderful Joe Cruden, was the first candidate I ever worked for, back in 1980 when I was a sixteen-year-old. And Pat Sorbara was my first boss in politics in the office of Premier David Peterson in 1986. Pat was also one of the first people I came out to a few years later. Rossi was never really a threat to win the mayoralty. His name recognition was too low for that. But he nonetheless changed the dynamic of the race. Using contacts he had enhanced during his very brief time as a federal Liberal functionary, he managed to raise $1 million. He spent most of that money attacking me, especially over eHealth. The media took him seriously and gave him equal air time and ink in their stories. A couple of newspapers were even poised to endorse him until he pulled out of the race at the last moment. Today, when people ask me about Rossi, I tell them to be wary of anyone who claims multiple epiphanies (which he does). I was delighted when Mike Colle beat him to a pulp when he showed his true colours by running as a Conservative in Toronto.

As for my former Liberal colleagues at Queen's Park, I didn't garner as much support from them as I had hoped, perhaps because my exit had been hasty and haphazard and because I hadn't adorned my campaign with Liberal contemporaries. I certainly reached out to many of them for their support, but the response was mixed at best. In retrospect I may have taken for granted that years in the trenches would have generated more enthusiasm for my candidacy. I was able to call in some IOUs, of course, because I had been beating the bushes around the province on behalf of various Liberal candidates for years. I almost never refused a request to attend a fundraiser for a fellow Liberal. But let me just say that, in a campaign where you put your political life on the line, you learn who your friends are. For example, Brad Duguid, a contemporary of mine since the 1980s, has always shown greater enthusiasm campaigning for John Tory than for me, a fellow Liberal.

Then there was Kathleen Wynne, minister of transportation in the McGuinty government at that time. One might expect that Kathleen, a fellow urban progressive and member of the LGBTQ community, would back me wholeheartedly. But she was initially very reserved in her response to my candidacy, mostly due to what she regarded as my stylistic deficiencies. She told me that she saw me as a member of the "old boys club" at Queen's Park, the McGuinty government's mostly male inner core from which she felt excluded. While Kathleen did come 'round and lend support to me both in her riding and at a fundraiser in the LGBTQ community, she was seemingly unable to influence others in her circle, such as Councillor Shelley Carroll, who indicated a preference for NDPer Joe Pantalone despite regularly touting her Liberal credentials. A few years later, when Kathleen ran for party leader, I returned the favour by backing Gerard Kennedy, whom I had long admired as a highly principled person.

* * *

As 2009 drew to a close, the field for the mayoral race was taking shape. Along with me and Rossi, the expectation was that at least one NDP councillor (Adam Giambrone or Pantalone) would enter. And there was heavy speculation that John Tory would run as the right-of-centre candidate. Rob Ford still was not in the picture. Then right after New Year's, Tory surprised everyone and declared he would not be a candidate, apparently after consulting with Bill Davis.

An aside: Talk of a Tory candidacy never really went away during the campaign, and Tory himself did not exactly stay on the sidelines. On his radio show, he really went after me on eHealth. He knew what he was doing. He had been opposition leader at Queen's Park. Today, he is a mostly well-regarded mayor. I am much more wary of John than many of my Liberal friends. You could see John's weak side at play when he got on board for a billion-dollar Rail Deck Park scheme without any apparent funding model. More telling yet was his reliance on Nick Kouvalis in his mayoral campaigns. (Kouvalis worked for Ford in 2010.)

I formally registered as a mayoral candidate in the first week of January, 2010. Ideally, I would have waited to register at least two months longer, but the ridiculous provincial law that governs the mayoral race in Toronto does not allow you to make any expenditure until registered. And I played by the rules. Meanwhile, the Fords ignored them, including the one that is designed to prevent businesses from floating campaigns. But Ford was not in the race in early January. And with Tory out, I was clearly the front-runner. An Angus Reid–*Toronto Star* poll showed that I had the support of 44 percent of decided voters, way ahead of Giambrone at 17 percent, Rossi at 15 percent, and Pantalone at 5 percent. But 58 percent of the voters were undecided.

Notwithstanding the undecideds, the political landscape looked very favourable for me. David Miller and John Tory were on the sidelines. Giambrone soon pulled himself out before his campaign really got started, after the *Star* published an interview with a young woman who said she had an ongoing affair with him while he was living with another woman. (I had insights into Giambrone's lifestyle and was not surprised by this.) So, besides myself, the mayoral field was effectively reduced to Joe Pantalone, a New Democrat and veteran city councillor who saw himself as Miller's rightful heir; Giorgio Mammoliti, another veteran councillor, whose platform called for creation of a red-light district; Sarah Thomson, publisher of a local monthly newspaper and a flake; and Rocco Rossi. None of them had much of a public profile, certainly not compared to mine. This was not entirely a blessing, however. The problem is that, once you are seen as the front-runner, the media look at you differently. They press you harder on the issues. And if you respond cautiously, they accuse you of ducking for cover or lacking any vision. Worse still, with Miller out of the race I was also viewed as the de facto incumbent, because I possessed the patina of government from my Queen's Park days. Unfortunately, I inherited none of the benefits of incumbency and all of the negatives. It raised the level of expectation around communication and policy for my campaign, especially because I had decided to look "mayoral."

We had policies by the bucketful, all costed out. My platform called for holding property-tax increases to the inflation rate; building a subway (not LRT) extension to Scarborough, largely utilizing the RT route; cutting the vehicle registration tax by one-third; freezing hiring at city hall to eliminate thirteen hundred jobs through attrition; contracting out some city services, including (possibly) garbage collection, ski hills, and even bus routes; keeping Toronto Hydro in public hands; investing in parks, recreation programs, and the arts; making transit free for seniors during off-peak hours; and much more. The irony is that a comprehensive plan came across as an incremental approach in contrast to a slogan that promised a revolution. I realized a little too slowly that when people asked me for my vision, what they really wanted was a slogan.

I also had government experience by the bucketful, especially compared to my opponents. Experience can be a two-edged sword, however. It can make a candidate look ready to govern, but it can also become the baggage that drags a candidate down. Ask Hillary Clinton, whose resumé made her one of the most qualified candidates ever to run for president but who lost to a buffoon with no government experience at all but a great slogan.

Still, in the early days of the campaign I was feeling confident. We were having good success at fundraising and, of course, the polls showed me way ahead. Wherever I went, people were referring to me as "the next mayor." The assumption was that I was a shoo-in for the job. Even Miller's staff, no supporters of mine, were heard saying that.

* * *

Just as the mayoral campaign was getting rolling in early February, my world was turned upside down by the arrival on short notice of a sixteen-month-old boy. The adoption process had been in the works for well over a year, but when it came, it came fast. Because Michael bonded so readily, the familiarization process proceeded quickly and gave us just a few days to prepare. Christopher and I went out to Vancouver for three nights to see some of the Winter Olympics and came back home to find our lives had changed dramatically.

The new normal was a house filled with energy and activity, with Michael taking full advantage of expansive and slippery polished linoleum floors to perfect his speedy sidesaddle crawling.

Christopher took a leave from his position at Lindt to stay home with Michael. In a dedicated way, he took to narrowing some of the developmental

The first-ever picture of me and Michael, within minutes of our meeting. February 2010.

gaps that Michael was experiencing, especially in terms of solid-food consumption. Those first few nights after taking Michael off formula were more than enough to test our patience and make us question our capability as parents. That particular self-doubt has never left me.

Our little Michael was born premature and after a tough experience in the womb. With a month in the loving care of the nurses at Humber River Hospital, Michael progressed to living in a loving environment with an extended foster family from Scarborough to Whitby. Despite his early hardships, he showed no inability to connect, and within seconds on our first visit he climbed into my lap. Our bond has been unbroken since.

The wonder of this little boy is a credit to Christopher's patient nurturing during those earliest days. And because I was running in the mayoral election, the job was shouldered mainly by him, with an incredible assist from Barbara Hall. (By then she was head of the Ontario Human Rights Commission, so she was prohibited from campaigning for me.) The Riverdale farm and the backyard pool at Barbara's helped to idle a hot summer away.

The G20 protests in 2010 had their start at Allan Gardens in our neighbourhood, and Michael, in his red stroller, and Christopher must have been quite imposing to have provoked the attention of Toronto Police, who conducted a hurried and, in Christopher's eyes, terrifying search, only to conclude that the only bombs being packed in the stroller were organic.

Michael and Christopher were regular attendees at my mayoral campaign office. But because the adoption had not been finalized, we weren't

Michael's adoption ceremony at the 311 Jarvis courthouse, with family, in October 2010. A week later, I lost the Toronto mayoral election to Rob Ford.

able to show Michael to the world. Many commented after seeing Michael on election night that I might have won if only I had introduced him to the campaign earlier. Fact is that just a week before the election, our family was formalized with a lovely private ceremony at the 311 Jarvis Street Family Court.

Watching Michael develop was far more interesting to me than running for mayor. With Michael's arrival, the election quickly took second place on my priority list. I recall such great delight in holding Michael aloft and looking out the window of our sixteenth-floor condo on Carlton Street down upon Maple Leaf Gardens and teaching him to say Toronto.

This is not to say that I mailed in the mayoral campaign. I worked hard at it and attended over one hundred all-candidates meetings and count-less other events. But there were problems within my campaign that never got resolved. The campaign team — a construct of prominent Liberals, Conservatives, and New Democrats — looked impressive but failed to gel. As a result, the campaign lacked strategic rigour. The chair was John Webster, a prominent Liberal who had run campaigns for Paul Martin, John Turner, and David Peterson. I was looking for a big gun to be in charge, and John was definitely a big gun. But as a senior bank executive, he was a distracted big gun and took little interest in the campaign. For campaign manager, I recruited Jeff Bangs, a Conservative who had been principal secretary to Ernie Eves when he was premier. Jeff and I did not hit it off and soon parted ways. I replaced him with Bruce Davis, a long-time Liberal acquaintance who had municipal experience from Mel Lastman's successful 1997 mayoral campaign. I hoped that Bruce would help to develop a ward-based operation capable of seeding a storyline about our campaign. But Bruce also had a busy day job as chair of the Toronto District School Board, and important campaign tasks remained unaddressed. In retrospect, I think everybody believed I was going to run my own campaign, so nobody was motivated to take on the job. And there was no inherited infrastructure, especially if you shed your partisan identification.

One area that gave rise to a lot of confidence was the fundraising com-ponent, headed up by dear friends like Pam Gutteridge, a skilled fundraiser and a woman who twice in my life helped to advance my career dramatically. After Tory dropped out of the race, Ralph Lean also joined the team. Lean is a Bay Street lawyer and Conservative who raises money in every mayoral campaign on one side or the other, depending which way the political wind is blowing. While the actual amount he brings in may vary, he is very skilled at dealing with the media. Accordingly, he got most of the credit for our fundraising success. But also highly effective was my own network, developed over the years. No person deserves more credit than the great Lawrence Bloomberg, who staked his very significant reputation in favour of my candidacy. We raised more than enough money to run the campaign and emerged with a surplus. Unfortunately, Toronto's outdated campaign spending limit does not allow for a full-fledged campaign. There's no room in the budget to buy TV advertising, for instance.

Fundraising aside, we were weak at the strategic level, where data is analyzed and a communication plan developed to advance the campaign's message. Not that the people involved were bad. In fact, the team included some very talented people: Gerald Butts, my first executive assistant, who was McGuinty's principal secretary and did the same job in Ottawa for Justin Trudeau; Bob Penner, a political consultant who has worked on more than thirty-five election campaigns at home and abroad, mostly for the NDP in Canada; and Greg Lyle, a pollster with strong Conservative credentials. These were very smart people, but the construct of my campaign left nobody in charge and nobody accountable.

Early in the campaign, we spent a ton of money on polling and focus groups, most of it to no avail. One focus group report in early February — from Jaime Watt and Navigator, a major political consulting firm — said my sexual orientation was unlikely to be an issue, which turned out not to be true. (More about that later.) The report also urged me to embrace my "furious George" image. "George Smitherman should not run away from his perception as a bull in a china shop but instead embrace it as a unique strength for times when a tougher approach is required," said the report. We largely ignored this advice. Instead, I tried to look like a statesman, not an insurgent. Maybe we went too far in that direction, but it would have been no easy task to outdo Mammoliti/Ford/Rossi on the outrage scale.

There were also two ominous warnings in the Navigator report. First of all, my presumed association with the eHealth "scandal" was a problem. "Our [focus group] participants were not willing to give George Smitherman a pass on his involvement with eHealth Ontario and gave stern warnings that the issue would be a serious one for many come October [election day]," said the report. "They [saw] Smitherman as the original health minister who dodged a bullet and let another minister take the fall." With hindsight, eHealth was to my campaign what emails were to Hillary Clinton's — a stark reminder of a problematic past in a political environment where the prevailing sentiment was to throw the bums out.

The second ominous note was that the voters were looking for other choices. "The electorate is largely unimpressed with the candidates and ideas already present in the race." Of course, this was a month before Ford declared his candidacy.

Still, I was well ahead in the race as winter turned to spring. Then, on March 25, a boulder was dropped into the campaign pond with the entry of Rob Ford into the race. Typical for Ford, he announced his candidacy on a radio hotline show. His campaign consisted mostly of a slogan ("Stop the gravy train"). When I first heard he might join the race, I wasn't too worried. Ford seemed to be a bit of a joke candidate. He had been a city councillor for a decade and had a high profile, but for all the wrong reasons. He was on the losing end of too many forty-four-to-one votes on council. He had publicly insulted fellow councillors — calling one (a woman) a "waste of skin" and another (an Italian Canadian) a "Gino boy." He had said outrageous things about immigrants and ethnic minorities. He had behaved disgracefully in public, once getting tossed from a Maple Leafs game for drunkenness. This was not a man fit for public office.

What I — and most of my team — didn't realize at the time was that Ford's candidacy represented a northern version of the Tea Party. He had hit a nerve in that segment of the public that was "mad as hell and didn't want to take it anymore," to borrow the old movie line. It should not have been a surprise to me that this sentiment would catch hold in Canada. But we did not anticipate that Ford, of all people, would effectively harness that energy and sloganize it. During the campaign, people kept asking me: What's your vision? What they really meant was: What's your slogan? Mine was "For a Toronto that works again." It lacked the punch and pithiness of "Stop the gravy train." Ford's slogan, when combined with his quirky habit of buying his own paperclips (instead of claiming office expenses as a councillor), gave his message an air of authenticity that his supporters could rally around.

The first in a long string of mayoral campaign debates was held in Scarborough several days after Ford entered the race. There were six of us on the platform — Ford, Pantalone, Mammoliti, Rossi, Thomson, and me. It was a format that would be adopted in practically all the one hundred-plus debates that followed. It proved to be both a liability for me and a benefit for Ford. With so many candidates on stage, none of us got enough time to make our points. That was bad for me but good for Ford. He did not have to answer a lot of pointed questions and could get away with merely repeating his slogans. And I didn't get enough opportunities to go after Ford directly. (For a point of reference, think of Donald Trump's performance during debates in the Republican primaries, when there were seventeen other candidates. He could inject himself into the proceedings with a quip or a nasty aside and then fade into the background while the rest of the candidates tore strips off each other.) To change the dynamic, I kept pressing Ford for a one-on-one debate with me. Ford once committed to do it: he reneged within twenty-four hours. Even though we hired a man in a chicken suit to stalk his events in an effort to goad him into fulfilling that commitment, we got nowhere.

At the first debate in March, Ford opened with a reference to his wife and kids, presumably to contrast himself with me. (He repeated this reference at all subsequent debates.) And he and Mammoliti echoed each other's ultra-conservative views of the world. Ford said he would make "customer service" his top priority as mayor. That is, he would personally answer everyone's phone call. (This is a promise he more or less kept, to the detriment of everything else.) And Rossi went after me on eHealth. "You certainly know how to spend money," he said. "You don't know how to save it." It was a line he would repeat at virtually every debate. Meanwhile, I had about six minutes out of two hours to make my thoughtful and complicated case for a more responsible government and my credentials to deliver it.

In these debates — and, indeed, during the whole campaign — I never found a mechanism to leverage my experience in government. The record was generally good. I had run the biggest government department in Canada (the Ontario Ministry of Health) for five years, had reduced wait times and doctor shortages, and had kept a lid on spending (especially on prescription drugs). But we didn't campaign on the good stuff in my record. Instead, we were pilloried — unfairly, I think — for the bad stuff (notably, eHealth). As for Ford, he won praise just for being authentic. As much as some of us might be inclined to write off his lack of intellectual depth, nobody should doubt the value of authenticity for a politician's message. After all, Ford had voted No on virtually every expenditure that came before city council.

By mid-June, I sensed my goose was cooked. A Forum Research poll showed me still ahead in the race, but my support had slipped to 29 percent, and Ford was just behind at 26 percent. (Everyone else was below 20 percent.) Ford had momentum, which is crucial in politics. We knew this inside my campaign, but we never quite got around to answering the question of how to deal with the new dynamic. Indeed, instead of confronting Ford and his slogan head-on, we appeared to be falling in line with his austerity message. I wasn't being insincere. I strongly believed that the city bureaucracy had become bloated under Mayor Miller and I said as much in November prior to my Board of Trade speech. But coming from me, that message was nuanced with new spending priorities and lacked authenticity, especially in light of eHealth's elevation thanks to advertising. By the time we figured out that this approach wasn't working, the ballot box question ("Who can best deliver change?") had already been framed.

Furthermore, it was difficult for me to get an arm free to attack the new front-runner (Ford) when I was still under attack myself from the rest of the pack (Rossi, Pantalone, Mammoliti, and to a lesser extent Thomson) because I stood in their path. We fell back on the same strategy deployed unsuccessfully against Trump in the U.S. presidential race: "faint hope." That is, we told ourselves that the next time Ford said something really stupid that would be the straw that broke the camel's back and people would realize he was unfit to be mayor. And it wasn't just my campaign that believed this. Media commentators were saying the same thing. It was yet another example of conventional wisdom being totally wrong. The elites were a little slow to realize that a lot of people were just happy that politics was entertaining for once.

On July 5, Mammoliti pulled out of the race. His support was in the single digits (white men who wanted a red-light district, I suppose). But it drifted to Ford and gave him another boost. Momentum remained on Ford's side. So in mid-July my campaign team had a strategy session at Bruce Davis's house in Mimico. At this time, our internal polling still showed it was a close race, but there were warning signs. For example, I was supported by just 26 percent of *Liberal* voters. A background document prepared by

Davis for the meeting described the political landscape in bleak terms: "Ford is riding an insurgent wave of discontent over government spending abuses. If the ballot question becomes, 'Who can best control spending?' he could win…. His anti-spending message is clearly resonating with voters…. An additional challenge for a centrist candidate is whether to grow by tacking to the right or the left. This tacking question has more or less divided the campaign strategy group and has left us lurching from week to week, issue to issue."

The document recommended a new narrative for the campaign: "Change for the better, with George being the only one who can do it…. We must stop being defensive about his experience because of eHealth and we must talk about his successes." As for Ford, the document recommended: "We need to define Ford not as the conservative or frugal candidate but as the candidate who is unfit for office…. [But] our campaign should not be involved directly or indirectly with this line of attack…. We must attack Ford's policies or lack thereof and the dumb things he has said by highlighting Ford in his own words. Do not attack his character."

Here were two fundamental issues that dogged my campaign that summer: whether to tack left or right, and whether to go directly after Ford. On the first, we continued a two-track approach, a bit left and a bit right, and ended up satisfying no one. For right-wing voters, it looked like a pale imitation of Ford. And for progressive-minded voters, I was betraying my roots. John Filion, the lefty city councillor, clearly thought I erred to the right. "George Smitherman had chased after Ford so far to the right that supporters of the left-wing candidate, Joe Pantalone, weren't inclined to move to him," writes Filion in his post-election book, *The Only Average Guy.*

This is a convenient argument for progressives who want to let themselves off the hook of the 2010 election result by suggesting that I was running like some big, bad, right-wing bear. Which of course is nonsense. Yes, I called for restraint on spending, which the city desperately needed, and for holding the line on property taxes, which the electorate wanted. But my platform also included calls for more investment in transit, parks, and the arts. Given my history, I thought progressives would cut me more slack than they did. Most telling for me was when a close ally in the LGBTQ community with whom I had collaborated on the relisting of sex reassignment surgery told me she voted for Pantalone because he was a New Democrat, as she was. But party labels were only a part of the problem. I think what really bothered many progressive voters was that I was critical of David Miller. A lot of the mayor's allies on council felt that any criticism of him was also a criticism of them. In other words, they took it personally.

I could hardly get any endorsements from city councillors, even though I met — mostly amicably — with all of them (except for the three I was running against). All the lefty councillors despised Ford, but some of them gravitated toward Pantalone, because of his NDP label, and most others just sat on the sidelines, a position the lack of municipal political parties largely encourages. And by the time those on the sidelines realized it had become a two-man race, they had already figured out Ford was going to win and decided it was not in their interests to try to stem that tide by backing me. Thus, my efforts to build a progressive coalition against Ford were frustrated. At one point, in desperation, I even reached out to Miller himself. But he never returned my call, which I can't exactly fault him for even though I personally bailed him out on a huge issue (funding for new streetcars). In the end, I was endorsed only by Kyle Rae and Pam McConnell (my seat-mates in Toronto Centre), Joe Mihevc (St. Paul's), and Chin Lee (Scarborough–Rouge River), although Adam Vaughan (Trinity-Spadina) and a few others provided some help behind the scenes.

* * *

After the election, the lefty councillors who backed Pantalone tried to make themselves feel better by saying his vote would not have gone to me anyway. But that was not the real issue. Rather, it was that even though Pantalone had zero chance of winning, his presence in the race prevented me from engaging in a head-to-head showdown with Ford. It was a selfish act by Pantalone, a man who made a life in Toronto politics mostly by messing around at Exhibition Place and keeping that place stuck in the 1980s.

If there was a failure in my campaign, it was that I did not go after Ford more on character issues and at every turn. I should have torched the landscape around him by constantly raising the issue of his public drunkenness, his racist and homophobic remarks, and his unsuitability for the mayoralty. Instead, I mostly pulled my punches and tried instead to look statesmanlike while depending on faint hope that Ford's unsuitability would shine through.

One exception to this rule occurred at an all-candidates meeting organized by the Toronto Real Estate Board (TREB). This looked like a trap for me, given the sponsors. Don't get me wrong; I know many realtors and respect them. But as a group they can be pretty self-serving. And Ford had promised to eliminate the city's land transfer tax (made possible by the McGuinty government through the City of Toronto Act). Elimination of that tax, which brings hundreds of millions of dollars a year into the city treasury, would wreak havoc on municipal services. It wasn't doable, and, indeed, Ford never did it. But the realtors loved the idea.

The TREB debate was held at that dreadful, low-ceiling convention barn that the Fords liked to frequent out on Dixon Road — the one where they hosted Prime Minister Stephen Harper (fittingly) for his last public event in the 2015 federal election. The audience this time was a single-issue advocacy group charged up for a particular candidate (Ford). To make it even worse for me, the organizers hired John Oakley, the small-time radio hotline host and Ford surrogate, as the emcee. I threatened not to attend, but TREB chair Richard Silver, who just happened to be my own personal realtor and an ally in AIDS fundraising, begged me to do it. I agreed for his sake. And since I knew it was pointless for me to try to woo the audience, I used the platform to set Ford on fire by recalling some of his most repulsive homophobic utterances and actions. (He had called gays "disgusting" and consistently voted against AIDS prevention measures.) Ford took the bait, and after the event he was swarmed by reporters questioning him on his views. Thrown off script, he looked very uncomfortable, his face dripping with sweat. In retrospect, I should have done it to him more often.

And with hindsight, Ford's drug use was another obvious angle of attack for me. We did not know the full extent of it at the time, but there were rumours. And during the campaign, someone released a bizarre audiotape of Ford seeming to give advice to somebody on where to buy OxyContin on the street. The story should have been very damaging to Ford. But his team successfully turned the narrative around by focusing the spotlight on me. They dishonestly got the guy featured in the audiotape, who happened to be gay (and obviously very vulnerable), to say, "Oh yeah, I used party drugs with George Smitherman." I didn't know this person, and what he said was absolutely untrue. Nonetheless, Newstalk 1010 and the other hotline radio stations accepted his story at face value. Fake news carried the day.

In my earlier life, as I mentioned, I did use party drugs. I openly acknowledged this without prompting when I was minister of health in 2006 and was speaking at the Courage to Come Back Awards Ceremony, an annual event staged by the Centre for Addiction and Mental Health (CAMH) to honour those who have beaten their own addictions and mental health challenges. I was trying to show empathy for the honorees. But my well-meaning admission of past drug use made it very tough for me to fight back against the Fords' thuggish tactics, because Ford's media cheerleaders would say his behaviour and mine were comparable. The irony, of course, is that Rob Ford dishonored Toronto by partying recklessly while he was in office and fessed up to it only after the smoking gun was discovered still smoking.

I describe these kinds of tactics as thuggish for good reason. I have no respect for Doug Ford (now premier) and Nick Kouvalis, who ran Rob's campaign. They are the lowest of the low. It was so telling that after the campaign the firefighters' union hired Kouvalis to forestall the cuts to fire halls implemented by Mayor Rob Ford — the candidate Kouvalis had helped to elect. And I laugh aloud when I think back to a lunch I had with Bonnie Crombie, who wanted to sound me out on whether she should hire Kouvalis to run her Mississauga mayoral campaign in 2014. In customary fashion, I let her know that I was the wrong person to ask. I said my personal view is that Kouvalis is a person who gets off on dividing people. I was and continue to be shocked that John Tory reduced himself to this level by hiring Kouvalis to run his 2014 mayoral campaign. Ironically, Tory, who thrives on being all things to all people, also hired Tom Allison, a Liberal Party contemporary who was my first campaign manager, one-time housemate, and someone with whom I shared progressive values.

Kouvalis went on to work for Kellie Leitch's Conservative leadership run in 2016–17, which featured an assault on immigrants seemingly inspired by Donald Trump. Not only did she promise to subject new immigrants to a "Canadian values" test, but she also suggested that the immigrants would be required to pay for the test themselves. Kouvalis must have concluded that, if making Mexicans pay for a wall was popular, then getting immigrants to pay for her proposed screening tool would also be popular.

As for Doug Ford, I cringe when I see him describing himself as Rob's best friend. In his book, *Ford Nation*, Doug says he was "stunned" when

Rob finally admitted to smoking crack cocaine. As Rob's brother, best friend, work colleague, and neighbour, how is it possible that Doug was unaware of his brother's reckless behaviour? And why didn't Doug intervene on behalf of both his family and the city?

Another person from the Ford campaign should be noted: Mark Towhey, the former army officer who went on to become Ford's chief of staff in the mayor's office. Towhey was Ford's enabler-in-chief. During the campaign debates, he would sit in the front row like a security blanket, always within reach to pacify the candidate. On several occasions, he even heckled me if I laid a glove on his boy. I was just so sick when I watched Towhey turn on Ford years later, after the crack cocaine video emerged. The media fell for it and made Towhey out to be some kind of hero for holding out against the dark side for as long as he could. Let's face the fact that Towhey was a key enabler and at best failed to respond to a series of obvious warning signs about Ford's erratic behaviour until near the very end.

* * *

Back to the campaign. In mid-August came what appeared to be a game-changer: a news story in the *Toronto Sun*, of all places, reporting that Ford had been arrested in Miami a decade earlier on charges of DUI and possession of marijuana. Confronted by the *Sun*, Ford at first tried to deny it, which only made him look worse. "When the joint story hit, I thought Rob was finished," says Doug Ford in his book. "I guess the media thought so, too. At our campaign office, the telephone lines were lighting up like a Christmas tree." But soon after the *Sun*'s story, an Ipsos Reid poll showed Ford still had a commanding lead over me, 32 percent to 21 percent. It appeared that Ford, like Trump six years later, was immune to negative publicity. In fact, as with Trump, damaging press may have helped him by reinforcing his campaign's narrative, which was that the attacks on Ford were coming from the very people who were trying to keep the gravy train rolling.

For my part I remember the street corner I was standing on in Kensington Market when I got tipped off the night before about the story. A friend had it on good authority that the *Sun* was running with the Florida arrest and he was breathless in anticipation that it would help me. I was blasé in my response because by this late date in the campaign I was convinced that the public wasn't concerned about the personal issues. The voters just wanted their vehicle registration tax money back and enjoyed a little entertainment along the way.

Was my sexual orientation an issue in the campaign? In at least three ethno-cultural communities, there were efforts to make it one. In the Bengali community, a picture of Christopher and me holding hands was posted on neighbourhood hydro poles. And on radio stations targeting the Tamil and Chinese communities, there were advertising spots that drew attention to my sexuality. For example, in an ad that aired on the Tamil radio station, one person asked another whom they would be voting for. "What kind of question is this?" said the other. "I am Tamil. We have a religion and culture. Take Rob Ford, for example. His wife is a woman." Ironically, no politician had spent more time in the Tamil and Bengali communities than me, seemingly all for nothing.

During the campaign, we did not make a big deal about incidents like this because my team felt it would only draw unwanted attention to my sexual orientation. This decision reflected a certain insecurity within my campaign. Even though I was the most well-known "out" politician in Canada at the time, some of my advisers did not want me to be photographed with Christopher by my side. Others counselled me against referring to him as "my husband." And I myself did not speak up as loudly as I should have against the homophobia that I had experienced. Kathleen Wynne did that much more effectively after she became premier.

My guiding principle of politics, informed by my own experience both as a minority and as a champion of the Charter of Rights, is that we are all in this together. Early in my political career I once spoke to a gathering at the Masjid mosque in my riding. I acknowledged they might have some issues with my sexual orientation. "But in a place like Toronto," I said, "if we all wake up in the morning focused on our differences rather than on the things we have in common, we're ruined. So I expect you to treat me with respect and, in turn, if your community is under attack, I will stand beside you." I received a warm reception, and in the days following 9/11 I spoke up quickly when ignorant people initiated attacks on Muslims. (Because the assailants were so ignorant, they targeted Sikhs and other minority communities, too.)

During the campaign Salma Zahid, now an MP, and Harpreet Hansra, two of my most loyal and trusted team members, organized a giant Iftar dinner at my Scarborough campaign office. It filled me with pride to know that my politics included hundreds of Muslims praying and then celebrating the daily breaking of the fast as guests in my house.

The lowest point in the campaign (aside from losing) involved my very estranged older brother Art, who was manipulated into endorsing Ford. Naturally the *Toronto Sun* put Art on its front page. I still remember the first time I saw his mug staring at me from a newspaper box as I arrived for a meeting on the Danforth. My first instinct was to kick the newspaper box over, but I somehow restrained myself. Art ran in 2010 as a candidate for council in a North York ward. (He got a grand total of 268 votes and came fourth.) During the campaign, the Fords staged a "Fordfest" and invited any and all candidates who wanted to have their photos taken with Rob. My brother showed up. Doug Ford is no slouch; he tipped off the *Sun*.

Whatever grief this might have meant for me is entirely secondary to the pain that it caused my mother. I called her that day, and she was crying on the phone. "I am so sorry for this," she said. "I wish I knew how to stop it." I think it is not well enough understood just how tough it is to be the family member of a politician, especially if the politician has a high public profile. This was one of many days when my mother paid a steep price for my participation in public life, but I know that there were many moments of joy and pride as well.

Later that day, Christopher broke the ice as only he could and drew a belly laugh from me when he critiqued the shirt my brother was wearing in the photo on the front of the *Sun*. Sometime earlier, we had seen a promo for the CFTO evening news featuring Ken Shaw wearing a casual item from his closet, which he must have kept for nostalgic purposes. It was out of place for Ken, who usually looks so dapper. Thereafter, whenever we saw a really retro item of clothing, we would say it looked like a piece from the Ken Shaw collection.

* * *

After Labour Day, the mayoral campaigns ramped up — or, at least, this is the conventional wisdom. By then I had attended dozens of all-candidates meetings and worked my butt off all summer; yet we had nothing to show for it. Ever want a lesson in humiliation and rejection? Try soliciting interest from people while they are jostling for souvlaki at the Taste of Danforth.

My campaign manager, Bruce Davis, and I had a long talk, and we agreed that the strategy of offering a balance of positions and sometimes skewing to the right (lest Ford open up too much distance between him and me) was not working. So I returned to my Liberal roots and began taking more progressive stands. I also got some key endorsements from several mainstream Conservatives who could not abide Ford: Isabel Bassett, Charles Harnick, and Dan Newman (all of whom had been ministers in Mike Harris's cabinet), and Jaime Watt, a key Conservative strategist. None of it seemed to help. A Nanos Research poll on September 19 showed me trailing Ford by a staggering 24.5 percentage points.

I soldiered on and got a small boost at the end of September when Sarah Thomson pulled out of the race and endorsed me. (I have referred to her as a flake, but I also consider her one of the most courageous retail campaigners I have witnessed.) But Pantalone and Rossi hung in there. It took Rossi until October 13 to leave the race — far too late to get his name off the ballot — and Pantalone stuck it through to the end.

Still, momentum appeared to be shifting back to me near the end of the campaign. On October 18, with just one week to go, a *Star*–City TV poll showed the race was a dead heat, with Ford at 41 percent, me at 40 percent, and Pantalone at 16 percent. On October 19, in the last mayoral debate of the campaign, I made one last pitch for Pantalone's votes by stressing my own "progressive values." And on October 23, I was endorsed by David Crombie, a progressive former mayor who is still revered in much of the city. He joined another former mayor, John Sewell, who had endorsed me earlier. (Barbara Hall was prohibited in her role as head of the Ontario Human Rights Commission from issuing a formal endorsement of me.)

On election day, I remember feeling a kind of serenity. Notwithstanding the late polls showing the race was tightening up, I knew I was going to lose. I remember killing time with Noble Chummar, a charismatic lawyer and law partner of David Peterson's. "Sometimes the awards just aren't proportionate to the effort," he told me. True enough. The night ended very quickly, with Ford declared the winner just thirteen minutes after the polls closed. He beat me by almost 95,000 votes, 383,501 to 289,832. It is fitting that Pantalone's vote represents Ford's margin of victory over me, leaving at least some to believe he played the role of spoiler.

Michael, reaching out at the end of my journey to be mayor of Toronto.

"It will be written that I lost an election that was mine to win, and I accept that," I said in my election night concession speech. "The only way to survive, especially in politics, is to have no regrets and not spend a lot of time second-guessing. I won't be spending a lot of time on regrets or second-guessing."

One footnote about election night: my campaign manager, Bruce Davis, barred Rocco Rossi from entrance to my would-be victory party. It was Bruce's finest hour in the campaign!

Did I think my political career was over that night? In politics, you never say never. But at the time I felt liberated. I had been a senior cabinet minister for six years, had allocated more than a quarter of a trillion dollars and experienced unrelenting pressure and media exposure. Now I no longer had to worry about being accosted while out doing errands. I didn't have to take media calls at strange hours. I could go looking for a house to buy in neighbourhoods outside my riding. I also felt a sense of relief after a year-long campaign that was both physically exhausting and emotionally draining. After a hundred all-candidates meetings with the likes of Ford and Rossi, I may have been suffering from post-traumatic stress disorder. There were times when the campaign felt like a death sentence that could not be carried out quickly enough, like trying to campaign at events such as Canada Day at Downsview Park or Taste of the Danforth rather than just attending them for fun.

* * *

What political lessons were learned? In the twenty-first century, conventional wisdom about campaigns needs to be thrown out. It used to be that to win a mayoral race you needed name recognition and money. I outspent Ford in the campaign by half a million dollars ($2.2 million to $1.7 million). But Ford could have won without spending a penny, thanks to social media. If you hit the vein just right, social media has so much potential to propel you forward. (Ask Trump.) The web is tailor-made for sloganeering, and as a society we have become more susceptible to slogans instead of substance. The more knowledge we get through the web, the less wisdom we have. It is the triumph of entertainment over news: it is "infotainment."

As for old-style media, I was battered by voices on the right, partic-ularly hotline radio hosts, but I got little or no help from the progressive side. Right-wing personalities always complain that liberals dominate the mainstream media. But it isn't really true, because the liberal or centrist media outlets mostly refuse to play a partisan game and perhaps sometimes set a higher bar for the candidates who share their values. Whereas the right-wingers in the media see a candidate they like and throw everything behind him, progressive candidates never get that sort of support. Yes, the *Toronto Star* gave me a strong editorial endorsement, but its news pages were filled with stories about Tory, Pantalone, and Rossi as well as me. Meanwhile, the *Globe and Mail* gave me a tepid endorsement after flirting with Rossi. The *Sun*'s endorsement of Ford was full-throated, and its news pages reflected that bias toward the end of the campaign and right up until today. In fact, a former paid apologist for Rob Ford currently serves as editor of the *Sun*.

Still, when you blow a big lead in a campaign, as I did, conventional wisdom would argue that you sat on your lead and became too cautious. From a policy standpoint, I would reject that analysis of my campaign. My platform was both comprehensive and ambitious and stands up to the test of time. However, I may have made a mistake by trying to look "mayoral" rather than defaulting to my "furious George" persona. Looking back, and boy have I ever, I have often wished that just once I had said: "How can a man who looks like he drinks from the gravy boat stop the gravy train?" My campaign team also shot down my proposal to project the movie *Tommy Boy*, with Chris Farley in the title role, onto the wall of a historic building as our contribution to the annual Nuit Blanche event. (I wanted to call it the "Rob Ford Film Festival," as Farley and Ford shared much in common.) But in my heart I know I did the right thing by not reverting to the role I had played in chasing Mike Harris out of Queen's Park or bringing unruly hospital CEOs to heel. My son, Michael, made the difference by motivating me to remain calm and keep my options open for an obvious next chapter.

My gentlemanly conduct was tested further when, after the campaign results were tallied, it became clear that each campaign except mine had a deficit. John Tory was among those who pushed me to participate in a big dinner that was organized to pay off the debts of Ford and the others, as doing this for Hall and Miller in an earlier tussle aided his reputation. To say the least, I was incredibly reluctant to take part and did so only because part of the proceeds were destined to help Sarah Thomson. Needless to say, I didn't hang around to get my picture taken with the mayor-elect, but etched in my mind is the image of many of those I knew doing so. As my father once told me after a hockey game where I came out on the losing end of a battle, "Sometimes the best you can do is take his number."

CHAPTER TEN

Worse Than Defeat

Conceding the election to a thug like Rob Ford was going to be tough enough to swallow emotionally. Accordingly, when I wrote my remarks (there was only one speech prepared), I planned to introduce Christopher and Michael in my final words so as not to belie my emotion and cue the crying. That careful preparation went for naught, however, as someone missed the cue and Christopher and Michael came on stage prematurely. That forced me off-script, which turned out perfectly. For a defeated politician, the outstretched arms of a not-yet-two-year-old, held by the man who stood beside me, offered sweet sanctuary. Let's face it, I was going to need it.

* * *

The one and only great transition from campaign loser to father took place just after the election at our condo's party room, where we celebrated Michael's second birthday. The opportunity to express sadness through joy, or some such formula, meant that the outpouring of material love was overwhelming, and I am sure it messed with Michael's sense of expectations for all time. There were so many presents that he kept opening them for days and days, to the point where his first Christmas with us, which was already destined to be over the top, became indistinguishable except for the seasonal wrapping paper. The birthday was a three-week run.

One of the points of liberation that came from being unelected was that our residence no longer needed to be tied to a particular political territory. (The law doesn't say you *must* live where you run, but as a rule of thumb I preferred to do that.) On top of that, we wanted a backyard to give our kid more room to roam. (By now in life, I think parks and the public realm matter more, and I long to return to a condo!) During the mayoral campaign, I knocked on a door and I was impressed by what I saw. The house was for sale, and I saw it online. In addition to being affordable, it was within walking distance of my tennis club. So we moved from our condo on Carlton Street to Davenport Road between Christie and Ossington.

The local parks and shopping were great, and the open-concept layout of the home allowed the kitchen and the dining room to emerge as the focus. This was so appropriate, because Christopher's best energies were saved for using food to make people happy (and for balloon fights, according to the kids, who remember them so fondly).

My new private-sector life had me out less in the evenings, although I was prone to a fair bit of travel to Asia. But once Christopher returned to work, our combined incomes allowed us a reasonably good quality of life. And George Brown's daycare at Scotia Plaza proved a convenient and accommodating venue for Michael, who despite his obvious charms is occasionally quite a handful.

When the September 2011 provincial election rolled around, I made a speech or two at the opening of campaign offices. But I skipped election day and took my family on a luxurious and long-dreamed-of return to Las Vegas. We stayed at the Four Seasons, where the staff pampered Michael and arranged care so Christopher and I could attend a One Republic concert with our feet dipped in a wave pool, followed by a fine dinner and some gambling. True to form, we came back to the room an hour before our curfew.

One of the most memorable things we did was use a multi-year bounty of Aeroplan points for the three of us to take a helicopter ride over the Hoover Dam and out to the Grand Canyon. The vibration put Michael to sleep instantly in both directions, so he can't fully recall the sensation of flying in a helicopter. But we have great photos taken that day. Returning to the Grand Canyon after having visited there as a kid was amazing for me. After Trump is gone, I may consider taking my family back.

* * *

We had heard from the nice staff at CAS that Michael's mom had had another baby — a little girl — and that mother and child were doing well. Of course, knowing that historically the mother had struggled to maintain connections despite her obvious love meant we might be called upon to expand our circle of love.

What hit me about Christopher's response to the opportunity to adopt Kayla (we dropped several other names she had been given but we liked the name Kayla a lot) was his insistence that, rather than take another leave from Lindt, he should quit altogether. I wish I could say I reluctantly went along with this, but I didn't put up the least resistance. Rather, I concluded that if there was a point in our life where I could afford to carry us, it was then. The part I was slow to get, and that Christopher discounted or missed entirely, was the extent to which his confidence was tied to his mastery of the retail chocolate environment. Oddly enough, his prior promotion meant that when he returned to the workplace his job had shifted from operationalizing the frontline to presenting the budget and plans for the frontline back at headquarters. Or, put another way, Christopher was shifting from day-to-day interaction with retail employees to a results-driven executive leadership team at head office. The latter was a tougher fit for Christopher.

Now I would like to say to anybody with one kid who is feeling pressure to acquire another: think about it long and hard. Because what seemed like more than ample resources for one kid quickly became a stretch to manage two. The added pressure seemed to create an uptick in Christopher's alcohol consumption. To try to spread the burden, I adjusted my own sleep and work patterns. I often exercised at 6 a.m. before heading to work, early enough to allow me to get back and take the kids to the wading pool late in the afternoon.

The deterioration of Christopher's mental health in this period was a real challenge, and his history of attempts at taking his own life resurfaced. Before eventually succumbing to his own devices, Christopher made two bold efforts to accomplish the same pain-ending feat. One of those, his disappearance and eventual discovery in a clump of bushes along a railway line, is well known. As is my memory of sitting down on my deck to pen some remarks that Barbara Hall was to deliver soon after to searchers on my behalf, only to have my privacy interrupted by a helicopter hovering directly overhead. It was as if they could see what I was writing.

Frankly, the shame Christopher suffered in realizing that he had created such a circus was nearly impossible for him to get over. Sad as it is to say, it was pretty much clear that at some point he would take his own life, and we had this conversation very openly in the company of his (and later my) psychiatrist. She reminded us that, if a person wishes to die, we are quite powerless to stop it.

After an earlier overdose attempt where his cellphone gave him away, Christopher expressed dismay that he had left his phone on. In the latter case, he did not share my enthusiasm, or that of the kids, that Ranger the police dog had found him where he lay after bouncing off a slow-moving freight train. That same meeting with the psychiatrist was our only real conversation about the underlying trauma that made Christopher's life so tormented. He confirmed that he had been sexually abused at the hands of a trusted figure in his youth, but he delved no further.

Around midafternoon the day before Christopher died, I pretty much knew the show was over when I received an email from him promising a final result. He asked us not to sound the alarm as precautions on his part were going to make this a recovery, not a rescue, mission. My fervent efforts to trace debit and credit card transactions were fruitless but were an outlet for my energy during a period that felt a lot like the final hours on election day when the outcome is in doubt. *Tick tick tick.*

My mother had swooped in and picked up the kids Sunday afternoon, and their ability to roll with the situation was tested once more. By 5:00 a.m. the next day, I got a confirming word from the coroner that Christopher had died. I spread the word to close family, dictated the fateful tweet, and called my mother for my children's return. By 9:00 a.m., I squeezed my children tightly and told Kayla, then age three-and-a-half, and Michael, five, that Dada wouldn't be coming home. That he was dead. Their grasp was at first limited to the practical with Michael asking, "Who is going to feed us?" From that day until now, my crew of two hugs-and-cuddles have filled the void and saved the day.

People have different strategies about how to approach the complicated matter of death with children. While I didn't then explicitly tell Michael and Kayla that their father had taken his own life, I did tell them that his brain let him down, not his body. It's not my style to bullshit around subjects to begin with, and so I have been gripped with fear trying to balance my need to be the first to tell them, with the attendant reality that another kid's Google search could lead to schoolyard humiliation. Get the spelling of the family name right and it's not too many clicks before you find the full story about Michael and Kayla's Dada.

Only more recently have I explained to Michael and Kayla that Dada took his own life because he was in pain and sometimes our brain can send us the wrong messages. "How did he die?" they asked. "He stopped breathing," I said. The real details of his death are left to be a burden shared between me and very few others, and I repeat what I said at Christopher's memorial about the good fortune I experienced by actually knowing the deputy coroner who attended to Christopher. About Christopher's taking of his own life, Kayla recently said as we crossed the street to school: "It's sad and it's a little bit mean."

In organizing the memorial for Christopher, I unearthed the really sad reality of his life: the underlying unwillingness on the part of his parents to let him be who he was and truly respect him for that. "Don't bother going to Toronto for his memorial," his parents told everyone in Sudbury. "We will do something for him here in Sudbury." And what they did for him in Sudbury was hold a Catholic funeral mass. This for a man who had a pronounced and undisguised disdain for the Catholic Church and was notably an atheist. I protested to his mother, who in the same sentence blamed me for his death and proclaimed that he was baptized with his god and that he shall be with his god in death. To say any more about the matter would not shed any more light on it.

Christopher's Toronto memorial was attended by hundreds, including dignitaries and, especially, the many he had touched professionally over the decades. Our yellow bird was free, but his flock was deeply burdened by the events. I don't really know how we have survived. The depth of despair I felt was intense, but the saving grace was the pitter-patter of feet on the floor. Because my kids are such good cuddlers, they wore my sadness away with the comfort of love.

We headed for Florida. Our customary twenty-four hours of driving put some real distance on the pain. Anxious as I was to get there in my stepmother's Chrysler 300, we attracted attention from two separate representatives of the constabulary. One, an OPP officer near London, took a look at my driver's licence, offered condolences on our loss, and wished us a good day. Not sure how exactly, but about ten hours later a similar courtesy was offered by the police as we slipped from Tennessee into Georgia. Perhaps my sadness was etched in my face.

My best advice to anybody facing the devastating impacts of trauma is to respect it for what it is, and I hope you have kids. The former is to help people escape the guilt they feel from having no motivation to do anything. The latter — having kids — is because, no matter how shitty you might feel, you can't just climb back under the duvet, or in my case chase a longish high down a funnel of self-fulfilling despair. The emotional needs of the kids forced me to adjust my work away from the office and toward home. The ideal of everyone finishing a night's sleep in his or her own bed was shattered, and despite the annoyance I needed the comfort as much as they did.

Our language has taught us to say things like, "We will be there for you" and "Anything we can do?" and "Don't worry." Almost all of those expressions are sincerely uttered but largely unfulfillable. I have personally skipped many funerals since Christopher passed because my trauma quotient has remained so high. But when I do attend, I try very hard to tell people: "Respect the trauma."

It's been tough on my little people. Michael quite understandably suffers from fears of abandonment, and Kayla longs for more attachment. For all that we have been through, however, we get stronger and better every day. But not a day goes by that we don't make note of how much we miss Christopher. He found his peace, and everywhere we see yellow birds we feel his presence.

There are just so many music anthems to rely upon, each one a soundtrack for my life inside and outside politics. The great gay anthem, Gloria Gaynor's "I Will Survive," comes to my mind often, as well as Kanye West's "Stronger," which paraphrases Friedrich Nietzsche's famous dictum that what doesn't kill you only makes you stronger. Michael certainly seems to identify with Shawn Mendes's song "There's Nothing Holdin' Me Back."

Christopher walking happily with his first daughter, Morgan, and Michael and Kayla.

At various times, I have had people tell me how great a man I am for sticking it out and not walking away from Michael and Kayla. It is the stupidest thing I have ever heard. The truth is that Christopher's death revealed to me that, without Michael and Kayla, I am nothing. Their existence is my sole purpose in life.

Others have told me that it is remarkable I don't view Christopher as having been selfish. Of course, in quiet moments of anger and despair, some of this sentiment might take hold, however briefly. But I love Christopher and I will forever hold him in that special place that views him as a great partner, lover, and father. As for his brain and the terrible tricks it played on him, it reminds me always of our need not to judge others too harshly. Not everyone is capable of processing the same facts and drawing the same conclusion.

CHAPTER ELEVEN

Carrying On

Finally, when I let it come, it came fast and hard. Renewed love that is. I'd been working at it for many months — well, years really — since Christopher's death in late 2013. Working to get to that point where I could give love a fighting chance, given that the life-experience quotient threatens to overwhelm the faint of heart.

I had a lot of life experience at this point in my life. I know "life experience" sounds like a whitewash term. But "baggage," another frequently used term, implies that even my darkest moments haven't been a source of strength and knowledge. On the contrary, they have given me a greater affinity with those suffering similar turmoil, defeat, and tragedy.

Long before my new relationship, I had been very open to Barbara Hall and others that I surely didn't intend to carry on alone forever in my family mission. Fact is that my kids needed to have a new family unit formed even more than I did. Not that there could be any replacement for Christopher, but commensurate levels of energy and creativity and nurturing remain much needed for these lively little kids to prosper. Daunting prospect, though, this dating thing in the online age, especially when your Google and Wiki profiles are hot even before you are asked to share your dick pic.

I spent a fair bit of time as an online voyeur, posting a profile without a photo just to gain access to what was on the market. Some of those sites were all about instant gratification and hook-ups, not that there's anything wrong with that. Others targeted the more long-term-relationship-oriented person.

Excitedly I pursued the paths toward those indicating they wanted to be part of a family. And I found nothing, and I mean nothing, that appealed to me. Even where a profile indicated that the person was interested in a partner with kids, it seemed mostly upon further evaluation that they had an ambivalence rather than a preference.

For my fifty-third birthday weekend in February 2017, I ventured to Havana for a brief trip. I knew from having visited Havana in 2004 with my friend Jason Grier that a good time could be had by all. Jason and I found an undercover gay scene that included a party at the Castillo fortress, which protects that harbour entrance; a rooftop drag show surely not sanctioned by the state; and an array of beautiful men lining the Malecón seawall who were keen to practise their English.

By 2017, a combination of gay-rights progress and economic reforms allowing private business to operate had created a burgeoning gay scene in Havana, complete with clubs. On my first night in Havana, my host arranged for a group of us to go to Club Las Vegas, located just metres from the Malecón meeting spot that was familiar from my earlier visit. There our party of five sat on a wall alongside the Ministry of Economics, downing a beer and delighting in the lovely evening sea breeze. It was at this very moment that I first made eye contact with Rolando Salomon Laurencio, and it was love at first sight. But it didn't play itself out quite the way one might have anticipated.

By the time I made eye contact with Rolando we had walked in a group a few kilometres along the Malecón en route to the club. During this walk, I learned that Rolando was a dentist and he learned that I was a former provincial minister of health. I will never forget the pride with which he showed me pictures from his cellphone of a tooth reconstruction he had completed earlier in the day.

Rolando arrived that evening with a friend to join our party, and I still don't know and don't care who the friend was. That's only important because, later in the evening, after having been thoroughly entertained by a great drag and traditional dance show, and after having consumed a lot of rum with everybody else, I picked up a very cute man who also wanted to practise his English.

Shortly thereafter our group, now numbering six, piled into a huge 1950s taxi. (Some of those 1950s cars in Havana are fixed up and featured in travel mags, but the majority of the fleet is much less glamorous.) We rambled through the deserted backstreets of Centro Habana until the driver's front tires proved no match for the patchwork replacement of water lines and accompanying ruts. Forced to disembark, we rocked this huge car out of the deep rut, Canadian snow-bank style. It was then that I made clear to Rolando that it was him and not my English student companion that I truly desired. I kissed him on the cheek and said, "I wish I was going home with you."

The next night, my evening plan was pretty much the same, but this time I travelled solo. The same scenario ensued: too much rum, a few English lessons, and a quick ride home. But on this night my BlackBerry outmatched my wits and didn't complete the journey. That is a bad enough scenario at the best of times, but it was made worse because I hadn't brought a computer with me. Very early the next morning, with my phone gone and utterly lacking the means to contact the network of people caring for my kids, I scrambled to get home. I rushed to a hotel on Central Park, where I confirmed that I could use a computer in the lobby. Then I diverted to get the internet access card essential in Cuba, paid a fee to skip the horrendous line, ran back to the hotel, logged onto the Air Canada site, and found I had nearly two hours until Air Canada's daily direct flight home. I bought a ticket and hailed a taxi, stopped by my accommodation, quickly packed, and headed home without hardly a word or a trace until I reached my computer in Toronto. It was February 11, the eve of my birthday, and I was home in Toronto safe and sound with my kids but feeling utterly depressed by the stupidity that led to the loss of my BlackBerry and cut short my brief liberation.

My fifty-third birthday hit me in a ho-hum kind of a way — that is, until I got an email from Rolando. None of my family members had reached out to share birthday greetings with me, but he did, to tell me that he had hoped to meet up and show me around Havana. "I'll take a rain check," I quickly told him. For days that followed, I ran up a massive phone bill as Rolando and I took up over the phone and on email. Many days, he and I would email back and forth as he was between patients; access to the internet for him was much better while he was at work. Remarkably, Cuba is mostly running the internet through some four hundred hotspots, mainly situated in parks.

Several weeks into our fledgling long-distance relationship, I made a bold move. I recognized that it was one thing for me to meet a man and be happy, but for practical purposes he needed to fall in love with my whole team. Without Rolando's permission, I booked a flight for me and the kids to spend March break in Cuba rather than have them go to the planned program at the local Boys and Girls Club. The kids were naturally ecstatic and seemed okay with my answer to their question, "Where will we stay?" I simply said: "I don't know yet, but I guarantee you a pool or the ocean." Good enough for them, but how would Rolando respond?

His first reaction was to immediately commit to taking the time off of work, which I had hoped for but not counted on. His second was to use all of his resources (stretching them) to help find the perfect accommodation for our fledgling family. He travelled to the eastern beaches of Havana and, after a few failed attempts, secured a beach house in Guanabo.

The kids and I are quite accustomed to rolling with whatever hand we are dealt, so we weren't nervous or trepidatious as we set off for Havana. I guess we should have been, but I told myself we were going to step off the plane and enter the terminal, meet Rolando, and continue as if it were day one thousand and one, not day one.

The strategy worked perfectly. Rolando, sitting in the middle of the back seat, was soon experiencing the double-cuddle effect that Michael and Kayla specialize in. The perfection was rounded out by the arrival of Rolando's spirited and lovely Chihuahua, Doby. In fact, the competition among the three of us for the dog's affections was significant.

Within minutes of our arrival, the kids witnessed a bit of the chaos that's possible when various forms of transport use a roadway at different speeds: a fast-charging motorcycle rider rode into the back of a slowing pickup truck taxi laden with passengers. Luckily the injuries, while very productive in terms of blood flow, weren't life-threatening.

The more challenging part of the whole visit was on the adult side of the equation, where the normal gay precaution of a "test drive" to ensure sexual compatibility hadn't transpired. Among the barriers to intimacy is lack of privacy, but the spacious casa, walled grounds, and plunge pool met everyone's needs.

Rolando, Michael, and Kayla in Havana within days of our forming as a family in March 2017.

Leaving Rolando at the airport was a very tough experience for all of us, especially Kayla. She benefited so much from the attention Rolando heaped on her. Rolando's fine motor skills produced results that have forever rendered me "useless at nails" in Kayla's eyes.

After a couple of more visits and having walked Havana very extensively, we found a modest apartmentio in Centro Havana, just a few minutes' walk

Our wedding day, December 23, 2017. Rolando and me with my stepmother, Marilyn Smitherman.

from Old Havana or the Malecón. I provided Rolando with the funds to make a home for us there. The kids travelled to Havana four times in 2017, and have made great friends with two of Rolando's cousins. They also met Rolando's mother, who lives a long way from Havana.

We tried numerous times to get a visa for Rolando to come and visit us in Canada but were denied over and over again. The system seemed biased toward the idea that every temporary visitor from Cuba is going to disappear upon arrival. However, we finally managed to get a temporary visa for Rolando to come to Toronto in December 2017 for a hastily planned wedding. The wedding came off without a hitch and was a joyous affair, with about eighty guests representing a broad cross-section of our lives, including our many new Cuban friends.

We didn't immediately head off on a honeymoon, but delayed that until the following March. But we did schedule a quick visit to Ottawa for a dinner with the Liberal caucus and a chance to meet and have our picture taken with the prime minister. Rolando also got to enjoy our cold winter. He probably won't ever forget the reading of minus thirty-four degrees as we travelled through Smiths Falls on a train at 6:00 a.m. Back in Toronto, it was most delightful watching Rolando trudge up and down our outdoor stairs to the laundry room wearing his flip-flops and walking in several inches of snow. We were very surprised that a Cuban would take so readily to walking with bare feet in snow.

Unfortunately the honeymoon was a completely different matter, on account of one of the biggest brain farts of my life. After weeks of intensive planning and an investment of well over $10,000, Rolando and I, accompanied by Michael and Kayla, arrived in China only to discover that I, who had travelled there about ten times prior, had arrived with an expired Chinese visa. More unsettling was that Chinese officials, instead of seeking to assist us in any way, gave us the bum's rush, with Air Canada's co-operation, and put all of us back on a return flight within two hours of landing in China after a thirteen-hour flight from Montreal.

Luckily for me, love prevailed. After a brief stopover in Toronto, which we pretended was Shanghai, and a visit to the CN Tower and the Ripley's Aquarium, we all departed for Cuba to make the best of the rest of the time that we had booked off. And while it's difficult to replace the kinds of things you can see in China, with its long and rich history, we thoroughly enjoyed the opportunity to travel outside of our home in Havana to the wonderful province of Pinar del Río and to spend several days of five-star living at Varadero.

Of course I couldn't stop kicking myself about the financial cost and the stupidity of my mistake, but on the other hand it proved to me the depth of the love of my family and their tremendous capability for forgiveness. What might have been an even more traumatic event for me I got over relatively easily because of their ceaseless love.

I really love China and had worked so hard to plan the perfect trip, all to culminate on the final day at Shanghai Disney. Until this day I can't help feeling sad about the lack of compassion shown to us in China. Neither Air Canada nor the Chinese government sought to aid us in any way. Rather, they collaborated to get us back on the airplane as fast as they could. All of this despite the fact that Shanghai is a place where one can land without a visa and be granted the privilege of staying for at least a few days. None of that was on offer to us, however.

CHAPTER TWELVE

Life After Politics?

After I left politics following the 2010 mayoral race, when people asked me what I was doing, I would say: a lot of parenting. That was simply to remind them that I was a solo parent, which is to say I was living life on the edge all the time. But to keep the lights on at my home and to broaden my own knowledge of the world, I began working in a variety of areas, including the recruitment of students from China to a private high school in Scarborough (New Oriental International College). The school is geared toward helping Chinese students gain admission to world-class universities. More than 80 percent of them end up going to the Universities of Toronto and Waterloo.

This recruiting role enabled me to visit at least twenty cities in China during ten different trips. I picked up a little Mandarin along the way, but I also gained a much deeper appreciation of Chinese culture and politics. At a gay night club in Shanghai after Christopher's passing, for example, I met a young gay man, an Uighur, from the primarily Muslim community in northwestern China. He was the son of a peasant family who had been sent to a technical institute in Shanghai. So he was a minority in various ways: cultural, religious, economic, and sexual. It was a most interesting conversation, and I enjoyed it so much that I had a secret rendezvous with him in Shanghai before he returned home.

Touring the Great Wall of China, where I worked on conquering my fear of heights, in March 2013.

China is very complex, with almost three hundred living languages and fifty-six officially recognized ethnic minorities. If that is not enough, there is the sheer scale of the place. China has twenty-two cities bigger than Toronto. And the buildings and other structures are awe-inspiring. Take, for instance, the Terracotta Army, located in Xi'an at the end of the Silk Road. It is estimated that the "army" of sculptures contains more than eight thousand figures guarding the tomb of China's first emperor, Qin Shi Huang. Or consider the Great Wall, which is some six thousand kilometres long, or more than double Trump's proposed Mexico wall. Construction on the wall began almost three thousand years ago.

Equally impressive is the modern rebirth of China, with massive investment in its infrastructure and cities. In Shanghai, now a city of twenty-five million people, a whole new district (Pudong) has been built to serve as the city's financial centre. Where once stood rice paddies and warehouses, there are now skyscrapers over one hundred storeys high.

All this has come with a price, of course. Civic life in China is constrained by restrictions on free association, free speech, internet access, and the rule of law. But what seems restrictive to us is normal for the average Chinese citizen.

Another pursuit for me was business start-ups. This interest sprang from Sheldon Levy, then president of Ryerson University and the only person who threw me a bone in my post-political life. He got me involved in the Digital Media Zone (DMZ), Ryerson's incubator for technology start-ups. While working there I helped the students prove their concepts, offered business model suggestions, and prodded their market concepts, including their various financing models. Truth is, I am sure I gained as much as I offered and sought to apply some of this learning to my own benefit. Looking back at my time at Ryerson, I can say that it informed my own business model and especially the desire to make income in nuggets or chunks rather than by the hour. In this way, I have been able to make a living without having to rely on becoming a lobbyist and begging for the attention of policy-makers on behalf of clients. Or, put another way, I have been able to maintain my independence.

Among the start-ups I can claim to having input at their infancy is Carrot Rewards, the successful behaviour-influencing app that is growing across Canada in leaps and bounds. I co-founded Social Change Rewards, Carrot's corporate predecessor.

Media presentation with Ryerson University president Sheldon Levy (left) and Tony Clement to announce infrastructure stimulus funds for Ryerson University.

Over the years I also served on the boards of public companies in sectors as distinct as medical marijuana and graphite mining. On several occasions, I provided witness support in various legal matters. The greatest fun of all was the chance to do a retrospective deep dive into areas where I had been legislatively active, especially Bill 102, Ontario's drug reform legislation.

* * *

While I found these pursuits rewarding, both financially and intellectually, the truth is that I missed politics almost every single day. And pretend as I might, it seemed to be what was expected of me. A lot of people still approached me even if I didn't know them, so I got asked a lot: "What have you been up to, George?" At an earlier stage in my life, I might have answered by saying, "240 pounds." But those days, I said, "A lot of parenting." (In the early years it was, "A lot of diaper changing.") I also got comments from people who hadn't seen me for a while and had concluded I must have been busy up in Ottawa. (Or enjoying my pension, another common misconception!) As I wrote earlier about my identity shift and the challenges that came with it for Christopher when he stopped working to raise our family, I, too, experienced quite a swirl of changes in those years after I left politics. But what I discovered is that, while I can do other things, I am and will forever be a politician.

I had a conversation with my son, Michael, who told me, surprisingly, that he wanted to be a politician when he grew up. "What does being a politician mean to you?" I asked. "Helping people," he said. This confirmed my thinking. Politics, at its best, involves helping individuals and communities reach their potential. Being a cabinet minister was a huge honour, but helping bring renewal to Regent Park, which I largely started during my time as an opposition MPP, is what remains with me as most satisfying. And helping to launch the careers of MPs Salma Zahid and Ahmed Hussen is an awesome reward, as well.

* * *

After losing to Ford in 2010, I mostly kept my views to myself. I did not spend time chirping against Rob Ford from the sidelines, even though there was a lot to chirp about. I tried hard to be a good father, experienced the joy of family, and endured the trauma of the deaths of my husband, my mother, and four cats. And I made a good enough living in the private sector. So why did I decide to get back in? There are many answers to this question, but the truth is that in my heart I never left.

The penny dropped for me in March 2017 in a conversation with my dear friend Pam McConnell, the long time Toronto city councillor. Despite our partisan differences, she had been a comrade in arms since we met through Barbara Hall in 1994, and we worked seamlessly together when I became an MPP and represented the same area. McConnell invited me to lunch to talk about our respective futures. She told me she was not going to stand for re-election and encouraged me to run for her council seat in the 2018 municipal election, with her endorsement. (Tragically, she died a few months later.) Now I had a place to land, and it would be political mecca.

But then in September 2017 Glen Murray, the Liberal MPP and cabinet minister who represented my old riding, resigned unexpectedly from the Legislature and created another opening. I was very tempted to run in his place. At the same time, I realized my candidacy would not be well received by the Liberal hierarchy at Queen's Park and my prospects for being appointed to cabinet would be slim.

There was no direct communication between me and Premier Kathleen Wynne. But I was told by her surrogates that I would be "big-footed" if I dared to run for that Liberal nomination in Toronto Centre. That is, the premier would bypass the nomination process by appointing another candidate in the riding. The Liberal Party even changed its rules to allow a leader to use his or her appointment power to derail a "controversial" candidate. (This will henceforth be known as the "Smitherman clause" in the Liberal rulebook.) No one had the courage or the courtesy to confront me directly on these matters. But I nonetheless got the message loud and clear.

Wynne had other ideas for the nomination in Toronto Centre, once a safe Liberal seat. She reached out to city councillor Kristyn Wong-Tam, former mayor David Miller, and former city planner Jennifer Keesmat. All three turned her down. The eventual nominee was David Morris, a policy adviser in the provincial ministry of health. He lost the riding to Suze Morrison, the NDP candidate, by almost twelve thousand votes.

Would I have done better, given my strong election team and deep roots in the riding? The margin would have been less, but it would be foolish to say I would have won the riding, given the province-wide swing against the Liberals. So in a sense Wynne did me a favour by opposing my candidacy. But I don't take any pleasure in this. And I took no delight in watching the party I love get decimated in the 2018 election. If I feel any vindication at all, it is over the name of the election winner: Doug Ford. All those people who have scorned me for losing to his brother in 2010 now understand that the Fords are not so easy to campaign against.

One last thought on the provincial election: It need not have been such a debacle for the Liberals. Kathleen Wynne gave Dalton McGuinty a shove out the door in 2013, but she was not smart enough to see that it was time for her to go five years later. Instead, she convinced herself that she was the messiah. She won unexpectedly in 2014 by running to the left of the NDP, and she thought that formula would work again in 2018. But it didn't, because by 2018 she was widely detested. This hatred sprang from cold places in the human heart — homophobia and misogyny. But that doesn't mean it could be ignored. It is doubtlessly true that, with a different leader, the Liberals would have done better in 2018. Now the Liberal Party faces actual extinction, thanks to her stubborn refusal to leave office before the election.

The Wynne government also made strategic errors in the run-up to the 2018 campaign. One was the constraint put on spending in the health sector. Wynne's greatest strength as a politician was her relentless progressiveness. But in attempting to balance the books while raising spending in other areas (education, infrastructure, the environment), she squeezed the health sector, which led to complaints about "hallway medicine." This undermined the Liberals' reputation for delivering public services.

The irony is that when I was health minister I kept the sector within budget — while improving services — with a variety of reforms, including accountability agreements with the hospitals. These same mechanisms were then used by Wynne to suppress spending on health care in spite of the demographic changes that were forcing demand up. She thus compromised the gains in quality of service (shorter wait times, including in emergency wards) that had been achieved in the McGuinty years.

Another error was the sell-off of Hydro One, a cherished public agency. For progressives, this was the single most offensive piece of public policy during the Wynne years. Hydro One and its sister company, Ontario Power Generation, were symbols of "public power," dating back more than a century to the time of Adam Beck. But Ed Clark, the former TD Bank head who became Wynne's senior economic adviser, persuaded her to sell off a majority share of Hydro One to raise money for investments in infrastructure. She thus caused public confusion about the government's agenda and provided an easy target for both opposition parties in the election campaign. They could attack the high executive salaries at the privatized Hydro One (Ford memorably labelled the CEO as the "six-million-dollar man") and suggest that privatization was the cause of higher hydro rates (totally false, but the argument resonated nonetheless with the electorate).

The last strategic error was the pre-election budget, which detoured from the track of a balanced budget and forecast six more years of deficits to pay for more social programs, including free daycare. Having spent five years bowing to the wishes of the bond-rating agencies and promising a balanced budget, the government had abruptly changed course. That left many Liberals, not to mention the general public, with their mouths agape. It also had the whiff of panic. In that respect, it was like the Peterson government's promise in the middle of the 1990 election campaign to reduce the provincial sales tax: desperation on steroids.

In the wake of all this, the 2018 campaign itself was almost an afterthought. The premier's bus arrived on time at all the scheduled stops, but in places where the Liberal Party barely existed on the ground. And in the last week of the campaign, Wynne delivered a premature concession speech. That further confused Liberal-inclined voters. The result was a Liberal caucus reduced to just seven seats — a historic low. If Wynne had stepped down eighteen months earlier, the Liberals could have saved twenty-five to forty seats. In the post-campaign bloodletting, many Liberals were pointing fingers and asking questions like: why was David Herle (Wynne's campaign chair) reportedly paid $70,000 a month to oversee this disaster?

But my focus was on the upcoming 2018 municipal campaign.

CHAPTER THIRTEEN

Run Over by a Ford Again
(Different Model)

As previously mentioned, my political career took another turn when, in early 2017, my dear friend Pam McConnell invited me to lunch. Pam was the city councillor for Ward 28 on the east side of downtown, comprising about half of the riding I used to represent in the Ontario Legislature (Toronto Centre–Rosedale). I had no idea why Pam wanted to see me. But I had known her for decades and, as I have noted in chapter 3 and elsewhere, we had worked together successfully and shared many local priorities, notably the redevelopment of Regent Park.

When I arrived for the meeting at a restaurant in the Eaton Centre on that March day in 2017, Pam hit me with a surprise: she told me she was in poor health and had decided not to stand for re-election, although she made it clear that she would have run if she could have. "It's only fitting that you run in my place to finish the job we started together in Regent Park," she said. I didn't commit immediately to run in her place, but I certainly left her with that impression. "I am sad for you and also humbled that you would choose me as the person to carry on your legacy," I replied.

Pam's pitch had come at a pivotal time for me. I was not enjoying the primary business relationship I was in, and I had already made the first $20,000 payment on a newly developed condo on Bloor Street in the ward.

This purchase was made NOT with an eye to returning to politics. Rather, I had recognized that my friends, my doctor, my bank, and so much else were all on the east side of downtown and I wanted to move back there. That being said, I also knew that in my heart and mind I had never entirely ruled out a return to politics.

What Pam did was give me licence to consider something that I had up until then pushed away. Pam also gave me some assurances that the New Democrats — with whom she was aligned — and her own team would abide by her wishes and support me because she had already discussed the matter with them and gained their support. In other words, I would be running with her blessing. (With hindsight, I should have gotten that in writing.)

It was an offer that was too good to refuse. So I decided to take Pam up on it and run for city council, thereby imposing on my family the adjustments that come with moving and switching schools in Grades 3 and 4.

I returned to politics better suited than ever, because I was humbled, informed, and inspired by my varied experiences — personal and business — since I had left the battlefield in 2010. My motto was "old and improved." The fundamental things that drive me — my sense of the need to fight injustice, my passion for progress, and my independence — were still the same. What had changed was my perspective. Take public parks, for example. As a parent, I appreciate them much more. The same for public education. Also, I have a greater concern for the need for affordable housing and the importance of limiting public debt so that it will not be a burden on my kids' backs.

Of course, politics has changed, too, at least at the provincial and federal levels. Within political parties, the grassroots have atrophied and a lot of campaign work has been professionalized. Accordingly, power has shifted, with all the parties adopting structures that emphasize central control. The parties have evolved around the all-important "data," and their emphasis has shifted from ground wars to air wars. There is a heavy reliance on ads (often negative), emails, and robocalls from centralized phone banks rather than on the door-to-door and street-corner engagement that are the hallmarks of grassroots politics.

But at the municipal level, grassroots politics still exists. And I looked forward to re-engaging on the east side of Toronto's downtown, where for more than a century the underprivileged and those just looking to make a fresh start have flocked in search of a community and have found it. I had been one of them. And I wanted to reconnect with the institutions there that are trying their best to help those in need face life's toughest challenges — like the Fred Victor Mission and Dixon Hall, Central Neighbourhood House, the Good Shepherd, and the Harbour Light; Sound Times, St. Jude's, Neighbourhood Information Post, Progress Place, 40 Oaks, the Christian Resource Centre, the Muslim Resource Centre, and so many others in between or not yet formed.

During the most rewarding years of my life, I dedicated myself to the service of these people and places, and they gave me the space, comfort, and love to do it. They taught me lessons about building community that I took elsewhere, especially Regent Park's community succession model, which simply but wisely proclaimed that as long as all the good jobs in the community are going to people from outside the community, the residents are screwed. There, focus was placed on educational achievement through Pathways, a national organization, rooted in Regent Park, that helps youth from low-income communities to graduate from high school and successfully transition into post-secondary education, training, or employment.

So, running on that turf wasn't a new experience for me. Nor was City Hall new to me, as I had been Mayor Barbara Hall's chief of staff from 1994 to 1996. (That's where I first met Pam McConnell.)

Before formally launching my campaign, I first had to align my private life and work with my political ambition. That meant I had to move myself and my children from our house in Toronto's west end to an apartment just north of Regent Park. (The condo on which I had made a down payment had not yet been built.) I had to place the kids in new schools and simplify my business activities to focus 100 percent on politics. As the sole income-earner in the family, I also had to survive for a while on less than we had become accustomed. Plus, I had just met Rolando in Cuba, so I was pursuing that relationship.

Then, in the summer of 2017, Pam McConnell died. This changed the political landscape dramatically, although I was not fully aware of it at the time. First, Toronto City Council had to appoint a replacement to fill the vacancy for a year before the election that would come in October 2018. I didn't put my own name forward for consideration for the appointment because I knew that one of the longstanding conditions was that potential nominees would have to commit not to run in 2018. (I lacked the audacity of Lucy Troisi, a former civil servant, who lied to everybody and said she wouldn't run and then ran anyway. But more about that later.)

There were thirty-one applicants for the open seat. Troisi won on the second ballot, mostly with the support of the right wing of council.

As the interim councillor, Troisi made a name for herself by, among other things, wildly opposing the establishment of a daycare centre in an under-used Victorian-era home in Cabbagetown, a constantly gentrifying part of the ward. The daycare was of industrial scale — up to eighty-two kids, with eighteen staff — and the proposal sharply split the community. Some residents called the proposed daycare centre an "outrage," "frankly ludicrous," and "completely incongruent" with the neighbourhood. Others were in favour of it, either because they had young children of their own or because they were embarrassed by the reaction of their neighbours.

Troisi sided with the antis. "The protection of this delicate neighbourhood is imperative," she said in opposing the daycare centre. The committee of adjustment, which had the final word, sided with her and killed the project.

Lucy emerged as a hero to some. But a more experienced councillor would have managed the scale of the project and the process without having Cabbagetown residents come off looking like jackass NIMBYs opposed to a daycare centre.

Enjoying the rapturous love created by taking stark positions favouring embattled constituents, Troisi moved on to oppose the expansion of services for intravenous drug users. To be sure, there were already five safe-injection sites in the ward, more than anywhere else in the city or in Canada. But Troisi's call for a moratorium in the ward contributed to opposition to the opening of badly needed services in other parts of the city, such as Parkdale.

Troisi took her moratorium message to all the affluent doors in the ward, but concerns of many other residents were ignored, and I saw problems in TCHC* communities that reflected neglect on her watch. If it had been just me against her in the eventual vote, I would have tagged her as "Lyin' Lucy" (because of her broken promise not to run) and won the election.

---

* Toronto Community Housing Corp., the city-owned provider of social housing. It is the largest publicly owned landlord in Canada, with 2,100 buildings and 110,000 residents.

However, events conspired against me. First, my campaign was slow to get off the ground. That's because in the early months of 2018 I was distracted by my efforts to exit a business, sell my house, and get Rolando, my new husband, back to Canada on a permanent basis. (After we married in December 2017, Rolando had to return to Cuba while we got his immigration paperwork sorted out, which required multiple meetings with lawyers.) And then there was my disastrous honeymoon with the kids in China, which I recounted in chapter 11. Suffice it to say that campaign mechanics took a back seat to these personal affairs.

To a certain extent, this was not a big problem for me, because the city has very strict rules limiting campaigns. Candidates are not allowed to raise or spend money until May 1 of the election year. They aren't even allowed to put up a sign until late September. Of course, these rules are designed to favour incumbents, who are permitted to keep sending mailers to their constituents and pad their name recognition. But name recognition was not an issue for me.

I did, however, have a problem with data — a crucial element in election campaigns today. My database from my old riding was eight years out of date. In an urban riding, with a high turnover in residents, that made it virtually useless. And I did not get much help from Bill Morneau, the federal finance minister and Liberal MP whose Toronto Centre riding included my ward. As for help from the provincial Liberals in the riding: my former machine was seriously diminished after Glen Murray exited in the summer of 2017 to run an environmentalist group, and Premier Kathleen Wynne had thought it best to keep the seat vacant.

I couldn't even get Pam McConnell's data. I asked Pam's daughter, Heather Ann, for it. "I'll see what I can do," she said. She never got back to me on that.

Undeterred, I forged ahead and formally launched my campaign in late June of 2018 with an event in Regent Park. Heather Ann McConnell — accompanied by her father, Jim — spoke at the event and teared up while noting that my chosen campaign colour was yellow, the same as Pam's. "I want to say how honoured we are to have George run under the yellow banner, which was both my mom's favourite colour and the colour that she chose to run under," she said. "For George to honour the legacy of my mother is very important to us."

My campaign team for the 2018 Toronto municipal election.

At this point in the campaign, I was very confident. I had seen Lucy Troisi in operation, and I thought I could easily beat her by rebuilding my data door-to-door.

Then, on July 25, Premier Doug Ford turned the election upside down. Out of the blue — there was no prior warning, unless you count a *Toronto Sun* column — Ford announced he was introducing legislation to cut Toronto City Council almost in half, from forty-seven members to just twenty-five. And he planned to implement this change immediately, for an election that had already begun and had just eighty-nine days left. In practical terms, this was head-shakingly ludicrous. It showed Ford lacked respect for our democratic traditions.

I was not reflexively opposed to the downsizing of council. I saw it as facilitating more focused decision-making at city hall; there would be fewer speeches and more action. I also thought it could lead to a much more robust citizen involvement in municipal politics, because it would drive decision-making down to the local level, with community councils made up of a mix of politicians and appointed citizens. (Indeed, that was an idea I had favoured in my mayoral campaign.) What I did oppose was the thuggish way that Ford imposed the downsized council on the city in the middle of an election campaign.

So, my first (short-lived) reaction to Ford's move was positive — I thought it might help me. First of all, the expanded ward (number 13, or

Toronto Centre) encompassed most of my old riding (except for affluent Yorkville and Rosedale) and I had run and won three straight provincial elections there (1999, 2003, and 2007). I had also done well there in my mayoral run in 2010.

I also naively assumed that Kristyn Wong-Tam — the incumbent councillor for the western half of the enlarged Ward 13 — would choose to run in the neighbouring new ward of University-Rosedale (number 11), where she was equally well-rooted.

My first warning that something might be amiss was an exchange of messages with Heather Ann McConnell, Pam's daughter. "Pam told me once that she liked Kristyn and would step aside for her if she had to," wrote Heather Ann. I slowly realized that Pam's personal endorsement of me could be posthumously revoked by her family.

Then I learned that the progressive councillors had worked out a deal among themselves so as not to face each other in the campaign: Joe Cressy would run in Spadina–Fort York, Mike Layton in University-Rosedale, and Wong-Tam against me in Toronto Centre. And she would have the backing of Cressy's and Layton's teams and all the special-interest, union, and NDP

My campaign photo for the 2018 Toronto municipal election.

resources that came with them. (Cressy and Layton are New Democrats; Wong-Tam says she is not a member of any party, but she votes consistently with the NDP bloc on council.)

At this point, I took a brief family vacation at a friend's beach house in Prince Edward Island. Instead of relaxing on the beach, I went through a terrible depression while I was there. I knew that I was sitting on the horns of a dilemma. If I stayed in the race, I would likely lose the election. If I quit, I would lose face, especially within my own family, whose lives had been disrupted so that I could pursue my dream.

I talked to my former boss and mentor, Barbara Hall. "Ford has given you an elegant way out," she advised me. I got the same advice from others, like Patrick Devine, the veteran municipal lawyer, who bluntly predicted I would be slaughtered in the election. But I decided to stay in the race. I couldn't bear the embarrassment of quitting. I also felt a weird shame that I had been hoodwinked again and had put my family through unnecessary upheaval. Getting out early would have been the easy and prudent thing to do. But I stayed in and worked hard to press the incumbent(s).

Shortly after returning from P.E.I., I started campaigning in the expanded parts of the ward. But I campaigned only half-heartedly, because the downsized council was being challenged in the courts and I held out hope it would be struck down and the forty-seven-ward election would be restored. That did happen, of course. The court ruled on September 10 that Ford's legislation was unconstitutional because the change it imposed would result in wards of such size that they infringed on citizens' rights "to cast a vote that can result in effective representation," and the unilateral changing of electoral boundaries in the middle of a campaign infringed on candidates' freedom of expression. But this decision was immediately trumped by Ford's unprecedented threat to use the notwithstanding clause in the Constitution.* Ford's threatened move was unnecessary, however, since the decision of the lower court was overturned by the Court of Appeal on September 19. All this legal and legislative wrangling created a weird political vacuum during which it was difficult to campaign. With the appeal court's decision, the twenty-five-seat council, my worst-case

---

* This clause allows governments to pre-empt portions of the Charter of Rights for up to five years, in order to pursue policies that they wish to implement.

scenario, was back in play — with the election just thirty-three days away. The whole experience exhausted me and my family. Imagine explaining to a newly arrived Cuban and two kids just how the law works and what the notwithstanding clause is all about.

* * *

I ran a very issues-oriented campaign, with five pledges: to champion afford-able housing, to tackle poverty, to protect our kids from gangs, to finish the redevelopment of Regent Park, and to run for no more than two terms on council. (Not coincidentally, Wong-Tam was running for a third term.) The platform resonated with those people who paid attention to the details, but there were not enough of them.

The cost of housing is an overarching problem in the ward, where Cabbagetown houses that used to provide shelter for low-income people are being sold for over $1 million. Displaced by this gentrification and by new apartment developments with higher rents, the tenants have been left with nowhere to go, as there are long wait lists for city-owned housing. I spent much of my campaign addressing this issue and insisting the city needed "deeply affordable" housing. I must have had some impact because by the end of the campaign Wong-Tam was using the exact same phrase.

The affordable housing that is available in the ward is, unfortunately, plagued by crime and drugs, and suffers from poor maintenance and inad-equate security. One example is 251 Sherbourne Street, a city-owned apart-ment building in the heart of the ward that is about 250 metres from my own home. I talked to many of the tenants there and discovered they were terrified by the drug dealing and violence on their premises. (A man had been shot dead in their building earlier in the year.)

"Think you're tough?" I asked in a campaign video, with the building looming behind me. "Imagine living at 251 Sherbourne with the city as your landlord. If getting to the front door meant fighting your way through drugs and crime, would you ever even leave your apartment? The current councillors have had years to fix this. Can you even trust them? I'm George Smitherman and I make positive change happen."

For this, Desmond Cole, a local activist, accused me of "racist attacks" on social housing tenants, and *NOW* magazine said I was "beating the crime drum to death." (I learned in this campaign that there are a lot of so-called progressives who think it is "racist" to point out that the tenants in city-owned housing are being neglected by their landlord.)

What I was seeking was housing that is both affordable and SAFE. My bold proposal was to use section 37 of the Planning Act, which allows the city to extract cash or other benefits from builders in exchange for higher-density developments. Wong-Tam had been using these section-37 dollars, which amount to millions, to improve parks and install fountains in her ward. This is what the "Chardonnay set" in the ward wants and that's where the votes are. But they aren't the people most affected by new development in the ward. Rather, the biggest impact is on those people who are already marginally housed. I wanted to use section 37 to buy a piece of all new developments for low-income housing. That would ensure mixed-income buildings on the co-op model. But the homeless, who would benefit most from such a move, don't vote.

The campaign had its highs and lows. Among the lows, beyond those inflicted by Doug Ford, was the decision by Pam McConnell's children, Heather Ann and Madelyn, and Pam's husband, Jim, to openly side with Wong-Tam. "Our family knows that Kristyn is the best person to serve Toronto Centre's diverse neighbourhood," they said in an endorsement published in KWT's campaign pamphlet. "She has a proven track record, cares deeply about people and the community and is highly effective at getting things done. Pam's legacy of hard work and love for the common city will be in great hands with Kristyn, who shares her values and worked so closely with her over the years." So much for my values and years of close co-operation with Pam, and so much for Heather Ann's teary-eyed endorsement at my own launch just weeks prior.

Another low was the decision by two former Toronto mayors, Art Eggleton (a Liberal) and David Crombie (a Red Tory), to go ahead with their pledge to hold a joint fundraiser for Wong-Tam. They had made the commitment before it became known that she would be running against me in the expanded ward, but the shifting political landscape didn't give them pause. (For the record, another former mayor, Barbara Hall, dropped out of the event.) And, to make matters worse, they deliberately shifted the venue for their fundraiser from Wong-Tam's old ward to my new turf, Regent Park, even before the Toronto Centre battle lines had been legally confirmed. Along with being deserted by the McConnell family, this was one of the most hurtful acts I have ever experienced in politics.

Nor were the provincial Liberals — with the exception of former cabinet minister Steve Del Duca — any help. That is not surprising because they had actively tried to recruit Wong-Tam to run for them in the provincial election earlier in the year. And after the June election debacle the provincial Liberals' resources were almost entirely extinguished.

In the end, few Liberals came to my aid in the campaign. One exception was federal immigration minister Ahmed Hussen, whose political career I had helped to launch. Another was Bob Rae, former Liberal MP for the riding. But current Liberal MPs Adam Vaughan (Spadina–Fort York) and Julie Dabrusin (Toronto-Danforth) both endorsed Wong-Tam. Bill Morneau did call me on the day before the election to inform me that the polls didn't look good for me. I abruptly ended the call and trudged along in the terrifying final hours of a losing battle. I will definitely remember those for whom I have sacrificed and those who abandoned me in my time of need.

Despite my disappointment with the lack of support from the federal and provincial wings of the Liberal Party, I wasn't trying to run a Liberal campaign, per se. Quite the contrary. As noted already, my campaign colour was yellow, not Liberal red. I do not like party politics at the municipal level. But I had hoped more Liberals would at least lend me a helping hand, as I had helped many of them over the decades.

The media largely shunned me as well. The *Toronto Star*, which had endorsed me for mayor in 2010, opted for Wong-Tam and smothered her with coverage. So did *NOW* magazine, which called my campaign an "embarrassment." The *Toronto Sun* backed Troisi, while at the same time noting she couldn't win and suggesting I might be the better bet to beat Wong-Tam. Go figure.

It didn't help me that there were so many candidates in the election for Toronto Centre — nineteen in total. (To run as a candidate you only need to pay $100 and have twenty-five people endorse you.) They represented every neighbourhood and virtually every ethnic and social group in the ward. That meant the campaign was chopped up into little pieces by the candidates, each with a claim on some neighbourhood or group, and it was hard for me to get any traction against a well-entrenched incumbent like Wong-Tam.

Everywhere I turned, along streets and into buildings that were once part of my political fortress, I found shifting allegiances. In the Gay Village, I was no longer the only gay politician in town. Wong-Tam is an out lesbian. And in Cabbagetown, a lot of my hard-core supporters peeled off to Troisi. Elsewhere, within ethno-cultural communities where I was well known, candidates from those communities challenged past loyalties to me.

With so many people running, all-candidates meetings — there were half-a-dozen of them during the campaign — were a bit of a zoo. Candidates were given only a few minutes to make their points. And most of the audience was filled with partisans from the camps of each of the candidates. That left only a handful of undecided voters in the room. So the meetings were basically a waste of time. Troisi actually skipped a couple of them in St. James Town, thereby avoiding accountability to the angry residents of 650 Parliament Street who had been displaced by a fire. And Wong-Tam approached them with dull, scripted messages that wouldn't offend anyone. When asked how she would address a problem, she would promise to order up a study or plug the issue into some established process.

As in my mayoral campaign against Rob Ford, I never got a chance to debate Wong-Tam head-to-head. I thought I was going to on CP24, a local news channel. But Troisi was included in the debate at the last minute, and the debate sort of fizzled. I did manage to make my point that Wong-Tam did not have a good relationship with Mayor John Tory. "I would work with Tory to deal with the issues in the ward," I said. Wong-Tam said she had a "proven track record" of working with everyone, a statement that belies the truth of her toxic relationship with the mayor.

Nonetheless, there were rewarding moments in the campaign for me. On the Thursday before the vote, for example, I ran into a woman who lived at 251 Sherbourne and was terrified by her experiences. "Thanks for having our backs," she said.

Far and away the most moving experience for me was a visit to Margaret's Place drop-in centre. It operates as a low-barrier shelter open 24/7 and accommodates people suffering from serious mental health issues or drug users currently under the influence. There I sat and talked with an older woman who refused my offer to help with her Old Age Security payments because she distrusted governments. I planned to return and offer myself as an individual case worker for her.

Another woman called me to complain bitterly because she had not been allowed to meet with me when I was health minister about a personal matter involving the misdiagnosis of her son. "But I have read your platform and agree with every word of it and I am going to vote for you," she said. "I just wanted you to know it has been a difficult journey for me."

I really enjoyed these human interactions. They were a reminder that much of politics is basically social work.

Two weeks before the election it became clear to me that I was going to lose, and possibly by a wider margin. The outside world — media, my old Liberal colleagues, my friends and acquaintances at the community level — had ruled me out of consideration. Help stopped arriving. Meanwhile, Wong-Tam got support from the unions, Progress Toronto (largely an NDP front), NDP councillors, and the McConnell family.

I don't want to sound like I was entirely outmatched. We put up a good fight and carried a lot of the debate in the campaign, because of my provocative online videos. Money was not a problem for my campaign. The city restricts spending in ward elections to just $65,000, and I was able to raise that amount without much difficulty. We delivered a hundred thousand pieces of campaign material, and I got hundreds of hugs from friends I had gathered over the years.

And in the same way that my mother and stepfather stepped up to help with my first campaign in 1999, my family played a huge hand in this one. My sister Joanne legged it out and fought the battles one by one. In Regent Park, she was subjected to severe homophobic remarks from the sign crew of an opposing candidate on account of my sexual orientation. My sister Christine and her partner, Marc, scoured the best vantage points for signs on many late-night missions.

I also received support from my political family, those who assembled to express their love for me as a candidate and my mission. Amazing women like Patti, Nancy, Hawaa, and none greater than Joyce Grigg, my most loyal supporter of all time, gave so much. As did wonderful new friends like Michael and Anthony.

In the end, I finished a poor second with just 15 percent of the vote. Wong-Tam got 50 percent, and Troisi was third with 9 percent. On election night, in my concession tweet I wholeheartedly congratulated Wong-Tam, and I thanked the voters "for giving me the chance to fall in love again."

Considering that my fate was clear long in advance, I surprised myself with how emotional I was when I rose to give my concession speech, after being introduced by none other than Barbara Hall. I choked up badly when I described the fortress-like fencing I had seen proliferating in my neighbourhood as a result of intensifying displacement and the income disparity that has created a cavernous gulf in vast swaths of Toronto's downtown.

Afterward, my reaction was decidedly mixed. On the one hand, I felt intellectually reinvented and re-energized. I had run an issues-based campaign, and I had lost to someone who is a "process politician," someone who I felt would push the paper but not drive solutions. Even though I took a shit-kicking at the polls, I felt more relevant. And in a way, Rolando and my kids know the real me much better now. Indeed, Rolando, who had come to Canada from Cuba with no similar campaign context, gained experience quickly and supported me in the textbook way of a political spouse, at home and on the campaign trail. I will always picture him crossing Parliament Street after the election to take down that last errant sign of my political career, which had been taped to a Cabbagetown storefront. And I will always remember my daughter, Kayla, gleefully running across Ontario Street to show me the Troisi flyer she had pinched.

On the other hand, the whole experience — being run over by a Ford again, being shunned by Liberal colleagues, and seeing an endorsement posthumously withdrawn — was painful.

Of course, I realize I will not get a lot of sympathy. I hope instead to channel the pain, find strength from the experience, and live to fight another day. As my father advised me after I got run over by an opponent in a hockey game, "Take the number, George."

Acknowledgements

Writing a book is not a task to be taken lightly. As with politics, it inevitably requires sacrifices — this is particularly true for the writer's family, who are asked to give of their time and privacy. This book was only made possible by the space and time — and love — given me by my husband, Rolando. I thank him for that. Sharing the gritty granularity of my life with him was difficult; his acceptance helped to draw us together.

The actual writing of this book involved collaboration with Ian Urquhart, the former *Toronto Star* editor and columnist. As a writing partner, Ian exceeded my wildest dreams. Bringing his craft and his enthusiasm, he drew from me the story of my life. These are my words and this is my life, but it is offered with the help of Ian's thoughtful hand.

I was fortunate to have Patrick Boyer, an author himself and a former MP, put in a good word with Kirk Howard, publisher emeritus of Dundurn Press, who threw me a lifeline and never wavered. And Dundurn editor Dominic Farrell provided thoughtful suggestions and amendments that enhanced the prospects for the book to be compelling to the reader.

Special mention goes to my friend and former assistant Chris Drew and the love of his life, Farah, for the constant sacrifice and friendship they provided to my family and me. Without their support during the writing process this book would not have been possible.

Any small royalties the book might produce will be dedicated to the Smitherman family commitment to Casey House in honour of my late husband, Christopher. From its earliest days, when June Callwood summoned up love and made a home for people who were infected with AIDS and dying at a stunningly rapid rate, Casey House has been known for its love and compassion. Today, the situation for people dealing with HIV and AIDS is different, but they need our support just as much.

And finally to my mother and grandmother, my sisters, my stepmother, and those women in politics named Bea, Simone, Marian, Pam, Barbara, and Libby, who knew better than me where to go and steered me there, I thank you.

Image Credits

Index

Page numbers in italics represent photos.

Abdi, Khadija, *67*
Acker, Carolyn, 70, 79
AECL, 140
Agostino, Dominic, 69
AIDS Committee of Toronto, 42
Albany Club, 163
Allison, Tom, 61–62, 177
Ambrozic, Cardinal, 73
Anderson, Colin, 135, 143
Anderson, Enza, 69
Ashworth, Gordon, 11, 83
Avro, 14

Babineau, Natalie, 132
Baird, John, 146–47, 163
Bangs, Jeff, 169
Basrur, Sheela, 84–86
Bassett, Isabel, 181
Beck, Max, 51, 56, 154

Beer, Charles, 81–82
Begin, Monique, 29, 98
Beltzner, Rainer, 115
Bennett, Carolyn, *50*
Berger, Phil, 60
Bernardo, Paul, 55
Bethel, Guy, 61
Bigliardi, George, 39
Bitove, John, 53
Blizzard, Christina, 47–48
Bloomberg, Lawrence,
    90, 133, 170
Bombardier, 146–47
Bonneville Salt Flats, 23
Bradley, Jim, 133
Bradley, Mike, 73
Braithwaite, Leonard, 31
Breithaupt, Jim, 30
Breslauer, Helen, 63–64

Brezhnev, Leonid, 23
Brockovich, Erin, 144
Brown, Mike, 154
Burnham, Libby, 51, 58–60
Burnhamthorpe Collegiate,
    22–23, 43
Butts, Gerald, 74, 77, 133, 170

Campbell, Archie, 84
CANDU, 140
Cansfield, Donna, 136
Caplan, David, 69, 89,
    97, 112, 145
Carbin, Dan, 82
Carr, Jan, 135–36
Carroll, Shelley, 164
CBC, 137
Centre for Addiction and Mental
    Health (CAMH), 46, 177
Chan, Ken, 82
Charnetski, Bill, 51
Chrétien, Jean, 56, 97
Chummar, Noble, 181
Clancy, Tamara, *108*
Clark, Ed, 205
Clark, Joe, 27–28
Clarke, John, 36
Clement, Tony, 60, 87, 146, *201*
Clinton, Hillary, 166, 171
Cohn, Martin Regg, 116
Cole, Desmond, 214
Colle, Mike, 163
Collenette, David, 56
Copps, Sheila, 30, *50*
Corbett, David, 72
Courtyard Group, 90

Cressy, Joe, 212–13
Crombie, Bonnie, 177
Crombie, David, 181, 215
Cruden, Joe, 28, 30, 163
Cunningham, Dianne, 39
Curling, Alvin, 76

Dabrusin, Julie, 216
Dagnone, Tony, 89–90
Darlington nuclear plant, 139–41
Davey, Keith, 51
Davis, Bill, 10, 30, 164
Davis, Bruce, 169, 173–
    74, 181–82
Daytona 500, 17
D'Cunha, Colin, 84
Dean, Tony, 83, 105
Del Duca, Steve, 216
Denison House, 153
DesRosiers, Claude, 71
Devine, Patrick, 213
Dewan, Phil, 33, 74
Diefenbaker government, 14
DiPede, Tony, 59–60
DJ TigerStyle, 154
Doncaster, Deb, 135
Donolo, Peter, 163
Douglas, Shirley, 119
Douglas, Tommy, 119
Dryden brothers (hockey), 15
Duguid, Brad, 164
Duncan, Dwight, 74, 136, 140

Eagen, Michael, 30
Ecker, Janet, 75
Eddie the Eagle, 33

Eggleton, Art, 215
Elgie, Bob, 32
Elliott, Douglas, 72
Elston, Murray, 32, 49
Enersource, 142
Erlick, Larry, 83
Etcheverry, Jose, 135
Etobicoke Centre
    riding, 10, 27, 30
Eves, Ernie, 75–77, 80, 87, 169
Ezrin, Hershell, 33

Farley, Chris, 184
Farrow, Ernest ("Pete"), 30–31
Farrow, Karli, 82
Faubert, Frank, 57
Filion, John, 174
Finnerty, Isobel, 33
Flaherty, Jim, 67, 146
Flahiff, Simone, 28
Fletcher, Paula, 143
Floyd, Gordon, 40, 48
Fonseca, Peter, 141
Ford, Doug, 10, 54, 69, 102, 177–
    78, 180, 204–5, 211, 213, 215
Ford, Rob, 45, 113, 159, 164,
    171–85, 202, 217
Fox, Charles, 152

Gallagher, Bob, 49
Galloway, Roger, 73
Geesink, Anton, 35
Giambrone, Adam, 164–65
Gibson, Brandon, 198–99
Gigantes, Evelyn, 37
Glenn, Peter, 98

Globe and Mail, 34, 66, 95, 183
Graham, Bill, 50, 50–51, 55, 103
Gray, Herb, 56
Great Wall of China, 200
Greedy, Jack, 15, 17
Grier, Jason, 56, 60–61, 82, 193
Grigg, Joyce, 62, 218
Grinspun, Doris, 83, 91, 91–92
Grossman, Larry, 59
Guerriere, Michael, 90
Gutteridge, Pam, 33–34, 39, 169

Hall, Barbara, 42, 51–57,
    61–63, 63, 65, 70, 107,
    152, 154, 156–57, 162–63,
    168, 181, 184, 188, 192,
    203, 208, 213, 215, 219
Hall, Marc, 72–73
Hampton, Howard, 73
Hansra, Harpreet, 179
Harding, Tonya, 65
Hardy, Meladina, 152
Harnick, Charles, 181
Harper, Stephen, 98, 102, 151, 176
Harris, Mike, 50, 54, 57–58,
    61–62, 63, 65, 73,
    75–76, 85, 87, 91
Hart, Christine, 32, 35
Harvey, Robin, 46
Haslam-Stroud, Linda, 91–92
Hassen, Phil, 83
Hawkes, Brent, 46, 61, 64, 68
Herle, David, 205
Hialop, George, 39
Hopkins, Janine, 82
Hudson, Alan, 97, 112

Hussen, Ahmed, 66, *67*, 70, 202, 216
Hydro One, 136, 204
Ignatieff, Michael, 163
Indianapolis 500, 17
Infrastructure Ontario, 146

Jakobek, Tom, 54
Jakobsh, Tom, 61
Jenner, Caitlyn, 132
Johnson, Molly, 154
Johnston, David, 111
Joy, Howard, 54

Kealey, Marc, 111
Keesmat, Jennifer, 203
Kelley, D'Arcy, 20–21, 25, *103*, *108*, 122
Kelley, Michael, 20
Kelly, Fraser, 30
Kelowna Accord, 102
Kennedy, Gerard, 164
Kennedy, John F., 13
Kirkey, Sean, 45
Klein, Ralph, 131
Korwin-Kuczynski, Chris, 54
Kouvalis, Nick, 165, 177
Kramer, Sarah, 97, 112

Lalonde, Marc, 29
Lang, Eugene, 56
Laroza, Nelia, 84
Lastman, Mel, 57–58, 169
Lauber, Michael, 111
Laurentian Lodge, 152
Lauzon, Jeff, 60

Layton, Mike, 212–13
Leach, Al, 61, 62–63
Lean, Ralph, 53, 169–70
Lee, Chin, 175
Leitch, Kellie, 177
Leluk, Nick, 30–31, 38n
Levy, Sheldon, *201*
Lewis, Michael, 51
London Centre riding, 36
London North riding, 39
Lopinski, Bob, 77
Lovell, Scott, 66, 82
Lumley, Ed, 29
Lyle, Greg, 170

MacDonald, David, 50
MacIsaac, Rob, 100
MacKay-Lassonde, Claudette, 32–33
MacLeod, Hugh, 83, 105
MacNaughton, David, 81
Maeda, Richard, 43–44
Magill, Dennis, 59–60
Malik, Abid, 107
Maloney, Marian, 28, 31
Mammoliti, Giorgio, 165, 172–73
Mandaman, Indian Ron, 152
Maple Leaf Sports and Entertainment (MLSE), 53
Marin, Andre, 95
Marland, Margaret, 33
Martin, Paul, 97–98, 169
Matthews, Deb, 115
Mazza, Chris, 113–17
McCallion, Hazel, *114*, 142–43
McConnell, Heather Ann, 210, 212, 215

McConnell, Pam, 54–55, *55*, 70, 148, 175, 203, 206–8, 210, 215

McGrath, Rita, 82

McGuinty, Dalton, 11–12, 47, 66, 73–75, *74*, 77–80, 83, 85, 94, 98, *103*, 103–4, 107–8, 113, 131, 140, 144–45, 147, 150, 157–58, 160–61, 176, 204

McLeod, Lyn, 40, 48–50, 81

McNeely, Phil, 75, 137

McPherson, James, 61–62

Meagher, Aileen, 59

Meech Lake Accord, 36

Meinzer, Gerry, 52

Mendes, Shawn, 191

Mihevc, Joe, 175

Miller, David, 85, 146–48, 156, 158–60, 163, 165–66, 173, 175, 184, 203

Millward, Robert, 53

Mississauga South riding, 32–33

Monty, Jean, 111

Morneau, Bill, 210, 216

Morris, David, 203

Morris, Jennifer, 52

Morrison, Suze, 203

Moses, Erika, 161

Mulroney, Brian, 36, 95

Munro, Lily, 40

Murphy, Tim, 50, 61, 62

Murray, Glen, 203, 210

National Post, 64

Naylor, David, 84

Neiman, Clem, 23, 28

Neiman, Joan, 23, 28

Newman, Dan, 181

New Oriental International College, 199

Nishnawbe Aski Nation, 99

Nixon, Robert, 32

NOW, 216

Nunziata, Frances, 57

Oakley, John, 176

Obama, Barack, 104

O'Brien, Dick, 30

O'Hagan, Dick, 61, 62, 153

O'Hagan, Wanda, 61

O'Neil, Hugh, 17, 33–37, 39, 40, 49, 82, 102, 153

Ontario Hospital Association, 90

Ontario Medical Association (OMA), 61, 83

Ontario Nurses Association, 91–92, 96

Ontario Place, 34

Ontario Power Authority, 141–44

Ontario Power Generation, 136, 141, 143

Orridge, Camille, 70

O'Shaughnessy, Thomas, 87

O'Toole, John, 85

Paech, Gail, 87

PanAm Games, 147–48

Pantalone, Joe, 164–65, 172–75, 181, 183

Pearce, Deb ("Dirk"), 73

Pearson, Lester B., 61, 153

Peloso, Christopher, 51, *103*, *108*, 149–55, 158, 166–69,

179–80, *181*, 185–92, 202

Penner, Bob, 170

Perks, Gord, 36

Peterson, David, 10–11, 30–31,
    33–39, 50, 53, 76, 87, 107,
    147, 152, 163, 169, 181, 205

Peterson, Jim, 152

Pickering nuclear plant, 144

Pirk, Herb, 54

Portlands Energy Centre, 143

Priest, Lisa, 95

Pupatello, Sandra, 74, *74*

Rae, Bob, 32, 37, 40–41,
    48–50, 63, 131, 216

Rae, Kyle, 54, 175

Rafi, Saad, 135

Rapin, John, 96

Rappolt, Marguerite, 83

Regent Park, 66–67, 70, 128,
    202, 206, 208, 214–15, 218

Registered Nurses Association
    of Ontario, 83, 91

Reid, Pat, 35

Rickard, Don, 59

Rickford, Greg, 146

Rock, Allan, 150

Roman, Stephen, 153

Romanow Report, 79–80, 97

Ronson, John, 90

Ross, Todd, 72–73

Rossi, Rocco, 163–65,
    172–73, 181–83

Rowlands, June, 51–52

Ryerson University, 201

Sachow, David, 87

Salomon Laurencio, Rolando, 193–
    98, *196*, *197*, 208, 210, 219

Samian, Ali, 82

Samsung, 137–38

Sapsford, Ron, 59–60,
    83, 90, 97, 105

Scheer, Hermann, 134–35

Scott, Ian, 40, 49, 51, 62, 73

Sewell, John, 63, 66, 181

Shack, Eddie, 19

Shaw, Ken, 180

Sheinbaum, Lana, 87

Sherman, Barry, 93

Silva, Mario, 54

Silver, Richard, 176

Simcoe West riding, 37

Simkhai, Joel, 48

Smith, David, 56

Smith, Don, 104

Smith, Kevin, 83

Smith, Monique, 154

Smith, Stuart, 30, 40

Smitherman, Arthur, Sr. (father),
    14, 17–22, 25, 43, 56, 184

Smitherman, Arthur, Jr.
    (brother), 14, 21–22, 180

Smitherman, Christine (sister),
    14, 20–21, *108*, 151, 218

Smitherman, George,
    adopting children, 154–55,
        166–69, 187
    AIDS awareness, 25, 42
    beginning in politics, 26–29
    Bill 7, 37–39
    Bill 167, 48–50

C. difficile, 118
childhood, 13–25
China, 198–200
Christopher's suicide, 187–92
City Council race,
    2018, 206–19
coming out, 39–40
Commitment to the Future of
    Medicare Act, 86–87
Curious George dolls, 12
deputy premier, 102–4
drug use, 44–48
early jobs, 25–26
eHealth, 105, 110–13, 117,
    170–72
energy and infrastructure
    minister, 134–45
father's death, 43
federal-provincial health deal,
    97–99
film processing shop, 43–44
Florida trips, 15, 18, 25, 190
marrying Christopher, 149–55
marrying Rolando, 193–98
gas plants, 141–45
Green Energy Act, 134–37, 139
health-care reform ideas, 119–30
health minister, 79–118, 131–34
hospital deficits, 80–81, 90–91
Local Health Integration
    Networks (LHINs),
    99–102, 106, 124, 127
long-term care, 132–33
mayoral race, 2010, 155–84
mental health reform, 95
nuclear power, 139–41

nurses, 91–92
Ornge, 101, 110, 113–17
P3s, 87–89, 145
parents' divorce, 19–21
prescription drugs, 92–95
primary care reform, 96, 124–25
promotion to cabinet, 11–12
provincial election, 1999,
    61–67
rookie MPP, 68–78
Samsung deal, 137–38
SARS, 84
sexual awakening, 24–25
Smoke-Free Ontario Act, 85
transgender people, 131–32
wait times for medical
    procedures, 97
weight, 23–24
Wellesley Hospital
    campaign, 58–60
working for Barbara Hall, 51–58
working for Herb Gray, 56–57
working for Hugh O'Neil, 33–37
working for Premier
    Peterson, 32–33
Smitherman, Joanne (sister), 14,
    17, *103*, 151, 153, 218
Smitherman, Kayla (daugh-
    ter), 90, 187, *191*,
    195–98, *196*, 219
Smitherman, Margaret (mother),
    13, 19–23, 25, 108, *163*, 188
Smitherman, Marilyn (step-
    mother), 21, *197*
Smitherman, Michael (son),
    90, 152, 166–69, *167*,

168, *182*, 184–86,188–91, *191*, 195–98, *196*, 202
Sobers, Tracey, 12
Solursh, Gerry, 152
Sorbara, Greg, 76, 97, 137, 159
Sorbara, Pat, 32, 39, 163
Sousa, Charles, 142
Souvalotis, Arthur, 47
Starr, Patti, 34–35
Steele, Andrew, 77
Steeve, Jamison, 82, 133
Stoudamire, Damon, 53
Sure-Way Transport, 15
Suzuki, David, 134
Sweeney, John, 30

Tabuns, Peter, 54, 133, 143
Thomas, Richard, 30
Thomson, Sarah, 165,
    172–73, 181, 184
Toldo, Tony, 153–54
Toronto Blue Jays, 15, 23
Toronto Centre–Rosedale riding,
    11, 50, 58, 61, 64–65, 76,
    161, 203, 206, 212, 215–16
Toronto Maple Leafs, 15, 53
Toronto Raptors, 53
Toronto Star, 23, 46, 52, 66,
    69, 91, 102, 105, 108,
    115, 132, 165, 183, 216
Toronto Sun, 47, 178, 180, 183, 216
Toronto Toros, 15
Tory, John, 133, 158–60,
    164–65, 177, 183–84, 217
Towhey, Mark, 178
Trans-Provincial Freight
    Carrier, 25–26

Troisi, Lucy, 209, 216–18
Trudeau, Justin, 64, 170
Trudeau, Pierre, 13, 23, 26–27, 36,
    61, 158
Trump, Donald, 137, 172–73,
    177, 183, 187
Turner, John, 169
Tweed, 92–93

Van Dette, Justin, 159
Van Horne, Ron, 39
Vaughan, Adam, 175, 216
Victoria-Haliburton riding, 49

Watt, Jaime, 67, 170, 181
Webster, John, 51, 169
Wellesley Hospital, 58–60,
    62, 64, 79
West Deane Public School, 19
Wilkinson, John, 75
Wilkinson, Peter, 103
Wilson, Michael, 27, 29–30, 95
Winkler, Doreen, 71
Witmer, Elizabeth, 75, 91, 100, 161
Wong-Rieger, Durhane, 63, 64, 87
Wong-Tam, Kristyn, 203, 212–19
Wynne, Kathleen, 10, 63, 104,
    113, 164, 203–5, 210

Yakimov, Bea, 28
Yetman, Bill, 40
York East riding, 32
York West riding, 30–31

Zahid, Salma, 179, 202
Zerucelli, John, 64
Zolf, Larry, 30

DISCARDED

Book Credits

Developmental Editor: Dominic Farrell

Project Editor: Elena Radic

Copy Editor: Laurie Miller

Proofreader: Patricia MacDonald

Designer: Sophie Paas-Lang

dundurn.com   dundurnpress

@dundurnpress   dundurnpress

dundurnpress   info@dundurn.com

FIND US ON NETGALLEY & GOODREADS TOO!

DUNDURN